CLINTON, INC.

CLINTON, INC.

THE
AUDACIOUS REBUILDING
OF A
POLITICAL MACHINE

DANIEL HALPER

An Imprint of HarperCollinsPublishers

HarperCollins books may be purchased for educational, business, or sales promotional use. For information, please e-mail the Special Markets Department at SPsales@harpercollins.com.

A hardcover edition of this book was published in 2014 by Broadside Books, an imprint of HarperCollins Publishers.

FIRST BROADSIDE BOOKS PAPERBACK EDITION PUBLISHED 2015

Designed by Leah Carlson-Stanisic

Library of Congress Cataloging-in-Publication Data has been applied for.

ISBN: 978-0-06-231122-1 (pbk.)

15 16 17 18 19   OV/RRD   10 9 8 7 6 5 4 3 2 1

To Lauren

CONTENTS

INTRODUCTION:
BRAND MANAGEMENT

"They were careless people, Tom and Daisy—they smashed up things and creatures and then retreated back into . . . whatever it was that kept them together, and let other people clean up the mess they had made."

—F. Scott Fitzgerald

Hillary Rodham Clinton was all smiles as she stood on a Pentagon stage in early 2013. Buoyant, almost girlish, she was rocking a shapeless deep red blazer with a Peter Pan collar and four large black buttons, as she prepared to take part in another moment of Clinton mythmaking. It was the kind of exquisite brand reinvention and choreographed stagecraft that had been a Clinton hallmark since their first campaign for national office in 1992.

Beside her was the colorless General Martin Dempsey, chairman of the Joint Chiefs of Staff, and Leon Panetta, Barack Obama's jovial secretary of defense. He had served as White House chief of staff for Hillary's husband in his first term as president and remained fiercely loyal to the family through the hard-fought 2008 Democratic primary campaign against Obama. Dressed in a dark suit with a blue-gray tie, Panetta had extolled the former first lady in ways that might make even the most studied Clintonite blush. The burly and gregarious Italian American gushed that Hillary was "one of the most informed, most passionate, and most dedicated public servants that I've had the privilege to serve alongside." He was, just as one would expect, a close ally of Clinton's all throughout their time serving at President Obama's request.

Panetta bestowed upon her the Distinguished Civilian Service Award, the Pentagon's highest honor, and then dropped a little news to the reporters gathered. "In many ways, I have to tell you, it was her inspiration that encouraged me to move forward to be able to bring down the last barriers for women in the Department of Defense and to give them the ability to have a chance to engage in combat." He turned to a beaming Hillary. "I thank you for that inspiration."

And so Leon Panetta added another talking point for the Hillary Clinton brand, Version 10 or 12 or 15 by now. The news nugget about Hillary's then-undisclosed role in allowing women to take on combat roles made headlines in U.S. newspapers and around the world. This time, as she gears up for the 2016 election, the outgoing secretary of state sought to be known as the inspirational crusader for the rights of women. Indeed, ever since leaving the State Department, she has urged a review of "women's rights" around the world, even partnering with her new best buddy, former first lady Laura Bush. That she paved the way for American women finally to serve in combat was just another sign of the impact she had had. Except for the fact that it wasn't technically true.

Contrary to Secretary Panetta's assertion onstage that February, national security policy in the Obama administration was not managed by the Department of Defense, or the State Department, for that matter—a source of enormous frustration for Secretary Clinton, as well as Panetta and his predecessor as defense secretary, Robert Gates, who in his 2013 memoir noted that Obama's White House "was by far the most centralized and controlling in national security of any I had seen since Richard Nixon and Henry Kissinger ruled the roost."[1] Instead, as Gates and other sources within the State and Defense departments have noted, all major policy matters were debated and decided among a small group of Obama loyalists at the White House—who lacked much, if any, substantive national security experience and operated almost totally through a political lens. Their decisions often were presented to cabinet secretaries as close to a fait accompli.

Also contrary to Panetta's boastful assertion, the controversial decision to place women into combat roles was not made as some homage to Hillary Clinton. Indeed, it really had nothing to do with Mrs. Clinton or Mr. Panetta, for that matter—both of whom Obama loyalists viewed with suspicion or disdain. One Obama appointee in the Defense Department, for example, denigrated Panetta as someone more interested in returning home to California every weekend than in running the massive Pentagon bureaucracy.

In 2013 the primary focus of the Obama National Security Council was political, national security sources have told me: reclaiming the House of Representatives in the 2014 midterm congressional elections. Losing the House to the Republicans in 2010 was an embarrassment to the Obama team. Obama's women-in-combat initiative was conceived to ensure that social issues remained front and center in the news. Moreover, women on the front lines would create a compelling visual as Obama Democrats continued to defend against the so-called War on Women, a rallying cry in the 2012 election that sent single female voters to the polls in overwhelming numbers for the Democratic Party.

Far more interesting about the Pentagon ceremony that day was not what was said on the platform but the set of questions surrounding it, those that few asked aloud.

The first, of course, was the state of the honoree's health. For one of the first times in weeks, Mrs. Clinton's lively brown eyes were finally freed from the strange greenish glasses she'd donned since her mysterious collapse the previous December. They had been outfitted with Fresnel prisms to help her see straight after what aides claimed was a concussion she suffered during a fall at home. One of the consequences of the strange adulation/suspicion dynamic that existed between the

Clintons and the Washington press corps was that a number of reporters didn't believe the concussion story for a minute.

For several weeks that December, the U.S. secretary of state had not been seen in public, a time when her own record and that of the administration she uncomfortably served had come under its sharpest attack, as a result of the deaths of State Department personnel on her watch in Benghazi, Libya. Some on the right openly speculated that Clinton had concocted this sudden malady to avoid testifying before Congress about Benghazi. However, as has often happened in the past, some of Hillary's wild-eyed enemies on the right seized the opportunity to propose a conspiratorial theory—in this case, that she had a drinking problem. The pretext for this canard was an incident in which she was photographed drinking and partying in Colombia—a scene that ABC News said "caused a stir." (The *New York Post* ran the story under the headline "SWILLARY.") After she inexplicably tumbled upon boarding her government plane—a moment repeatedly played on YouTube—right-wing bloggers had a field day. Rumors of her drinking became so pervasive that even President Obama joked about Hillary "drunk texting" him. Others believed her health scare was more serious than was publicly known, so serious that it could threaten her large ambitions.

Whether by design or incompetence, the Clinton press team did not help douse speculation. First, reporters were told Mrs. Clinton had disappeared from the public scene because she was "under the weather," as if she had a mild cold.[2] Then they said she was severely dehydrated from a stomach bug, which caused her to fall and suffer a concussion.[3] Only days later did they report she was being hospitalized for a blood clot in the brain.[4] The latter malady, in fact, is a common definition of a stroke. According to WebMD, those symptoms include "sudden dizziness, loss of balance or loss of coordination . . . trouble with speaking and understanding . . . paralysis or numbness of the face, arm or leg . . . blurred or blackened vision in one or both eyes, or you may see double . . . a sudden, severe headache, which may be accompanied by vomiting, dizziness or altered consciousness." Concealing these symptoms likely would require a patient to be out of public sight for weeks.

"She did not have a stroke," an aide pronounced at one point. Which made reporters familiar with the Clintons believe exactly the opposite.

"Of course, it was a stroke," one veteran reporter from a mainstream news network ruminates. "It's the only thing that makes sense." Such a revelation, if true, would almost certainly doom the future presidential aspirations of anyone who would be nearly seventy on her first Inauguration Day.

Reporters point to a number of factors that support their theory. For one, there was the simple fact that she was completely out of public sight for weeks without a convincing explanation. For another, Mrs. Clinton had a family history of stroke, which had killed her father in 1993 at the age of eighty-two. The Fresnel prism glasses she wore for her concussion also are commonly prescribed for stroke patients to improve visual perception. Reporters noted the look of worry, even panic, on Chelsea's face after visiting her mother at a New York hospital. Days before her collapse, Clinton had canceled a foreign trip, citing a stomach virus—which was the same excuse she used in 2005 after collapsing during a speech in Buffalo, New York.[5] Though not unprecedented, fainting is not a common symptom of stomach flu. After she was hospitalized in New York, Mrs. Clinton's doctors and the hospital delayed releasing a medical statement to the press, allowing not always forthright Clinton aides total control of the flow of information.

The chief science and health correspondent for NBC News, for example, was among those publicly questioning a statement from Clinton aides that the secretary was being treated with blood thinners. "The problem," Dr. Robert Bazell said on NBC's *Today* show, "is that usually when blood clots come from concussions, they can't be treated with blood [thinners]. So either it's not really related to the concussion and she's got a blood clot in her leg or something, or there's something else going on that we're not being told."[6]

Reporters on the Clinton beat knew it was nearly impossible to get actual news, or facts, from Hillary Clinton's primary spokesman, Philippe Reines, who was known to feed carefully scripted information to favored reporters—a number that could be counted on one hand, such as Amy Chozick of the *New York Times*, who once detailed her many long lunches with Reines in a lengthy *Times*, magazine piece, and Bloomberg's Jonathan Allen, who was a staffer for Democratic National Committee chairwoman Debbie Wasserman Schultz—and then freeze out everyone else. Absent some revelation from Secretary Clinton's doctors, which medical canons would prevent, this was another of many mysteries about the Clintons destined to remain unsolved.

The second mystery offered at the Pentagon that day was even more tantalizing to longtime Clinton watchers. While Hillary was receiving such a singular honor, from her husband's former chief of staff, and on Valentine's Day to boot, where in the world was her adoring husband?

Wherever William Jefferson Clinton was—giving a highly compensated lecture under the guise of his foundation, schmoozing with former enemies like Newt Gingrich, or coaching Democrats on Capitol Hill—he was making news. On that day alone, the *New York Post* was reporting that Bill privately had "confirmed" to a longtime Clinton donor that Hillary was all but certain to run for president in 2016.[7] This was only the latest of umpteen stories in which Bill had been caught openly speculating about his wife's ambitions, whether she liked it or not. (She didn't.) Meanwhile, the Associated Press was breaking news on a series of secret correspondences between then-president Clinton and his onetime foe Richard Nixon.[8] The exchanges, none particularly notable, were yet another example of Clinton's unrivaled ability to shift his opinions of people as it suited him, to forge useful alliances with the most unlikely of people, and, of course, to steal headlines from his wife.

For anyone at the Pentagon that day, the conspicuous absence of Bill Clinton offered another chance for one of Washington's favorite parlor games to begin anew—the usual speculation over what may well be the most talked-about, gossiped-about, history-making marriage since Henry VIII and Catherine of Aragon. One that may soon accomplish what once seemed an unthinkable, even preposterous, task only a decade or so ago when the Clintons left the White House burdened by scandal: the establishment of the first husband-and-wife presidencies in American history.

Over the years many metaphors have been used to describe the Clintons. Among the most common is their similarities to the mafia. Former Clinton cabinet secretary Bill Richardson, for example, talks about the perils of breaking the Clintons' omertà when he endorsed Barack Obama over Hillary in 2008. Similar mafia imagery has been invoked to me by other former senior Clinton aides who fear retribution about being quoted on the record. The writer Christopher Hitchens referred to Bill and Hillary as if they were leaders of a suicide cult. "They act like cult members while they are still under the spell," he once noted of the Clintonites he'd encountered in his less than impartial biography of the First Family, *No One Left to Lie To*, "and talk like ex-cult members as soon as they have broken away."[9]

My own reporting and analysis lead me to a different analogy, one that explains the title of this book. It is commonly said that marriages are in many ways like business partnerships. And after thirty-eight years of marriage, that is what the Clintons are these days: dueling CEOs of a multimillion-dollar empire, Clinton, Inc.

A source who has worked closely with both Clintons for years shares this view. "I think the word *partnership* has been used before," he tells me. "It's a pretty fair word."

Like any corporate entity, Clinton, Inc. embarks on a variety of potentially profitable endeavors. The company adjusts strategies and cuts its losses. It fends off rival brands—other Democratic factions or Republican challengers—and sometimes it partners with them to mutual advantage, such as surprising collaborations with the Bush family that until this book have not been fully known. At the upper levels of management there are fierce battles for the attention and patronage of the two CEOs at the top.

The duo at the top have different lines of authority within the company. For the past decade, for example, Bill was in charge of bringing in the money. His net worth alone is said to be over $100 million. Hillary improved the family's political fortunes in the Senate and then the Obama administration. These various responsibilities have allowed them to live comfortably, even happily, as well as to lead largely separate lives with different aides, different entourages. Differences in temperament, style, and their involvement in various scandals and indiscretions have tested their partnership, but both concluded that the sum is stronger than its individual parts. Their myriad efforts share a singular goal: to help the Clintons profit, politically and financially, from their various endeavors. To improve, in effect, the company's value, or its stock price.

"It's the most unusual but very productive relationship," former senator Joseph Lieberman tells me in an interview. Lieberman, of course, was selected as Al Gore's running mate in 2000 largely due to his very public condemnation of Bill Clinton's affair with White House intern Monica Lewinsky. The denunciation by the respected Democrat, an Orthodox Jew, allowed a conflicted Gore to put some distance between himself and the scandal. Years later, even Lieberman seems surprised by the strength and endurance of the Bill and Hillary partnership—one, notably, that outlasted that of Al and Tipper Gore. Lieberman tells me of overhearing a phone conversation between the two, during which Bill greeted his wife with "Hi, sweetheart" and they chatted amiably about their respective activities. It seemed a marvel to him, especially after all the scandals, the adultery, the gossip. "You go through different chapters in a marriage," he notes with a shrug as we sit together in his New York City office. "But they seem very devoted to each other."

Former Clinton nemesis Newt Gingrich puts it more clinically when I interview him on the same subject. "She married him because he was going to be somebody," he tells me in his Arlington, Virginia, office, expressing a common view among Republicans. "And he married her because she's going to help him be somebody. And they decided to be somebody together. And it's been a mutually beneficial relationship.

"They must have at some point had a very tough period of talking through—what the ground rules are, and how they relate to each other.

[Daniel] Yankelovich used to have a formula he called 'the giving and getting strategy': What do I give, and what do I get for it. . . . Clearly they reached a very clear agreement on how they would operate and what they would do."

Ever the college professor—he taught at what was then West Georgia College before entering politics—Gingrich even offered me title suggestions for this book. "I think the title's already been used, but in a sense, *The Power Couple* almost begs to be the title of something about the two of them." Later, he reflected, "He wouldn't have survived without her. So maybe the title is *Mutual Survival, Mutual Prosperity*."

In this mutually beneficial partnership, only one other person is allowed to cast a decisive vote. As this book will detail, their daughter, Chelsea, over the years has slowly emerged as Clinton, Inc.'s tough and ambitious senior vice president. As her parents age and they look far into the future, Chelsea's portfolio expands by the day. Recently, for example, she was added to the masthead of the Clinton Foundation, which was rechristened the Bill, Hillary and Chelsea Clinton Foundation in 2013. She is poised to take over the family business one day.

After Chelsea comes a large and varied board of kibitzers and advisors who run the gamut from well-known figures such as James Carville, Paul Begala, and Rahm Emanuel to lesser-known personalities such as Maggie Williams, Huma Abedin, and Cheryl Mills. Those who offer total loyalty to the Clintons, defend them in the press, and help them solve problems are rewarded—with attention, financial assistance, connections, and access.

One omnipresent Clinton backer is Lanny Davis, a friend of the Clintons since their shared law school days. Within the Clinton circle, Davis has something of a notorious reputation of one who frequently talks to reporters without authorization and trades on his decades-long associations, not only with the Clintons but with George W. Bush, another friend of his from their days together at Yale. Many Clinton insiders send me to Davis for quotes and gossip, labeling him a "self-promoter" and a gadfly. Davis is in fact a very likable presence, earnest and apparently sincere in his devotion to the former first couple. In his office, adorned with accouterments from his associations with the Clintons and Bushes, he offers this: "I think [Hillary] was destined for public service since the first time I met her." He adds helpfully, "That's on the record."

Those kinds of quotes are acceptable in ClintonWorld. Others leave Clinton associates vulnerable to a company purge. As in any good corporation, investors in Clinton, Inc. jealously guard the company brand and police insiders who might put it at risk. "They have an infrastructure," a former Clinton cabinet official tells me, insisting that he be quoted without attribution. "A political infrastructure, political consultants, a press infrastructure, a business infrastructure." And they have a network of spies, informants, and enforcers.

All of which leads to a note about sourcing for this book. Wherever I could I have tried to quote sources on the record. In many cases, however, I have agreed to quote prominent Clinton aides on background, or without attribution. I approached many of them at the outset with a liability, my work as a writer and editor for the *Weekly Standard*, which was rightly seen as a right-of-center magazine often critical of the Clintons. As a result, many people were initially reluctant to speak to me.

"Write something interesting and surprising that will not be as predictable as what the *Weekly Standard* has become," former White House press secretary Mike McCurry advised me. "I used to read it with great interest and even contributed a letter to the editor once. But the conservative critique of Obama . . . and I fear what will be said of Hillary Clinton . . . will be predictably snarky, and designed to add to the current polarization of our politics rather than figuring out how to overcome it. Write something that will make conservatives say, 'You know, I never thought I could see that in Bill/Hillary Clinton but this made me think . . .'"

The subtext of course is that my book was intended to be unflattering of the Clintons. In some ways, the reporting has borne that out. But as I've learned more about Bill and Hillary (and Chelsea), a more complicated portrait has emerged of each of them that is sometimes sharply at odds with their public personas. The private Hillary, for example, is warmer, more likable, and in some ways sadder than her public persona suggests. She's the more sympathetic and relatable one. Her biggest asset and her biggest vulnerability are one and the same: her husband. Contrary to his emotive Bubba persona, the private Bill Clinton is colder, more calculating, and more compulsive. Many people love his company, at least over the short term, yet he lacks real lifelong friends in a way his wife doesn't. His charm is legendary but has its limits. Clinton, for example, long admired Arkansas senator J. William Fulbright. A Fulbright relation told me that the senator was never fooled by the aspiring and self-serving politico—who was once the senator's driver. He related a story at Fulbright's funeral, in which then-President Clinton insisted on inserting himself into a Fulbright family photo. The suggestion was that the famously fatherless Clinton was clumsily still trying to form ties that existed only in his head. It should be noted that I made repeated efforts to interview both Bill and Hillary Clinton for this book. In one letter sent, I wrote, "I want to give the former President Clinton the chance to answer some of the questions that have been raised by employees, friends, and aides and to give him a platform to put things in context." The Clintons' "story deserves to be told. And I'd like to interview President Clinton in order for him to have his say—and in order to get his take." (Through spokespersons, the Clintons ignored my requests.)

Over time, I have managed to meet with a large number of people within the Clinton orbits, including a number of friends, colleagues, and aides who dealt with Bill and Hillary and Chelsea on a daily basis. I have had the opportunity to review thousands of pages of documents collected by political operatives, private investigators, and legal teams never disclosed to the public. And I've conducted dozens of interviews with Clinton aides, past and present, former cabinet officials (who served in the Clinton, Bush, and Obama administrations), and a fair number of onetime Clinton adversaries. This has not always proved an easy task. Nearly everyone in Washington has a Clinton story, or two, or two hundred, but many are afraid to air them publicly or on the record, out of fear of retribution or attack from ruthless Clinton aides and their media allies. This is often true these days, contrary to conventional wisdom, even of Republicans.

Among the first to feel the sting of Clinton attacks is former aide George Stephanopoulos, who in 2000 published a critical and unauthorized memoir about the Clintons, which won their fierce condemnation and enmity. Stephanopoulos's bracing assessment of the Clintons and himself was a bit too bracing for them. The book included lines such as "I came to see how Clinton's shamelessness is a key to his political success, how his capacity for denial is tied to the optimism that is his greatest political strength. He exploits the weaknesses of himself and those around him masterfully, but he taps his and their talents as well."[10] While there is not much damage that can be a done to a multimillionaire and well-liked TV personality—Stephanopoulos is now of course the anchor of ABC's *Good Morning America*—the pain inflicted on Stephanopoulos has been more personal. After publication of his memoir, he lost a number of friendships that were important to him. Though some longtime friends such as Emanuel and Carville still talk with him regularly, the Clintons themselves have proven unforgiving, according to several close associates of Stephanopoulos with whom I spoke.

"We had a big staff reunion and the Clintons invited everyone no matter how disgraced they were," a former Clinton press aide recalls. "And George was one of the few people that somehow didn't make that list."

To this day the ABC News host is trying to gain their forgiveness while Bill Clinton in particular seems to take joy in denigrating his former aide in private settings.

"Bill still hates him," says a source.

A similar psychological toll has taken hold of Bill Richardson, who took the risk of endorsing Barack Obama over Hillary in the 2008 Democratic presidential primary. Bill Clinton has never forgiven him, and that clearly stings Richardson.

"He has no interest in healing the breach," Richardson told me during an interview. "I think that sends a message to me that every relationship that he has is mainly about him and not about the other person. . . . He expects total loyalty. It's his way or the highway in the end in a relationship. I wish his forgiveness, his spirit of forgiveness were there and apparently it isn't."

The personal loss hurts the most. "I just want to hear him say, 'I love you' again," Richardson wrote.[11]

Even former vice president Al Gore has paid the price for his break with the Clintons over his 2000 loss, which Gore blamed in part on the Monica Lewinsky scandal. Though he and Clinton had a faux reconciliation a few years back, "it's still really bad," a close friend says. Gore to this day is all but a nonfactor in the Democratic Party, and rarely consulted by the Clintons.

In contrast to his wife and according to people who know him well, Bill Clinton has few personal friends. "He has cyclical friends, transactional friends," says one close associate, people who circle in and out of his orbit without forming long, meaningful connections. Two exceptions during his postpresidential life were billionaire Ron Burkle and a young aide named Doug Band. Both have since felt the dark side of a friendship with the former president.

Burkle used to treat Clinton to rides aboard his private Boeing 757.[12] But as the *Daily Beast* reported in 2010, Clinton has consistently been "badmouthing" Burkle in Democratic circles after a business deal between the two went bad, with Clinton accusing his former friend of owing him $20 million. Burkle told *BusinessWeek* that entering a partnership with Clinton was "the dumbest thing I ever did."[13]

And throughout much of 2013, Doug Band has been the recipient of scores of attacks on his character in newspapers and magazines, such as the *New York Times* and the liberal *New Republic*, for his alleged role in the financial mismanagement of Bill's various enterprises. "[C]oncern was rising inside and outside the [Clinton] organization about Douglas J. Band, a onetime personal assistant to Mr. Clinton who had started a lucrative corporate consulting firm—which Mr. Clinton joined as a paid advisor—while overseeing the Clinton Global Initiative, the foundation's glitzy annual gathering of chief executives, heads of state, and celebrities," the *Times* reported in a lengthy piece in 2013.[14] Former Clinton aides tell me that the attacks have been "hypercoordinated."

As for Hillary, a book released in 2014 reported on her State Department "enemies list" of those who didn't support her campaign in 2008 and merited punishment.[15] Though that revelation won a number of headlines, it in fact was not actually all that new. It already was commonly known in Washington that her State Department blackballed Obama political appointees who'd worked against her in 2008. The new revelation only underscored what is well known among Democrats in Washington, D.C.: You cross the Clintons at your peril. They are watching you.

A source tells me that Bill Richardson, the former ambassador to the United Nations and former secretary of energy, was blackballed by the Clinton team from having any serious role in the Obama administration. And that Hillary's aides, or Hillary herself, blocked an effort by Obama to appoint the veteran diplomat to negotiate the release of an American held hostage in North Korea. Bill Clinton was sent instead.

Thus it is pretty clear why less powerful figures inside Clinton, Inc. insist on anonymity. The panic among Clintonites, past and present, is palpable. "Don't fuck me," one well-known Clintonite once begged me after our interview, despite my repeated assurances of anonymity. "You aren't going to fuck me, right?" He asked this multiple times, on more than one occasion.

Clintonites are known to scour through magazine articles and books to try to decipher blind quotes and tie them to a suspect. For example, a well-known Clinton aide, Jay Carson, was fingered as a source for gossip on Hillary's 2008 campaign and ire toward Obama in the bestselling book *Game Change*. Former press secretary Jake Siewert was tsk-tsked for being quoted on the record in a 2008 book about Bill's activities called *Clinton in Exile*. As a result, Siewert is reluctant to be quoted elsewhere.

Adding to the paranoia, Clinton associates are masters at cultivating an aura of knowing everything before others do. One author of an unauthorized book on the Clintons, Sally Bedell Smith, tells me of attending a party with veteran Clinton hand (and now Virginia governor) Terry McAuliffe, whom she had interviewed. McAuliffe, a Washington fixture and fierce Clinton partisan known for his overcaffeinated, staccato style, came up to Smith to say hello and drop a bit of news.

"You know he has your book," McAuliffe said.

"He has my book?" she asked.

"Yeah, the president has your book."

Smith was shocked—and rattled. The manuscript was not yet released to the public and had been tightly held by the publisher so its details would not be leaked. "That can't be," she protested. "There aren't any copies out. There are no galleys."

"He's got it," McAuliffe said, delivering a message with an intimidating glance. "I saw him, he's read it, and he was devastated." (True to ClintonWorld code, when the details of this encounter leaked to a reporter, McAuliffe denied the conversation ever took place.)

When another book that touched on the Clintons was set to be published in 2013, Clinton operative James Carville got in on the act. Claiming to be good friends with the book's author, Carville asked the publisher for an advance copy. The author in question had neither met Carville nor worked with him. The conversation between the publisher and Carville had been a simple ruse to allow ClintonWorld to get an early edition of the book—so they could try to discredit the contents ahead of time, in the event that there was damning stuff about the Clintons in the pages. The manuscript turned out to be relatively harmless.

Even my reporting for this book has not been immune to curious activities in recent months. A top executive at Knopf, the publisher of Bill Clinton's memoir, *My Life*, has quizzed editors in New York about this book and whether it was "legitimate." I've received a phone call from James Carville's office asking whom I might be reporting on. Reporters from Democratic-leaning publications, such as media reporter Dylan

Byers of the Virginia-based trade publication *Politico* and Michael Cal-
derone of the left-leaning website *Huffington Post*, called me up well in
advance of the publication of this book to ask about its sourcing. They
told me that they have been hearing I haven't been able to get access.
Who might be spreading these rumors? The reporters following up on
gossip won't say.

Reporters, Washington reporters especially, have a keen sense of self-
preservation. Indeed, many of the things described in this book are well
known among Washington journalists, and have been openly gossiped
about in private settings. But much of this has never been shared with
the general public, for fear of Clintonian retribution.

If they print stories that reflect negatively on the Clintons, they
know that any access they have will instantly vanish. Sources inside the
Clinton camp have to be extremely careful about who they talk to. For
someone most Beltway reporters think will be the next president of the
United States, dishing on the Clintons and divulging stories—even ones
that are common knowledge among Washington insiders and yet never
find their way into print—is career suicide.

One former Clinton lawyer tried to discourage me from writing too
negatively because he said it could affect my career. A CNN producer
said she could never have my book on her program for fear that the Clinton people would punish the network by denying them access. In an interview with me, Howard Dean made the case that there isn't anything
new about Hillary that can be written. "There's nothing anybody's going
to write about Hilary Clinton that either isn't true or isn't already well
known," Dean told me.

I knew something of this when I wanted to write a piece for the *Weekly
Standard*, where I work, and ran afoul of Hillary Clinton's spokesman
Philippe Reines.

In response to my query about Mrs. Clinton's release from a hospital
after her December 2012 collapse, he sent me a pointed reply. "You and I
have to come to an understanding," he wrote. "This routine of you only
checking in when you need something isn't working and isn't the way

it's supposed to work." It was his attempt to strike a deal with me—a deal on how Clinton would be covered. I never responded. And he never answered my question.

If there is a coldhearted, capitalistic nature to many of the Clintons' transactions, it is not inadvertent. For the Clintons, politics is just business and one they happen to be very good at. But it is made clear to anyone joining this entity that it exists for the sole protection of Bill, Hillary, and Chelsea. No one else is a member for life. No one else is indispensable, and those who leave the company or expose trade secrets risk punishment while others who prove inconvenient or insufficiently loyal are expendable. Perhaps this is why so many sources keep right on talking to reporters like me. They feel the need to unload. They feel a sense of unfairness and entitlement in how the Clintons deal with their friends—and those who threaten them.

In short, for such reasons, most of my sources were afraid of crossing the Clintons. To alleviate their fear, I promised to protect their anonymity. In their recklessness toward others, they harkened back to a memory of another famous fictional couple, brought to life by F. Scott Fitzgerald. "They were careless people, Tom and Daisy—they smashed up things and creatures and then retreated back into . . . whatever it was that kept them together, and let other people clean up the mess they had made."

CLINTON, INC.

1

HILLARY'S REDEMPTION

"Sick but brilliant."

—a senior Clinton aide on the Bill and Hillary relationship

"The most difficult decisions I have made in my life were to stay married to Bill and to run for the Senate from New York," Hillary Clinton once wrote in her bestselling memoir, discussing the aftermath of her husband's affair with Monica Lewinsky.[1] In retrospect, neither of those statements appears to be true. Even as her husband was facing the biggest scandal of his life, Mrs. Clinton's mind was not on divorce but political survival. Hers, not his.

On February 12, 1999, the very day the Senate was voting on whether to impeach her husband on charges of perjury and obstruction of justice stemming from his lying about an extramarital relationship with former White House intern Monica Lewinsky, Hillary Clinton huddled with her longtime confidant Harold Ickes, the thin-haired deputy chief of staff to her husband, to plot her course. If the Clintons were a business enterprise, this would be Hillary's chance to launch a brand of her own.

The First Lady and Ickes met in the residence at the White House, where Ickes sold her on a New York run, a state where she had never actually lived, but which offered lots of promise.

The Clintons' private residence was decorated with personal touches. Framed pictures of the Clintons lying together in a hammock, or enjoying a lunch with Chelsea. Board games, such as Boggle, and a deck of cards. And there were other touches that seemed a bit tackier: Russian nesting dolls that featured the Clintons, a Beanie Baby collection on display. In one of the Clintons' bedrooms was an embroidered pillow that quoted Albert Einstein: "Great spirits have always encountered violent opposition from mediocre minds." (Bill and Hillary, according to at least one biographer, hadn't shared the same bedroom in seven years.)[2]

White House servants occasionally loitered in and out. The majority of them never much cared for the Clintons, whose haphazard and chaotic scheduling often left the official White House staff scrambling to attend to their whims. The Clintons stood in sharp contrast to their beloved predecessors, the Bushes, who had long experience in dealing with servants.

Seated together, Ickes explained to Hillary the intricacies of what would soon become her "home state"—its politics, its divisions and unions, and her (likely) opponent, New York City mayor Rudy Giuliani. It was all foreign to her—but native to Ickes. They talked much of the morning and when they moved into the private dining room for lunch, they were briefly joined by Bill Clinton, who was wearing a sweat suit and trying out lines that he'd be using in a couple of hours when he would address the nation after his all-but-certain acquittal in the Senate's impeachment vote. "Hillary rolled her eyes and indulged him briefly before turning the conversation back to upstate electoral tallies," biographer Sally Bedell Smith details.[3]

"I remember that moment when the Senate was voting on whether to impeach Clinton, her husband, and she was sitting up in the East Wing with Harold Ickes, plotting out her Senate strategy, and somebody came in and said the motion to convict was defeated, and she just sort of said, 'Thanks,' and kept moving with her own plans," a close observer of the Clintons tells me as she thinks back to this moment.

Ickes, who had led the Bill Clinton presidential campaign effort in New York in 1992, was determined to be by her side for this effort. ("A longtime friend and confidant of Clinton's, Ickes has been surrounded by scandal, misconduct, abuse of office and questions of virtue," the Republican National Committee had claimed in a briefing book designed to portray President Clinton as "Shameless.")

It was Ickes who told her that the Monica scandal was playing well for her, though that was already obvious. As pollster John Zogby said at the time, her rebound in public approval was "a sign of the public's support for her handling of the Lewinsky issue." Americans, particularly women, felt sorry for her. She had become the world's most famous jilted wife and she would work it for all that it was worth. The one true thing that even her enemies granted Hillary Clinton was that she was the loyal, aggrieved spouse blindsided by her husband's adultery.

Contrary to the popular notion that she never had political aspirations of her own—"I don't think she even fantasized about that for herself," says law school friend Michael Medved, now a conservative radio host, in an interview for this book—Hillary's own ambitions were never far from her mind. In 1988, when Bill first considered a run for the presidency, he and Hillary had also considered the idea that she replace him as governor of Arkansas. By the time of his first inaugural four years later, the White House clearly was in her sights. This was part of the understanding she always had with Bill Clinton. He'd get his turn. She'd put up with his crap. And then she'd get her chance. And he'd do what he could to help her. Clinton aides told me they were astonished after Bill's taking office, at a time when Mrs. Clinton was viewed by a significant segment of the country as a shrill, polarizing radical, that this idea was such an active notion in the administration.

"Hillaryland was always, always, always a force," a senior Clinton aide recalls in a wide-ranging interview for this book. He worked within steps of the Oval Office during the administration and, like pretty much everyone else who hopes to have a career in Democratic politics, will speak only without attribution. "If you fucked up and were found out by [Bill] Clinton, you got a promotion. If you fucked up and were found out by Hillary, your throat was slit and you were left on the tarmac with no ticket home. It was brutal."

In those early days, Clinton critics were demanding the release of Hillary Clinton's records from her days as a partner at the Rose Law Firm in Little Rock as part of the investigation of a now largely forgotten early scandal known as Whitewater. Mrs. Clinton was reluctant to release documents or to comply with the requests of the special prosecutor in the case.

One aide approached the First Lady's press secretary, Lisa Caputo, then in her midtwenties. "Why doesn't she just come fucking forward and release them? The president had no business in the matter. It won't hurt him."

"We can't," Caputo replied. "Hillary's got her own ambitions."

"What do you mean?" he asked. "It doesn't get better than First Lady."

"Well, there's '04. Or '08."

It's always been known that Mrs. Clinton had political ambitions, but never before had an aide confirmed with such assurance that she was envisioning the presidency for herself, even as her husband was just settling in. Hillary Clinton wanted the keys to the White House herself and, as a former aide put it in an exclusive interview for this book, conjuring images of the popular movie *The Shawshank Redemption*, "She was willing to slog through all of [his] shit" to get there.

Hillary has been "the one to always play a long game, and she started playing that long game at the end of the second term, and I think she thought the Senate would lead directly to her own presidency in 2008," another close observer of the Clintons tells me, again insisting on anonymity.

As her husband's second term came to a close, the question was: Where to start? She was born in Illinois, went to college in Massachusetts, law school in Connecticut, had brief stints in California and Washington, D.C., and had moved to Arkansas to be with her future husband, Bill Clinton. Now she was back in Washington, D.C.—the nation's capital, living in the White House. Along the way Hillary had picked up friends and networks across the country and even a pronounced southern accent that she mysteriously lost shortly after she arrived in Washington in 1993. In other words, she had no strong roots anywhere—which, she believed, gave her license to represent people as an elected official from . . . just about anywhere.

When Hillary and Harold Ickes first strategized about her Senate run, both knew at least in the back of their minds that she couldn't win the election simply by being the shattered wife. As the *New York Times Magazine* wrote, "[F]or four hours, as she and Ickes—a scarred veteran of New York politics and a former aide to her husband—moved from the living room to lunch in the family dining room and back to the living room, she plumbed the risks of a race for the Senate seat that Daniel Patrick Moynihan had decided to vacate. Would she really want to be one of a hundred senators? Could she survive a street fight with a nasty opponent? Could she stand the pawing of New York City's feral reporters?" How did she counter the sentiment, as one reporter covering the campaign summarized it to me years later, that her candidacy was "naked in its political ambition—the fact it came after Lewinsky." That, in other words, she was in fact using Bill's humiliation as justification for being in the Senate.

As Ickes and Hillary conspired, one thought kept coming back to them. The "bottom line" of the First Lady's run for Senate, as first reported in the book *Hillary's Choice*, was "for redemption."[4] From what? Take the scandals: There was Whitewater, the investment deal in which they lost a fair bit of money—and probably should've lost more had it not been for their good friends James and Susan McDougal. The documents surrounding this mysterious deal—and Hillary's insistence on fighting to keep them sealed—led to the appointment of Special Prosecutor Ken Starr in the first place, whose portfolio would grow and grow—and finally led to embarrassing allegations of her husband's sexual misconduct toward an Arkansas state employee, Paula Jones, which then led to revelations about an alleged cover-up of the president's affair with Monica Lewinsky.

While the president remained politically popular due to a robust economy, on a personal level the Clinton brand was increasingly viewed by the public as unethical, immoral, and just plain icky. A Senate election would erase all that—it would not only salvage the Clinton brand, but give Hillary a chance to be the kind of leader she was destined to be. No longer would she have to suffer in comparison to Bill, or deal with his crap. This would be her achievement and her chance to show the world what she could do. On her own. And so Hillary did what she always did. She went to work.

One way she decided to counter the expected criticism of her bid was to play the reluctant candidate for as long as possible—a stance she will likely echo in her 2016 presidential run. One story leaked out that it was a veteran New Yorker, the outspoken African American congressman Charlie Rangel, who in October 1998 first mischievously suggested to Hillary that she run for a Senate seat. Hillary, according to the reports, laughed the idea off. But, as I've learned in my reporting, there's more to the story. Hillary in fact had been looking at the race ever since she'd heard rumors of Moynihan's retirement. Long before that chance conversation with Rangel, she had spent more time than was necessary that year campaigning throughout New York State in the 1998 midterm elections, getting to meet the major party figures and donors.

One member of Clinton's senior administration happened to cross paths with the First Lady during a retreat at Camp David and shared his encounter with me. As he recalled it, the First Lady, still playing Hamlet in the New York media, pulled the official aside.

"What do you think?" she asked. "Should I run for the Senate?"

"No," he replied. "I think you should be a college president, head of a foundation. I think you'll have more of a platform."

The First Lady looked stricken, and quickly turned away.

"She was pissed at me for that advice," says the former high-level official, who believes Hillary holds his honest advice against him to this day. She didn't want his opinion, he says, unless it was to tell her what a great senator she would be.

Further assisting the "reluctant candidate" narrative, reporters from the *New York Times* wrote any number of stories about state Democrats who were "begging her to run."[5] That too was an exaggeration. New York Democrats in fact already had a suitable candidate for the job, a woman who'd been waiting her turn—Representative Nita Lowey of Westchester County.

Among the real power players in New York politics there was a noted lack of enthusiasm for a Hillary bid—particularly among Senators Chuck Schumer and Daniel Patrick Moynihan, the man Hillary would replace. Moynihan was an intellectual giant in the United States Senate, a former aide to Kennedy, LBJ, and Nixon who was respected on both sides of the aisle. From the outset, the wry, bespectacled legislator seemed reserved, at best, about the idea that Hillary Clinton might replace him. "He had not much use for the Clintons," one reporter who covered that race tells me bluntly.

Although they have since mended fences, at least superficially, Schumer secretly opposed Hillary's political career from its start, as she eyed a bid for a New York U.S. Senate seat in 2000. Like most every other political observer, Schumer was initially shocked by the audacity of a first lady from Arkansas, who was born in Illinois, deciding she was entitled to a seat held by such a heavyweight as the retiring Democrat Moynihan. And in Schumer's state, too. Where she'd never lived.

"Schumer is a man of great ambitions," a Senate colleague tells me with obvious understatement. "I'm sure that living in the shadow of Hillary Clinton wasn't the most pleasant position for him."

Michael Medved recalls a dinner between the then-senators where he observed the interaction between Schumer and Clinton. "I will tell you what was evident was a lot of eye rolling," he said, on both of their parts.

With Moynihan's retirement, Schumer was to become the state's senior senator. That title—which means something, at least, within the clubby otherworldliness of the U.S. Senate—would be severely undercut if his junior colleague were Hillary Clinton. She would outshine him and outdo him. She was a celebrity, after all, who wouldn't need Schumer's help to shine—and wouldn't need him to be her lodestar in the U.S. Senate. She would steal New York newspaper headlines without even trying. She'd only have to show up. Schumer at best would be her understudy. Chuck Schumer, man of destiny, didn't care for that one bit. And like many other Democrats, he wondered if the country really owed her a Senate seat from a state she never lived in simply because her husband couldn't keep his pants on in the Oval Office.

As for the carpetbagger charge, Hillary was convinced she could overcome it through sheer endurance and persistence, long underappreciated qualities that are the Clintons' hallmarks. The state was too perfect a choice for Hillary to do otherwise.

In an expansive interview for this book, Mrs. Clinton's eventual opponent, Republican congressman Rick Lazio, summed up the advantages the state offered her: "A solidly Democratic state, big union organizations, big cities with machine politics where you could turn out the vote, and the biggest media stage maybe in the world.

"It was a pretty compelling case that they come to New York," Lazio recalls, "although she had absolutely no attachment to New York before that. She had never lived there, she had never worked there, she never paid taxes there. But New York is a very forgiving place. I think Hillary and their team knew that they would be able to get over on that hurdle, although there might be some resistance to that."

There was also a greater attraction for the overly ambitious Hillary: Assuming she became a senator from New York she'd be connected to arguably the richest and most powerful Democratic base in the country (with the possible exception of California). Which is to say, in order to win, she'd have to raise money, which she would do from New Yorkers. These rich and powerful New Yorkers would form an ideal financial base for a presidential run.

The final rationale for her campaign—and its secret driving force—was largely mystical. Harold Ickes was a junior. His father, Harold Ickes Sr., was a cabinet officer for Franklin Delano Roosevelt and, far more important, an advisor to Hillary's idol, Eleanor. It was the senior Ickes who'd urged Mrs. Roosevelt to seek a Senate seat in New York, an idea she'd considered and then dismissed. As other biographers have noted, Hillary could not resist the parallel, except in this story she'd fulfill the mission meant for Eleanor. The Hillary-Eleanor comparison was so strong in the First Lady's mind that some Clinton aides told me they referenced Eleanor's example to get Hillary to do what they wanted. Clinton, for example, once decided to write a column, titled "Talking It Over," thereby, as she put it, "following once again the footsteps of Eleanor Roosevelt."[6]

Because of the Eleanor connection, the Senate run appeared to be destined. But not to every keeper of the Roosevelt flame. After Hillary visited Eleanor's childhood home, Val-Kill, in Hyde Park, New York, and another round of Hillary-Eleanor stories appeared in the press, one veteran Democrat had had enough. "Her trying to coyly cuddle up to Eleanor Roosevelt is obscene," said Richard Wade, who ran Robert F. Kennedy's 1964 Senate race. "It's like comparing a thoroughbred race horse and an ordinary jackass."[7]

It was perhaps a cruel irony that Monica Lewinsky was one of the best things that ever happened to Hillary Clinton. Until the revelation that her husband had been carousing with a twenty-two-year-old woman, just a few yards from their bedroom in the White House, the growing caricature of the First Lady was that of a congenital liar.

It didn't help that, in the words of the well-respected independent counsel Robert W. Ray, Hillary made "factually inaccurate" statements to the investigators about her involvement in the controversial Arkansas land deal known as Whitewater. The *New York Times* columnist William Safire, in a January 1996 op-ed titled "Blizzard of Lies," cited a series of instances of dishonesty and alleged obstruction of justice on the part of the First Lady. "Americans of all political persuasions are coming to the sad realization that our First Lady—a woman of undoubted talents who was a role model for many in her generation—is a congenital liar," he wrote.[8] The writer Christopher Hitchens, no right-wing partisan, would title a book on the Clintons *No One Left to Lie To.*

That image was fading now—at least a bit—after Monica. The First Lady was receiving sympathetic looks from reporters who'd come to challenge her every assertion, and friendly receptions from people who used to hate her. Everything she said had a renewed power just because she was saying it. Just because she was still standing. She took a joy in it. Her close friend Diane Blair, who died in 2000, revealed in a collection of papers that the First Lady was almost taking joy in the predicament. "[Hillary] sounded very up, almost jolly," wrote Blair. "Told me how she and Bill and Chelsea had been to church, to a Chinese restaurant, to a Shakespeare play, greeted everywhere with wild applause and cheers— this, she said is what drives their adversaries totally nuts, that they don't bend, do not appear to be suffering."[9]

At the same time, she milked the victim role. At an appearance before six hundred New Yorkers at Buffalo State College, when she was still an unannounced Senate candidate, she took questions for an hour from her largely female fan base. She couldn't resist engaging in quint-essential Clinton pandering, at one point mentioning, "You know, ever since I first came to Buffalo when I was a young girl . . ."[10]

Clutching a microphone, she delved into a wide range of policy issues. At one point, she touched awkwardly on the subject of divorce. "I know that there are problems," she said. "I mean, marriage is hard. It is hard work, and I'd be the first to tell ya." She smiled and the au-dience rewarded her with sympathetic cheers. When they were again silent, she added one more killer line. "When you have a child," she said, "you have a special obligation." The crowd responded with tears and more applause for the woman wronged. The wounded mother who persevered and held her family together. But despite the many carefully dropped hints, public and private, that she might be contemplating divorce, that was never really on the table. All throughout the Lewinsky ordeal, Hillary was far more concerned about her own career than her marriage.

In the late summer of 1998, as he prepared to confess his affair with Monica Lewinsky in a live address to the nation, Bill Clinton was out of his element. Strikingly so. As eyewitnesses recalled the scene for me, the president's complexion was gray, his speech unusually slow, his demeanor almost disoriented. He was "practically carried into the room" by longtime Arkansas friends and Hollywood producers Harry and Linda Bloodworth-Thomason, one observer recalls. Absent from Bill Clinton's moment of ultimate humiliation was his wife, his daughter, and even his press secretary, Mike McCurry, who, according to a reporter he spoke to, was so disgusted with his boss's behavior that he could barely look at him. In an email, McCurry claimed to me that he was present, but admits to having been "frustrated" with the president. "I was not central to deciding what he should say because that was not my role," McCurry disclosed, a somewhat bizarre statement for a president's communication director. "But some part of me said, 'You got to handle this on your own, big guy, because it is about you and not about the White House, the presidency, or our country.'"

Propping up the president by holding his arms, the Thomasons bucked up their fellow Arkansan much as a manager would a wounded prize fighter. "You can do this," they reassured the gray and sedate president. "You can do it."

And so Bill Clinton finally did what he almost never had to do in his life: admit he had lied repeatedly and been caught red-handed. For months the president had blamed everyone and everything for the Lewinsky affair. The Republicans had been mean to him. His mother died. Vince Foster died. Yitzhak Rabin had been assassinated. Newt Gingrich and the GOP's "Contract with America" had defamed him. The "mean-spirited" investigations of his own conduct and of Hillary's. And, as his staff did, he tried to frame Lewinsky as the problem—the unstoppable predator who pulled a reluctant president into a tawdry affair. He felt sorry for himself, and as such could sometimes be a pathetic sight. "I just cracked," he told friends. "I just cracked."

After the speech, the first family headed to Martha's Vineyard for a family vacation and what appeared to be a very public flogging of the president by a furious wife and daughter. News cameras showed the president walking with only his dog, Buddy, at his side, while Hillary and Chelsea visibly shunned him. Aides let it be known that Mrs. Clinton and her family were doing their best to start "healing" over the revelations—with the not-so-subtle implication that if they could deal with this, then so could the country.[11] Among the leaders of the "let's move on" caucus were feminists, who all but ignored the president's workplace seduction of a woman barely out of her teens. They applauded their icon Hillary Clinton for standing by her man.[12]

At the time, there were endless stories about the fate of the Clintons' marriage, many seeming to originate from sources close to the First Couple. Bill was left to sleep on the couch. His family wouldn't talk to him. Bill spent hours talking to his dog as if he were a real person. At his 1999 State of the Union address, the president offered a long tribute to his wife and her good works. As he looked up at her in the visitors' balcony of the House chamber, and on camera, he mouthed the words "I love you" to Hillary. She sat impassive.

This of course was the official story—shame, then forgiveness, then eventual redemption. It's what the country was meant to see. But others in the Clinton orbit tend toward the cynical. Most of the drama between the two was for public consumption. It wasn't really what was going on behind closed doors.

"They understand that politics is all about narrative," a senior Clinton aide tells me. It was Bill Clinton who orchestrated his own public whipping, "the chief scriptwriter," as the aide describes him. Recalling the scene with Clinton alone with Buddy, an aide laughs. "He had to go to the doghouse—literally," he says, smiling at the mastery. "That wasn't spontaneous!" To one friend of Hillary's, the only believable aspect of

the Bill Clinton pity party involved his dog. "The most emotional relationship in Bill's life was Buddy the dog," he says without a hint of a grin.

Though it was to her advantage to stick with Bill, Hillary would've
done it in any case and for a larger rationale. It was the same reason that
led her to give up a high-powered law career in New York or Chicago
more than two and a half decades earlier to toil in remote Little Rock and
gamely fake a southern accent in the backward towns of the Ozarks to
appeal to the Bubba vote. She was still, even then, deeply in love with her
husband. Hillary felt the same thrill as when she first came across him as
a student at Yale Law School, where she overheard a bearded, unkempt
young man bragging about the watermelons in Arkansas as "the biggest . . . in the world."

"Who is that?" she asked a friend.

"That's Bill Clinton. He's from Arkansas and that's all he ever talks
about."[13]

"He's really a difficult person, you know, and certainly difficult
when you're going to be a woman who is totally focused on him," says
Michael Medved, the conservative radio show host, who back then was
an unapologetic liberal and a friend of Hillary's in law school. He was
among a number who begged Hillary not to date the guy, whom they
saw as a brilliant but self-important ass. "She had the world's most enormous crush on him," Medved says. "You couldn't say anything against
him. Bill is without any question the love of her life. Attraction is mysterious."

Years of his adultery did tend to make Mrs. Clinton a little less goo-
goo eyed about her husband, however, and she was anything but a wild-
eyed romantic. Diane Blair was Hillary Clinton's best friend, going back
to the 1970s. (Blair died in 2000 of lung cancer at the age of sixty-one.)
A friend of Blair's recalled for me a story in the 1990s in which Mrs.
Clinton became almost obsessed with the book *The Bridges of Madison
County.* The book, by Robert James Waller, was a nationwide bestseller
and would later become a film starring Meryl Streep. The First Lady's
interest in the book seemed unusual, but she kept prodding Blair to read

it. Finally, Blair agreed while staying overnight at the White House. At two or three in the morning, according to this friend's account, the First Lady burst into Blair's bedroom.

"Did you finish it yet?" she asked.

"Yes," Blair replied.

"Well, what did you think?"

Blair didn't want to disappoint the First Lady, but responded truthfully that she didn't really think the book was that well written.

Hearing the news, Hillary grinned, satisfied. "I *knew* it was a piece of shit," she said.

Though long aware of Bill's limitations in the husband department, the First Lady seemed to have made a sort of peace with them, through willful ignorance. "[T]he Clintons must carry many scars between them, but we found the marriage anything but loveless," recalls Clinton biographer Taylor Branch, who recounted a conversation with longtime Clinton associate Strobe Talbott. "Their private partnership still seemed warm and eager, never cold, with a spark from somewhere if not libido. This struck Strobe and me as an abiding mystery."[14]

In what should have, but didn't, shock her feminist supporters, Hillary shared her husband's tendency toward blame shifting and justification for his sexual misconduct. After the Lewinsky disclosures, Hillary's close friend Blair recorded the First Lady as saying, "Ever since he took office they've been going through personal tragedy ([the death of] Vince [Foster], her dad, his mom) and immediately all the ugly forces started making up hateful things about them, pounding on them."[15] The First Lady also indicated to Blair that her husband's unhappy, fatherless childhood played a role. She insisted on the creation of an "enemies list" of all those out to get her husband.

Hillary in short was still trying to protect him, and take control of his life, whether he liked it or not. A senior aide offers perhaps a fitting metaphor for the relationship. During the White House years, at a public event, Hillary would often depart ahead of her husband, waiting for him in their motorcade. After several minutes passed, the First Lady would send someone back into the event to urge her husband to get moving. The president, in response, would stay an extra fifteen minutes longer. The aide's point: She was seeking to control him and he wouldn't let her, which would make her want him even more. "That's really the crux of the relationship," the aide tells me. "She was basically the one always in the car trying to get him to come to her. He won't until he decides it's time." How Bill handles Hillary, as the aide described it, is "sick but brilliant."

After Monica, according to a multitude of aides and observers, that dynamic changed. Hillary was no longer the one in constant pursuit of Bill's love and attention. He now needed her in a way he never did before. She and she alone would determine the fate of his presidency. Though determined to save his political fortunes as well as her own, Hillary finally saw her husband for the lout he really was. The scandal liberated Hillary to pursue her own career and her own future. And it put Bill in her eternal debt. As Gail Sheehy, a sympathetic biographer of Mrs. Clinton, once put it, the decision to stay with Bill was "easy." Perhaps unintentionally evoking references to a business partnership, Sheehy noted, citing a source, simply that Hillary "had an investment in this marriage and his career."[16]

Nonetheless Hillary was "legitimately pissed," a senior Clinton aide says, about Monica. But not for the reasons one might expect. "It wasn't that he was fucking someone else. It was that he got caught and so rubbed her nose in it. And she had to appear pissed in public in order to save herself." That was Bill's (all but) unforgivable sin.

One source widely known to be very close to Bill Clinton said the former president "is paying the price for the rest of his life." Hillary, like the classic "scorned woman," is, according to the source, "still sort of pissed off all of the time." Whether explicit or understood, the First Couple had a new deal, a new spin on their partnership, from then on out. A close friend of the Clintons told biographer Jerry Oppenheimer her attitude when announcing her plans to her husband: "It's my turn, my day in the sun. You better support me, or else. And by the way, go fuck yourself."[17] (The psychological effect on the daughter who worshipped them both could also prove long-lasting and consequential.)

The stop in Buffalo, where Hillary waxed poetic about the difficulties of marriage, was before the kickoff of a "listening tour" of the state, a savvy ploy to show New Yorkers, especially the often forgotten upstaters, that she was intent on hearing their concerns and that she would be a good proxy in Washington.

Republicans tried to block her run, introducing legislation in the state to prevent her from "carpetbagging." The law, which was sponsored by Republican assemblywoman Nancy Calhoun, would've required Hillary to have lived in the state for five years before being able to represent it. "I thought carpetbagging went out in the 1860s," Calhoun told the *New York Post*. "We have lots of talent in both parties within this state, and certainly our next senator should come from New York."[18]

"The word 'carpetbagger' has crept into Mr. Giuliani's speeches as he and Mrs. Clinton crisscross the state, each exploring a run for the same United States Senate seat next year," the *New York Times* noted.[19]

But the paper and other Democrats would do their part to mold Mrs. Clinton as the second coming of Robert F. Kennedy, welcoming the celebrity politician as a token of the greatness of New York.

Yet, despite the sympathy Mrs. Clinton was engendering, the Kennedy example proved an apt one for her. Just not in the way she had been expecting. As the *New York Times* noted in a piece in 2000, "For Robert Kennedy in 1964, and for Mrs. Clinton today, the label 'carpetbagger' was really shorthand for a general condemnation, expressed in startlingly similar terms: they were, according to their critics, ambitious, opportunistic, ruthless (for Kennedy) and untrustworthy (for Mrs. Clinton)."[20]

Robert Kennedy Jr. reflected to reporters that year on "The intensity of feeling with my father's race, and the almost inexplicable intensity of feeling toward Hillary Clinton. People who ought to like Hillary Clinton, but don't, and can't really explain why, but just kind of have a visceral reaction to her—that's the same kind of thing that I remember from my father."[21]

For the first time in her life Hillary needed to campaign for herself, and the dirty secret was that she wasn't good at it, especially when compared to her husband.

"I've seen her and him in rooms, and she doesn't have the whirr," veteran Democratic campaign consultant Bob Shrum tells me in an interview. "Your eyes aren't constantly drawn to her the way they are to him."

Similarly, a former Clinton aide compared Hillary to Al Gore, a policy wonk who could be famously stiff and awkward in public settings and whose campaign style Clinton once compared to Mussolini. "Gore hated Clinton because Clinton was everything that Gore wasn't," he told me. At the funeral for Democratic operative Bob Squier, a close Gore friend, the vice president watched with envy and resentment as Clinton, who didn't know Squier as well, delivered the moving, crowd-pleasing eulogy that Gore knew he could never have managed.

"It's the same thing with Hillary," said the aide. "She knows that she's probably better than him on the intellectual stuff—though not a lot—but he blows her away on the retail."

A former presidential press aide similarly noted the contrast between the nimble Bill and the more programmed Hillary. "He was constantly improvising speeches right up to the very last second even in the middle of the speech," he recalled during our interview. "There's nothing like sitting next to him watching him give a speech, and watching a new speechwriter who's written this thing just flip through the pages and try to find where he's talking about. She's written speeches in advance, pretty much has it committed to memory, and wouldn't improvise a word, frankly much more like Bush or Obama."

From the start, she faced stumbles. For one, there was the purchase of her house. New York, as one journalist put it at the time, "had a residency 'requirement' so lax that it was more of a suggestion."[22] So it was relatively easy for the First Family to find digs that allowed her to comply with state law in a timely fashion.

They settled on Chappaqua, with a population of less than ten thousand, just north of New York City in Westchester County. The house was listed at $1.7 million in 1999. The trouble was the Clintons were broke—owing a fortune in legal fees from the many investigations into their personal lives. Terry McAuliffe, a longtime friend known for allegations of questionable business and legal dealings, offered to front them the bulk of the money, $1.3 million. The loan raised questions as to whether the Clintons were evading campaign and gift laws and made for an unneeded reminder of what the *New York Times* in an editorial labeled the "ethical sloppiness of the Clinton White House."[23] The Clintons eventually opted for a conventional mortgage.

For the first time in decades the Clintons were not living in public housing, but their personal taste had not seemed to mature with the times. A former White House press aide remembers the house search with a mix of humor and horror.

"We went to look at these houses, and the houses that they liked had shag rugs and gold walls," the aide tells me. Everything Bill and Hillary favored seemed like it had come from the 1970s, the last time they were ordinary citizens. "It was horrible and I just remember being with the press pool and thinking, 'Oh God. Do not say out loud how much you like this house,'" the aide says. "I think it just says a lot. Can you imagine living in this bubble for so long and then all of a sudden being let out of it?"

Further troubles came when the First Lady got quickly out of sorts with Jewish voters by sitting and smiling through an anti-Israel diatribe by the wife of Yasser Arafat, Suha Arafat, whom Hillary kissed at the event's close. She also clumsily announced that "I've always been a Yankees fan"—which no one believed of a girl from Chicago, who actually grew up rooting for the Cubs.

Bill Clinton, of course, was an enthusiastic booster of Hillary's fortunes. In part, this was because he always saw her in public office. It could also have helped alleviate some of his guilt over Monica. Or perhaps it was because he didn't have any choice. On the day of her Senate campaign announcement, the president did something unusual, if not unprecedented. He sat onstage for forty minutes and never said a word.

Ever the political analyst, the president was all but chomping at the bit for Hillary to face off against Rudy Giuliani. When Lazio signaled early on that in deference to Giuliani he wasn't going to join the race, Clinton pulled him aside during an encounter in the Oval Office.

As Lazio recalls in our interview, the president engaged in his usual practice with potential adversaries—flattery. Clinton's ability for "charm offensives" has long been considered a strategic asset to the Clinton brand.

"You know what the very best day in Hillary's campaign has been?" Lazio recalls Clinton asking him. "The day you decided to pull out of the race."

Clearly studying polls of the race, the president assessed Giuliani as polarizing and unlikable. (This was the pre-9/11 Rudy, who as mayor could be an abrasive combatant with his many enemies in the city.) "Giuliani is an easy person to run against," Clinton told Lazio. "He's got a lot of negatives." Lazio, by contrast, was forty-two years old, an attractive and likable Roman Catholic who had built a reputation in Washington as a moderate who won elections by wide margins in his Long Island district.

Lazio thinks back on that encounter and concedes, "Maybe he was just being Clinton and just being charming. I don't know. Maybe that, in fact, was the way they were thinking. The moderate who was well liked and wasn't easy to shoot at, there wasn't much negative that they could say about me. Of course they did end up trying to morph me into Newt Gingrich, relying on media ads and thinking people don't know that much. Actually, I thought the ads were very cynical but very effective."

Indeed, once Giuliani dropped out of the Senate race and Lazio announced a Senate bid, the Clinton team went after him with ruthlessness and relish. "They were the first to go negative and went negative hard," Lazio recalls, and the president was quick to use his position to help Mrs. Clinton make her moves. President Clinton held up legislation until after the election and made the White House photography office an arm of the Hillary Senate campaign.

"I had gone over to Israel as part of a congressional delegation—two House members, two Senate members, and the president, and Hillary. One of the lunches that we were at was with Yasser Arafat and the Palestinian Authority," Lazio recalls. Hillary "at the time was totally effusive with Arafat and his wife, [but] an official White House photographer had gotten a picture of, on the reception line, of me shaking the hand of Yasser Arafat and smiling. Her campaign got that, got access to that, and used that . . . certainly the media never called her out on that."

To the contrary, the media, in Lazio's retelling, played right along, making it an issue that Lazio had been photographed with a top terrorist and enemy of the Jewish state. In all, it was an "absolutely ruthless campaign operation," remembers Lazio.

Leading the charge for Hillary was her communications director, Howard Wolfson. Many Democrats have questioned his loyalty to their president, their party, and their principles—Wolfson would later go on to serve as chief spokesman for Republican-turned-independent New York City mayor Michael Bloomberg—but no one on either side of the aisle has ever questioned his loyalty to Hillary Clinton. An intense, neurotic, and foul-mouthed workaholic, Wolfson was a natural commander of the rapid-response Clinton campaign operation. His cutthroat operatives ran opposition research, fought back against criticisms, and tracked almost every word written or spoken about the campaign, searching for opportunities to exploit. Wolfson was the living, breathing embodiment of the *Untouchables*-inspired line he told his team: "If he uses a fist, you use a bat. If he uses a knife, you use a gun."[24]

Wolfson is loud and aggressive at work, but can be quiet and extremely shy in social settings. He's part of the establishment, but loves indie rock (and writes about it frequently). He's polished and professional in his rhetoric, but Spartan in his dress and personal tastes. Throughout the 2000 Senate campaign, Wolfson's living room had a single piece of furniture (a couch); his bedroom had only a bed; and his television sat on the cardboard box it came in. When Clinton's Secret Service detail gave him identification pins, the agent said, "I'm giving you two—one for each of your suits."[25]

The ferocity of the attack on Lazio was necessary. Hillary Clinton was not going over as well with New Yorkers as she had hoped. In an eerie precursor of her 2008 primary campaign, she was statistically tied in the polls with a legislator who was relatively unknown outside his congressional district.

Hillary Clinton might well have lost that Senate race—and dashed her presidential hopes—had she not gotten a bit of good luck and an assist from the media. A turning point came during a highly anticipated television debate with moderator Tim Russert, the respected NBC News bureau chief, former Moynihan aide, and host of *Meet the Press*.

During Clinton's debate preparations, her dear friend Bob Barnett, the Washington lawyer and book agent, portrayed Lazio. But nothing in those practice sessions had prepared Hillary for the shock of being onstage with a baby-faced, little-known congressman who considered himself her equal. "She had a completely offended look on her face," recalls Lazio. "I didn't believe it because of my particular point of view. I think it was the mere idea that it was the first time anybody had really publicly challenged her."

Russert, too, turned out to be an aggressive questioner of Clinton, which the Democrat did not appreciate.

"Hillary appeared offended at times that she was being challenged," says her opponent. "When I pressed her and challenged her on different things, different policy issues, she looked at me like how dare you even question me on these things."

It was in that debate, where Hillary, wearing a classic teal pantsuit, met the telegenic Lazio, who was amped up for a fight. She had never herself debated in an election setting. And here she was, being challenged on taking allegedly dirty campaign money and being asked to sign a pledge not to take so-called soft money.

Looking for a dramatic flourish, Lazio reached into a breast pocket inside his suit jacket and pulled out a pledge against soft money in the race. "Well, why don't you just sign it?" Lazio said, challenging Hillary. She stammered.

"I'm not asking you to admire it; I'm asking you to sign it." Lazio could see he was successfully putting her in an uncomfortable position. And her next words would give him, he thought, an opening.

"Well, I would be happy to—when you give me the signed—"

The camera panned out from its close shot of Hillary and caught Lazio darting from his podium toward hers.

"Well, right here," he said, sticking out a bundle of papers. "Right here. Right here, sign it right now." He was physically putting the pledge on her podium—and in the process coming inches from her.

Hillary looked immediately flustered and turned to her opponent, who was at this point mere inches from her. "We'll shake on this," she said, sticking out her right hand.

"No, no," Lazio said, instinctively shaking her held-out hand, but then quickly pulling his hand away from hers. "I want your signature." He used his just-released hand to start pointing at the documents. "Because I think everybody wants to see you signing something you said you were for. I'm for it. I haven't done it. You've been violating it."

His finger was no longer pointing at the papers. It was pointing directly at her. "Why don't you do something important for America. While America is looking at New York, why don't you show some leadership because it goes to trust and character." Lazio turned his back toward her as he finally returned to his podium.

Lazio finished the debate thinking he had won. He went to the spin room to say so. Hillary was nowhere to be found. "It was very interesting. When that debate ended, Hillary stormed out of there. She did not take the traditional questions from the press afterwards in the spin room." It was, according to Lazio, a sign that Hillary, too, believed he had won this round.

But within hours, what Lazio thought was a victory quickly turned into a defeat. Hillary Clinton did what she would often do when it worked to her political advantage—she played the gender card. The Clinton campaign latched on to the moment Lazio stepped into Hillary's space as threatening, invasive, and sexist.

"They had gotten the clip out" in nearly no time, Lazio says, and were "suggesting it was misogynistic to challenge Hillary on the debate set." Lazio laments, "We completely got mauled in the media by the Clinton machine, who just drove this message relentlessly, again at a very supportive media."

It was Hillary's first debate—and a sign of what would come. It *was* possible to defy reality, the Hillary campaign learned. It was possible to take a debate loss and turn it into a win. It just took a *single* moment to seize and that could eclipse everything else. And it took some friends in the press to push that narrative. Which they did. Before long, polls put Hillary into the lead.

Once she got the hang of New York, she was a meticulous campaigner. One former Secret Service officer on her detail remembers driving her around and learning very quickly that Mrs. Clinton is a backseat driver. "She's a bit of a micromanager. She'd always kind of tell us . . . thought she knew New York really well and didn't know the streets, I think, as well as we did."

They were driving around New York in an armored brown van, "which we had called the mystery machine, the Scooby Doo van, which was an interesting thing to drive and learn to manipulate," the agent tells me in an interview. That's because Hillary and her staff objected to the customary limo the First Lady would normally use. They complained the "optics" weren't right for an aspiring senator who wanted to look like she was a woman of the people—and not a product of the White House.

Her celebrity helped her. Not many first-time candidates for Senate have their own military jet and Secret Service detail, an immediate attention grabber wherever she might go. Lazio contends that her presence alone—and one must credit her: she showed up in the smallest New York towns—helped turn what otherwise might be right-of-center voters toward her side. "When she pulls into town with this media entourage and with the Secret Service entourage and she's the sitting First Lady of the United States and she's coming to the Chamber of Commerce event with fifty people or one hundred people, the usual audience, they're star-struck," he says.

Hillary won the election handily. She'd get 55 percent of the vote, while Lazio got only 43 percent. She'd get the support of nearly 3.75 million voters, while Lazio would get close to a million votes fewer—2.9 million. Interestingly, at the end of the day, Hillary Clinton lagged behind Al Gore's margin of victory over George W. Bush in New York—a sign perhaps of timid but not overwhelming support in the heavily blue state.

"She grinds it out," Republican strategist Mike Murphy, who worked for Lazio during that election, recalls in an interview. "She was very tough and just relentless. She just keeps going. That's how they do it. That's what the old pros do who won and lost before. She's been through winning and losing in Arkansas with him and that's a useful skill to have, ring-wise. But there's no flash of inspiration or genius; she just ground it out and the Democrat won the Democratic state."

The victory thrilled some New York Democrats, but not all of them.

Her victory party that night at the Grand Hyatt Hotel on Forty-Second Street in Manhattan demonstrated the less than comfortable relationship she had with many Democrats, most of them weary of a decade of defending the Clintons and worried about what new trouble they'd find themselves in now.

Reporters present at the event recalled a rather perfunctory affair, though Moynihan, for one, seemed to acquit himself with grace of the chore of handing over his seat to a person he thought an unworthy carpet-bagger. As did other prominent Democrats who privately looked askance at the audacity of the run—the New York branch of the Kennedys among them. Officially, so did her would-be colleague, Chuck Schumer.

What has never been revealed, until now, is the subversive role the would-be senior senator from New York—Chuck Schumer—was play-ing from the outset of Hillary's pursuit of public office. The Clinton-

Schumer tension had been the subject of rumors and speculation for years. "Chuck Schumer hatched secret plan to get Obama to run," a *New York Post* headline blared in 2010.[26] A book at the time described the senator's efforts to "betray" his colleague by recruiting Obama for the White House. "Schumer and the others were concerned about Clinton's political vulnerabilities," the book argued, according to the *Post*.[27]

But what was not well known is that the tensions between the two went back even further than the 2008 race. Schumer had served with Lazio in the House of Representatives and, as members of the same state delegation, they knew each other well. Schumer took an unexpected interest in Lazio's Senate campaign from the outset, finding opportunities to chat with the Republican on shuttle flights to Washington or when they encountered each other on the grounds of the U.S. Capitol. Schumer would offer Lazio unsolicited advice.

"I thought he was generally . . . he was supportive," Lazio recalls. "Quite helpful to me behind the scenes and encouraging. I just would say that it was clear to me anyway that he would not have been disappointed if I had been elected."

Pressed as to whether Schumer actually devised lines of attack against Clinton, Lazio demurs. "I don't really want to get into that or answer that question," he says. "I think I would just say he was generally supportive and, in my informal discussions, encouraging."

The revelation of Schumer's role makes sense to longtime Democratic strategist Bob Shrum. "Look, if you were the other senator from New York and she was in the Senate, you just sort of have to resign yourself to the fact that, you know, you might be called the senior senator, but in a way you weren't," he says.

What is more puzzling is that Schumer's offensive against Clinton continued even after she was elected. He was known to leak damaging information about his Senate colleague to the Rupert Murdoch–owned *New York Post*. Most likely this was done as much to ingratiate himself to the influential tabloid as it was to undermine Hillary. But the continued Schumer-Clinton rivalry underscored an interesting aspect of Hillary

Clinton's Senate career—and potential second run for the White House. Like her husband in his postpresidential life, she tended to have more of a knack for building bridges with her enemies than she did with her friends.

Soon after Hillary Clinton beat Rick Lazio to win the Senate seat in 2000, Lazio remembers finding himself in the Oval Office with her husband, President Bill Clinton. The president was then a lame duck—he was finishing his tumultuous second term and getting ready to transition from being the commander in chief to life as a political spouse, now that his wife was going to be the junior senator from New York and he was going to be an officially unemployed husband in a foreign state.

The meeting wasn't awkward, though, as one might expect when the political loser comes face to face with the spouse of his opponent who just beat him. It was quite the opposite: friendly and fun. They were sharing jokes.

Lazio was there because the president, finally, was going to sign a couple of bills that he had held until after Lazio's election against his wife. Lazio thought the timing was suspicious. "They wanted to deny me that photo-op," Lazio remembers thinking, over a decade later in an interview, until after the election.

One of the bills he remembers being in there to speak about was regarding breast cancer treatment or perhaps it was the environmental bill they were to celebrate.

Either way, Lazio thinks, Clinton had performed his duty as husband—by denying Lazio the image of being the moderate Republican able to work with the Democratic president. And now that that duty had expired, Clinton was performing the next duty: signing the bills that Congress passed into law.

But then something dramatic happened to change the mood. "Unexpectedly she came in to the Oval Office," Lazio tells me with a little laugh. "He [Bill Clinton] froze like a deer in the headlights and backed away from me as if I was uranium."

Winning a Senate seat meant Hillary needed a place to live in Washington, since the Clintons would be moving out of the White House. She settled on a 5,152-square-foot brick structure on Whitehaven Street, just around the corner from the vice president's residence at the U.S. Naval Observatory in Northwest Washington, D.C. It was in this house that Hillary Clinton would later film her 2007 video announcing her bid for the 2008 Democratic nomination.

With three stories, attractive black shutters, four bedrooms, and seven bathrooms, the home cost the Clintons $2.85 million in 2001—considerably less than the asking price of $3.5 million. The District of Columbia now assesses its value at around $4.5 million, which puts the Clintons' annual property tax bill close to $40,000, about the same as the salary of the average American. (In 2012, the Clintons got slapped with a $1,883.75 penalty for paying taxes on the home late, according to real estate records, and had to pay an additional $445.04 in interest on the late payment.)

When the time came to renovate Hillary's new home, her interior decorator, Rosemarie Howe, expected the senator to be too busy to care about a lot of decorating details. Clinton wasn't. Referring to an interview with Howe, the *Washington Post* reported in 2007 that "the senator from New York has been very involved in updating the Whitehaven Street property, which they're swatching through room by room. Howe has finished the living room, dining room and kitchen, yet is always searching for special pieces and fabrics to update the look. Upstairs, she has redecorated the bedrooms, including Chelsea's digs when she's in town. Downstairs, she has added storage to the basement."[28]

Howe says Hillary "makes decisions quickly but does it with enjoyment"—perhaps because the decisions are far easier and much less important than the political, personal, and public-policy choices she would have to make in her eight years as senator.[29]

While Hillary was preparing to enter the Senate, Bill was closing out his time at the White House—and scandal continued to dog him and tarnish his wife's own efforts. At the center of the latest controversy was Clinton's never-ending quest for money and the potential compromises he was willing to make to get it.

Toward the end of the Clinton administration, the president sought to close out business and prepare for life beyond the walls of the White House. So did the many, many political appointees, from across government agencies, whose work would come to an end when George Walker Bush was sworn in and the Democrats handed over power to their Republican counterparts.

One of those bureaucrats seeking another line of work was Louis Freeh, the former director of the Federal Bureau of Investigation. Had it been up to Bill Clinton, Freeh would've been out of work years earlier. He was a constant thorn in the side of the president. It had been Freeh's job to keep appropriate distance from the person who was both effectively his boss and who was at the center of a series of investigations that were faithfully carried out by the FBI. And since he was investigating the president, it wasn't as though Clinton could fire Freeh; it in fact heightened his job security in a way not comparable to any other government bureaucrat.

As FBI director, Freeh had had the unprecedented task of taking a DNA sample from the president of the United States so that it could be compared to the DNA in the semen stain on Lewinsky's infamous blue Gap dress. The exchange took place in secret—the president was at an official event when he pretended to have official business in the other room and slipped out momentarily to provide his sample to awaiting FBI agents. That Bill Clinton suffered such an indignity in front of a man who despised him only furthered the level of enmity between the two.

Freeh was in office during a terrorist attack on the Khobar Towers in Saudi Arabia on June 25, 1996. The towers had been used as a housing installation for members of the U.S. armed forces. The blast killed nearly twenty members of the U.S. forces and injured close to five hundred. It was a massive explosion—a sign, especially in hindsight, of the threat terrorists posed to Americans and what would consume American foreign policy for the next decade and a half.

At a meeting with surviving spouses while investigating the disaster, Freeh was asked by a wife of a fallen airman "to promise me to my face, and use my name . . . that you will pursue this until you catch the people" responsible for the terrorism. Freeh promised the group that day that he would pursue justice. But, he explained, he would be facing difficulties: The suspects were being held by the Saudi government, and the Saudis were refusing to let U.S. investigators interview them directly. He needed the help of the president of the United States. He needed the commander in chief to intervene and impress upon the Saudis how important it was that these terrorists be brought in for killing Americans.

Determined to keep his promise to the grieving widow, Freeh later met with Prince Bandar, Saudi Arabia's then ambassador to the United States. In the 1990s, despite his nervous breakdown, Bandar was an institution in Washington—popular, powerful, and long serving.

"They had some suspects, but the FBI wasn't allowed to interrogate them directly, they had to submit the questions to the Saudi investigation unit or something like that. It was annoying and they needed permission from somebody high up in Saudi Arabia for the FBI to directly talk to these people or the suspects," says a source familiar with the situation. "It was important to Freeh that he get [Saudi crown prince Abdullah's] permission to allow the FBI to interrogate the suspects in the bombing."

Bandar told Freeh that the Saudis would give Americans access to the suspects "if Clinton will ask" the crown prince, who was scheduled to visit Washington soon. "I will warn the prince that Clinton is going to," Bandar said, "if you can set up Clinton." It was up to the heads of the two states to work it out in person.

After his conversation with Prince Bandar, Freeh asked Clinton to request access to the Khobar Towers suspects, and Clinton said he would.

Freeh had made the request to National Security Advisor Sandy Berger, who made assurances to Freeh that his request would be granted.

So after a meeting between Clinton and Abdullah, Freeh went over to Bandar's posh house in McLean, Virginia, to follow up on the conversation that was supposed to have taken place between Clinton and the Saudi crown prince. Freeh also wanted to thank the Saudi crown prince, through Bandar, for helping to make sure that the Arab nation would help the Americans in their terror investigation.

But "it didn't seem to work and he didn't know why," a source close to Freeh explains. The Saudis had decided not to let the Americans in. And Freeh couldn't understand why. He thought he had done everything by the book—and that he had covered his bases by setting up both sides, the Americans, through Clinton, and the Saudis, through their ambassador. The request at that point would only be a formality, one that he had been assured would be granted when Clinton asked.

Bandar thanked Freeh for coming by and after chatting for a bit, walked the soon-to-be-outgoing FBI director to the door and then to his awaiting mini-motorcade.

Bandar followed him out and stopped him on the steps.

"I have to be honest with you," Bandar confessed to Freeh. "Um, Clinton never mentioned it." He hadn't said a word about the Khobar Towers bombing.

A source says, "Clinton raised the subject only to tell the crown prince that he understood the Saudis' reluctance to cooperate, and then he hit Abdullah up for a contribution to the Clinton Presidential Library."

Ten years after the bombings, in 2006, Freeh would out President Clinton in a signed *Wall Street Journal* opinion article—an uncommon act of indiscretion for a former FBI director, but a man clearly outraged by the president's handling of the entire situation. Freeh wrote, "The 19 Americans murdered were members of the 4404th Wing, who were risking their lives to enforce the no-fly zone over southern Iraq. This was a U.N.-mandated mission after the 1991 Gulf War to stop Saddam Hussein from killing his Shiite people. The Khobar victims, along with the courageous families and friends who will mourn them this weekend in Washington, deserve our respect and honor. More importantly, they must be remembered, because American justice has still been denied."[30]

The subtext of the op-ed was clear. The Clinton administration had its chance to help. And they blew it. Why? Because Bill Clinton would rather have used his opportunity with the head of Saudi Arabia to help his own cause and not the cause of bringing to justice in America the Iranian terrorists being held by the Saudis in conjunction with the terror attack. (Clinton has denied Freeh's version of events.)

Well, the Saudis did give. Eight years later it would be revealed that they had given quite generously. "The royal family of Saudi Arabia gave the Clinton facility in Little Rock about $10 million," the *Washington Post* would report.[31] It went toward the building of the Clinton Presidential Library in Little Rock, Arkansas. "In addition, a handful of Middle Eastern business executives and officials also gave at least $1 million each, according to the interviews. They include Saudi businessmen Abdullah al-Dabbagh, Nasser al-Rashid and Walid Juffali, as well as Issam Fares, a U.S. citizen who previously served as deputy prime minister of Lebanon. Spokesmen for Kuwait and Taiwan confirmed that each government has given the library $1 million."[32]

Clinton saw the generosity from abroad as support for him personally. "As president, he was beloved around the world, so it should come as no surprise that there has been an outpouring of financial support from around the world to sustain his post-presidential work," a statement from the William J. Clinton Foundation would read, defending the foreign donations to the $165 million project.[33]

He was "beloved" then, too, by the family of Marc Rich, which gave him $450,000—before the president pardoned the criminal financier on his way out of office.

This isn't the only anecdote that shows the Clintons were interested in, even obsessed with, money.

The Clintons' hunt for money had led to other scandals. In the president's first term, for example, he accepted $450,000 in contributions to his legal defense fund that were solicited by Little Rock restaurateur Charlie Trie. Suspecting that the money was illegally coming from China, the Democratic National Committee hired a private investigator, Terry Lenzner, to determine the true source of the funds.

According to Lenzner, "red flags were obvious. For example, the money orders had different names on them, but the word 'presidential' was misspelled on all of them—in the exact same way and in the same handwriting." Lenzner discovered that, in an attempt to hide the true source of the funds, many sizable contributions had been made in the name of people who in reality were highly unlikely, and even unable, to contribute large amounts of money. Many made only between $20,000 and $30,000 a year.[34]

Lenzner recommended returning the contributions, and the DNC agreed. Bill Clinton, however, didn't. Only after the former attorney general and the Catholic priest who cochaired his legal defense fund threatened to resign did Clinton begrudgingly agree to give back the (probably illegal) contributions.

During his presidency, Clinton largely emerged from these scandals, perhaps because there were so many others. But his financial dealings would finally come to haunt him—in a big way—on his last day in office.

In an interview for this book, Ari Fleischer remembers the outgoing president's notorious difficulties with time management and basic courtesy. "On Inauguration Day 2001, President-elect Bush was at a ceremony at the small church across the street from the White House," Bush's incoming press secretary recalled. "It is a beautiful old yellow church, the other side of Lafayette Park. At any rate, he was scheduled to be there for the morning service, and then we were going to leave the church and go straight to the White House for the ceremonial coffee with the president and the vice president, and then the president, vice president, president-elect, and vice president–elect would travel in four motorcades up to Capitol Hill for the swearing in of the new president, President Bush. As we were leaving the church, our advance people came to us, kind of sheepishly, and said, 'You have to hold, Mr. President-elect.'"

Bush, who was both punctual and notoriously impatient, seemed surprised. "Why do we have to hold?" The party was told that Bill Clinton was running behind schedule. On inauguration morning, he just couldn't seem to leave the Oval Office he loved. One need not have been present that day to guess the new president's reaction as he sat and waited.

"What it turned out to be, later, as I was told, was he was busy signing the pardons that he had issued in his last hours of the presidency," Fleischer tells me. "That is just one anecdote about life with President Clinton."

Of particular note that day was Clinton's last-minute pardon of Marc Rich, a wealthy financier and oil trader whose customers, clients, and sellers included Fidel Castro, Muammar Qaddafi, and Ayatollah Khomeini. Rich was facing a possible 325 years in prison. He illegally traded with the ayatollah while Iran was holding American hostages, and he was later indicted in the biggest tax evasion case in history, owing $48 million to the U.S. government in back taxes. After he fled to Switzerland, Rich was put on the FBI's Ten Most Wanted list.

Rich was pardoned only after his ex-wife, Denise Rich, an attractive middle-aged Austrian with big blond-highlighted hair, donated $100,000 to Hillary Clinton's 2000 New York Senate campaign, $450,000 to the Clinton Library, and $1 million to the Democratic Party. Later, Ms. Rich would invoke the Fifth Amendment when called to testify before the House Government Oversight Committee on her role in the pardon scandal. The donations were likely a prominent reason that Bill decided to approve the pardons. But there was also pressure being applied by the Israelis (Rich had long been an intelligence source for Israel). Since Clinton was still reluctant to release convicted spy Jonathan Pollard, even under the threat of leaking the Lewinsky tapes, might Rich have been their consolation prize?

The fracas over the pardons made a lifelong enemy of Eric Holder. Before he assumed his eventual role as attorney general to Barack Obama, Judge Holder was no one's idea of an ideological lightning rod. In the 1980s he had been appointed to the Superior Court of the District of Columbia by President Ronald Reagan. A lifelong public servant,

Holder had worked his way up the Justice Department ladder, starting off as an assistant U.S. attorney, before becoming deputy to the powerful attorney general Janet Reno. (Former colleagues of Reno at the Justice Department tell me that her health has declined to the point that she no longer talks to the press.) Inside the Clinton Justice Department, his motivations tended to be more pragmatic than ideological. That's the kind of guy the Clintons liked.

In 2001, the ambitious Holder was on the receiving end of a deal with the Clintons. It was the kind of deal Holder could not refuse. And that's mainly because he realized what had been struck only after it was too late.

Just as things were winding down for the administration, White House officials made arrangements for Holder to ride with the president aboard Air Force One. This was a big deal—a rare treat for anyone, especially a government bureaucrat below a cabinet-level position and not in the White House. Holder of course was thrilled.

Finally, Holder thought, President Clinton was showing him the respect his many years of service had rightfully earned the middle-aged lawyer with familial roots in Barbados. He flew halfway across the country and rather enjoyed it. With Gore's loss, he wasn't going to realize his personal goal of being the nation's first black attorney general, at least not yet. But maybe, Holder hoped, he would get his chance the next time around—when a Democrat returned to the White House. Maybe that's what this trip was about—to burnish a relationship with Clinton for next time around.

Indeed, Clinton seemed game. At an education event at James Ward Elementary School in Chicago, Clinton went out of his way to introduce his now-honored guest. "I brought the deputy attorney general, Eric Holder, all the way from Washington," he said. "He had never been on one of these trips for me, and he's been working like a dog for years, so I asked him to come." The shout-out was more for the benefit of Holder than the crowd, but they applauded anyway.

"To continue our school analogy," Clinton continued, "this is recess for him today."[35] The crowd clapped again.

Public praise from the president of the United States. And a ride on Air Force One. Holder was thinking to himself that he had finally arrived. But Holder later realized what this was really about. He wasn't being courted for some role in the distant future. He was being softened up for something Clinton wanted now.

There had been talk about a possible pardon of financier Marc Rich. But nothing had come of it. That is, until Clinton's last full day in office, January 19, 2001. Then the president's White House counsel contacted Holder and asked for his take on the controversial idea. Full of good feeling toward the president, Holder, by his own admission, was unprepared for the call.

"The full dimension of who this guy was and what he was charged with didn't come in evidence even after those initial news stories," Holder later said. "It was not something that ever commanded a lot of my attention while I was there."[36]

Holder was under the impression that the Rich application had been thoroughly vetted within the Justice Department. "It was almost unimaginable to Eric that an unvetted pardon could be under consideration at that late date and time," a colleague says. But that is in fact what happened.

Holder told the White House, in words that would come back to haunt him, that he was "neutral, leaning toward favorable" about a pardon in the Rich case.[37] Whatever that meant. That was all Clinton needed—he seized upon the "approval" of the Justice Department as one of the factors helping him make his decisions. (The $1 million he received from Denise was, of course, never mentioned.)

Rich's was not the only controversial pardon. In 1999, Clinton commuted the sentences of sixteen Puerto Rican terrorists, a move interpreted by some as an attempt to help Hillary's Senate campaign by pandering to New York's Puerto Rican voters. Then, in 2000, Clinton pardoned fraudsters Edgar and Vonna Jo Gregory, who were friends of Hillary's brother Tony Rodham and who may have compensated Rodham with more than $100,000 in loans that were not repaid. Finally, in the last hours before Clinton left office, he commuted the sentence of cocaine trafficker Carlos Vignali and pardoned fraudster Almon Glenn Braswell, who each paid Hillary's other brother Hugh Rodham $200,000 to argue for their clemency.[38]

Though the pardons clearly seemed influenced by her Senate campaign, Hillary and her new spokesman, Howard Wolfson, said the pardon decisions were strictly Bill's decisions. Because of Monica, it was easier for the public to believe that Hillary was in a completely different orbit.

The Rich pardon in particular clouded Clinton's legacy. It was a low point—one even lower than the Lewinsky scandal. "This was an official act that was as sordid as anything he did in four years," says a high-level former government official. "Probably more so."

It wasn't just Republicans who thought this. The Marc Rich case seemed to finally unleash a pent-up frustration among once-reliable Clinton defenders over his personal ethics and behavior. Feelings they'd contained even during Monica.

Erstwhile Clinton defenders like MSNBC's Chris Matthews berated the Clintons for their "pig fest . . . on their way out the door."[39] The columnist Maureen Dowd labeled them "grifters,"[40] and the *New York Times* chided the president for his "outrageous abuse of the pardoning power."[41] The *Washington Post* remarked on what the newspaper called the "defining characteristic" of Bill and Hillary Clinton: "They have no capacity for embarrassment."[42] Even Democratic stalwart Jimmy Carter called the pardons "disgraceful."[43] With the Clintons on their way out of the White House, it was finally safe to dump on them.

Eric Holder never forgave them for making him the fall guy in their latest sordid mess. After receiving a fierce rain of bipartisan criticism during Senate Judiciary Committee hearings, Holder told reporters that he wanted to "crawl into bed and pull the covers up over my head."[44] He believed at the time that his public life was over—all thanks to the Clintons. "Eric hates them," a former colleague of Holder's says. But he would get a chance to pay them back.

2

ON THEIR OWN

"Those were difficult early years. All everyone cared about was what woman was sitting at a table with him or what he was eating."

—senior Clinton aide on Bill's post-presidential exile

Freed from the confines of the White House, Bill and Hillary Clinton were unleashed on the world in 2001. Bill left the White House, by many accounts, including his own, with a great sense of reluctance. A feeling that things weren't finished. That he could have been elected to a third term of office in 2000, if the Constitution had allowed it. That was possible, since his job approval ratings remained high, largely attributable to a seemingly robust economy. A January 2001 poll taken by Gallup days before leaving office showed the president with astonishingly high favorables: 66 percent approved, while a measly 29 percent disapproved.[1]

Under the surface, however, the widespread view of Clinton among the general public was negative. He was seen as unethical, amoral, and sleazy. Ari Fleischer, who was entering the White House as press secretary to the newly elected George W. Bush, recalled the public sentiment keenly. "[Clinton] left office with a lot of ill will, and a bit of it was generated by those last-minute pardons that were highly controversial, on his way out," Fleischer told me in an interview.

Looking back, Fleischer marvels at how far Bill Clinton had personally come in terms of public esteem. "It is a remarkable story because President Clinton really did leave in a cloud of controversy," he said. "He had to cut a deal with the prosecutor [investigating the Paula Jones sexual misconduct allegations] because he did commit perjury under oath. As a result, his license was suspended. People forget that the United States president was barred from practicing law for a period of time as a plea bargain. That happened on his way out, at the end of 2000. It is also worth noting that the press, when they write about President Clinton, they never harken back to that."

Indeed, on January 19, 2001, his last full day as president, Bill Clinton "accepted and acknowledged" that "he knowingly gave evasive and misleading answers" to a judge "concerning his relationship with Ms. Lewinsky" and "he engaged in conduct that is prejudicial to the administration of justice" in regards to the Paula Jones sexual harassment case against him.[2] As a result, it was "the decision and order of [an Arkansas] Court that William Jefferson Clinton, Arkansas Bar ID #73019, be, and hereby is, SUSPENDED for FIVE YEARS for his conduct in this matter, and the payment of fine in the amount of $25,000," read the Circuit Court of Pulaski County, Arkansas, agreement. "The suspension shall become effective as of the date of January 19, 2001. IT IS SO ORDERED."[3] Clinton, with two of his lawyers and two of the plaintiff's lawyers, signed the document and filed it with the Arkansas court.

That historic agreement, to strip the law privileges of Clinton, who was a sitting president when he signed the document, coupled with the aftereffects of the Marc Rich pardon, stung Bill Clinton hard, especially the rebuke he received from liberal elites. As a result, he went to their main organ of communication, the editorial pages of the New York Times, to offer another defense, this time written in his own hand.[4] His op-ed, dated February 18, 2001, contained a number of factual misstatements—so much so that the *Times* felt obliged to append an "Editor's Note" to Clinton's version of events, which unwittingly chronicled the Clinton team's talent for parsing words and obfuscation. It read as follows:

An Op-Ed article by former President Bill Clinton yesterday about the pardons of Marc Rich and Pincus Green stated erroneously in some editions that "the applications were reviewed and advocated" by three prominent lawyers, Leonard Garment, William Bradford Reynolds and Lewis Libby. Mr. Clinton's office and the lawyers are in agreement that none of the three men, former lawyers for Mr. Rich, reviewed the pardon applications or advocated for the pardons. During the press run, Mr. Clinton's office asked that the reference to "applications" be changed to "the case for the pardons" to try to clarify Mr. Clinton's point. Even the revised wording, however, could be read as leaving the impression that the lawyers were involved in the pardon process, which Mr. Clinton's spokesmen said was not the intended meaning.

The revised wording, according to those spokesmen, was meant to refer to the underlying legal case developed by Mr. Garment, Mr. Reynolds and Mr. Libby, among others, in past years that argued that the criminal indictment of Mr. Rich was flawed. That legal analysis, according to Mr. Clinton's spokesmen, formed part of the argument that Mr. Rich's lawyer, Jack Quinn, adopted in applying to Mr. Clinton for the pardon.[5]

Clinton's favorability nosedived, clocking in at an abysmal 39 percent, much lower than it had been months before as he was packing his bags to leave the White House. Angered and embarrassed by his latest scandal, Clinton brooded at the family home in Chappaqua. A former high-level press aide who visited the former president there describes a "pretty modest" five-bedroom, four-bathroom suburban home, located at 15 Old House Lane. "He's very proud of retrofitting it," the former aide tells me. "It's very energy efficient." In exile, Bill continued planning his presidential library in Little Rock and the opening of an office in New

York City. But foremost in his mind was restoring his reputation and returning to his place in the sun. The whole thing made him depressed.

He missed the action, missed being in the mix. Aides recall how Clinton would watch everything—Sunday-morning talk shows, cable news channels, *The Daily Show*—to seize on anything he might use in conversation or in kibitzing with former allies, and rivals. His reading habits are legendary. When he left the White House, aides packed up eight thousand books (he'd give a thousand away).[6] He fretted constantly about what people were saying about him.

Acting with almost Howard Hughes–like obsession, the former president will see someone on television mischaracterizing some aspect of his administration and reach for the telephone demanding someone go out and correct the record. No issue is too trivial or too time-consuming for his small staff.

"You get frustrated with him," one former aide says. "He'd see some washed-up Republican or Democratic strategist that no one gives a shit about and he'd insist someone has to get out there." The aide pauses and shakes her head as if repeating a conversation she's wanted to have with him for years. "I mean, why do you fucking care?"

A close associate of Clinton's in his immediate postpresidential life reflected to me on the circumstances at the time—the beginning of the arc of Bill Clinton's remarkable comeback, which he believes people have forgotten. "He couldn't get a mortgage. He owed all this money to the lawyers. I mean he was getting killed for doing a paid speech for Morgan Stanley. His daughter had gone back to school. His wife had moved to Washington. He was accused of stealing rugs and things off of Air Force One that didn't exist. I mean it was a very, very difficult time. I don't think people ever really grasped how dark those days were."

"Those were difficult early years," the source says, as Bill Clinton was pursued by tabloid reporters and gossips. "All everyone cared about was what woman was sitting at a table with him" or his weight. "There were a lot of awful hangers-on," the source adds, citing by name people like Harry and Linda Bloodworth-Thomason.

Hillary, meanwhile, was forging her own path. The new senator would spend much of her time at Whitehaven, her home near Georgetown, during Senate sessions, leaving there to visit the home in Chappaqua on weekends or during congressional recesses. Bill, according to a different former Clinton aide, rarely spent much time in Washington, at least on overnight visits, a habit that continues to this day. "He's not in Whitehaven," an aide tells me. "Like at all."

Often living cities apart for the first time in decades, they immediately went through the process of building separate identities and, with the exception of holidays and other family occasions, leading largely separate lives. For Hillary that meant work. She was now a political figure all on her own. Her first important decision was how best to use her celebrity. She was, after all, the most recognizable person in the body of one hundred. And, while they say that every senator looks in the mirror and sees a president, she was the only one there who had actually lived at 1600 Pennsylvania Avenue for eight years. Indeed, the only one who had ever lived there and then gone on to serve in what is ridiculously called "the world's greatest deliberative body."

There were a few false starts. She made an early effort to try to rally the Democratic caucus. Senator Dianne Feinstein, a California Democrat, offers a gauzy recollection of the Clinton Senate sojourn. "In 2000, shortly after Hillary Clinton was elected to represent New York in the Senate, I was honored when she called seeking my advice," she wrote in a 2013 article in a *Politico*-sponsored series called "Women Rule." "As a senator, Hillary committed herself completely to the nuts and bolts of legislating that separates the show horses from the workhorses in today's Senate."[7]

In 2001, however, relations were more turbulent. Senior Senate staffers recalled for me a testy exchange Clinton and then-senator Mark Dayton had with Feinstein during a closed-door meeting of Senate Democrats. Clinton excoriated Feinstein for voting in support of a Republican-led initiative so ferociously that the veteran California politician left the meeting close to tears.

"A lot of people didn't like Hillary on the Democratic side," says a longtime Republican senator who served on committees with Hillary Clinton. He requested that his comments remain anonymous so he could be more forthcoming about his former colleagues.

The body's internal power structure is based on seniority—on years served in the body. So she had to be careful not to ruffle the egos of senators who had been there for years and pay what they deemed as proper deference. Among them was the Democrat stalwart Edward M. Kennedy. Though Kennedy would famously endorse Obama over Clinton in 2008, what was not commonly known was how much Mrs. Clinton rubbed the Kennedys the wrong way from the start. According to a former Senate aide, Kennedy held the view attributed to his former colleague Pat Moynihan that the Clintons were entitled climbers. The veteran Massachusetts legislator was known to roll his eyes at the junior senator from New York as she held forth in various meetings—especially when Clinton would encroach on issues like education that he felt he had spent years leading the liberal charge on.

"I would think that he may have felt that she was calculating and putting her personal agenda ahead of Kennedy's agenda, or of the Democratic Party," the Republican senator who shared committees with Clinton surmises. "Kennedy was a pretty loyal Democrat to the team, and I suspect she was maneuvering ambitiously."

Quickly souring on the effort to be the leader of the Senate Democrats—a self-interested, fickle assortment of egomaniacs—Clinton opted for the role of the dogged workhorse, cultivating allies where she could.

One close friend of Hillary Clinton, who also worked for her husband, President Clinton, recalls how she early on approached Democratic leaders like Robert Byrd for a tutorial on constitutional issues. The pompous, prideful Byrd, now deceased, was an easy target for ego stroking. "I know that Senator Byrd, who had his doubts about her when she ran for the Senate, was impressed with her enough that he called her a workhorse not a show horse," says the longtime Clinton friend.

She also went to work building up a formidable entourage that was loyal to her and not necessarily her husband. This was a team, many with national political experience, who would be ready to help her excel in the Senate and eventually move back to the White House.

One of the aides most gossiped about was Huma Abedin, a glamorous woman once dubbed Hillary's "secret weapon" and from whom the senator was said to be inseparable. Abedin, starting out as a Senate aide at twenty-five, was an attractive woman with long dark hair, impeccable skin, and a perfectly fit physique. She was a legend among her friends and colleagues for her designer clothes, unflappable composure, and quiet confidence. She spoke three languages, had traveled the globe, and was able to make one of the most taxing jobs in the world look easy.

During this time, Abedin's role in Clinton, Inc. would probably be parallel to that of an executive assistant on track to becoming corporate vice president (unheard-of, but not impossible), with daily duties maintaining Hillary's image in the Senate, traveling with her constantly between New York and Washington (and abroad, when called for), and doing small tasks like getting her boss a bottle of water when her mouth was parched. She earned about $15,000 her first year working in Hillary's Senate office. Her title was the lowest in the office: staff assistant.

Abedin's circuitous journey to national prominence began when she was born to two academics in Kalamazoo, Michigan. After her Indian father taught briefly at Western Michigan University, he and Abedin's Pakistani mother moved the family to Jeddah, Saudi Arabia, where Abedin lived until she left for George Washington University (GWU) in Washington, D.C. Her Muslim parents' approach to their faith, Abedin's membership in her college's Muslim Students Association, and her work on the *Journal of Muslim Minority Affairs* have all been reported as consistent with, depending on the source, either the practices of peace-loving moderate Muslims or the record of violent Islamic extremists. *Vogue* reported that Abedin's father "founded an institute devoted to fostering religious understanding between East and West."[8] *National Review* said he was recruited by "a top al-Qaeda financier" to run the *Journal of Muslim Minority Affairs*, which "promotes Islamic-supremacist ideology."[9] Her mother is either "a sociology professor" who "helped create one of the first private women's colleges in" Saudi Arabia, or an "influential sharia activist" whose book *Women in Islam* "claims man-made laws enslave women." It "reportedly provides sharia justifications for such practices as female-genital mutilation, the death penalty for apostates from Islam, the legal subordination of women, and the participation of women in violent jihad."[10] On the one hand, Abedin's GWU Muslim Students Association was a popular, utterly ordinary social group for Muslims at college looking to meet other Muslims—no different from a college Republicans club or a black students association. On the other hand, after Abedin graduated, her group chose as its spiritual guide a senior al-Qaeda terrorist (and American citizen) named Anwar al-Awlaki. Known as the "bin Laden of the Internet," al-Awlaki was targeted and killed in 2011 by an American drone strike in Yemen.[11] (To be sure, no one who knows Abedin believes she's a jihadist. Quite the opposite. Even Senator John McCain has blasted such attacks as an "unwarranted and unfounded attack on a honorable woman, a dedicated American, and a loyal public servant.")

Hired as a White House intern in the first lady's office in 1996, the twenty-year-old turned heads with her polish and professionalism. She became the backup to Hillary Clinton's personal aide before taking over the job in time for Clinton's 2000 Senate campaign. In that role, Abedin spent almost every minute of the day with her boss, and with only a few brief sabbaticals since then, she hasn't left Clinton's side. "I only have one daughter," said Hillary, "but if I had a second daughter, it would [be] Huma."

"They basically coexisted," a former Hillary Clinton aide tells me. "There were very few minutes of the day they weren't together."

Abedin's friend Mike Feldman once called the relationship between Abedin and Clinton "unique," noting that the two could communicate with "as little as a glance." Clinton's longtime media consultant Mandy Grunwald once said, "I'm not sure Hillary could walk out the door without Huma. She's a little like Radar on *M*A*S*H*. If the air-conditioning is too cold, Huma is there with the shawl. She's always thinking three steps ahead of Hillary."[12] One might think Abedin lived a charmed life until one considers her choice of husbands—a man she would meet while working for Hillary. He was New York congressman Anthony Weiner. But that story would come later.

As her legislative director, Senator Clinton tapped Neera Tanden, who first worked with her in the White House as a senior policy advisor at the age of twenty-seven. Tanden, a well-spoken committed liberal spinner, the child of Indian immigrants, and a graduate of the University of California, Los Angeles, and Yale Law School, would become one of Clinton's most trusted advisors and a staunch promoter of sharply liberal policies.

In a sign of her distrust for the press and near paranoia about her public image, Senator Clinton hired as her spokesman Philippe Reines. An unmarried man then in his thirties, Reines was known for his contempt for the press corps and willingness to mislead, obfuscate, and freeze out anyone challenging his boss. Sharp-elbowed and abrasive, Reines had quickly come to be loathed and feared by many D.C. reporters.

He proved quick to send terse nastygrams to those offering even the slightest insinuation of negative coverage of his boss. Years later, for example, Reines would call a reporter at a news website "an unmitigated asshole" and then taunt him by asking, "How's that for a non-bullshit response? Now that we've gotten that out of our systems, have a good day. And by good day, I mean Fuck Off."[13] He is "a master practitioner of self-preservation and the beneficiary of Clinton's almost maternal protection . . . Hillaryland's ultimate survivor," the *Washington Post* would declare in a self-serving profile of the man.[14]

One well-known Washington reporter who worked with Reines and requested anonymity because he might work with him in the future summed up for me what was a common view among many D.C. reporters. Working with Reines, he said, "was a very unpleasant experience. He carries himself with a kind of amateur theatrics and tries to physically block people from gaining access to people and information."

He was, like Howard Wolfson, exactly the kind of press officer the Clintons seemed to prefer: a bully and a brute who often got his way.

Even the standard complaints of reporters—over logistics, or schedule, or seats on the plane—were treated like life-or-death offenses against the Clinton regime. "He has a pride of craft to the elaborate and offensive emails he sends to reporters," the journalist tells me. Reines loved to mock, abuse, and go to war with the press.

"One of the interesting things that has been historically true about president and Mrs. Clinton's approach to the press is the staff is very forceful and muscular," says Ari Fleischer. "The staff is aggressive in dealing with reporters, especially with Mrs. Clinton. They guard her reputation like the crown jewels are guarded. They don't want anyone to touch it. That's why I say it's a fascinating story to me in how it's going to play out, with how mainstream media will cover Mrs. Clinton's campaign, because from my experience schizophrenia is the right word to use. They alternate between loving her and hating her."

The usual rules of decorum didn't seem to apply when it came to Reines's boss, who also demonstrated a knack for bending the usual rules and norms to her own advantage.

Like many Senate offices, where staff changes are common as people move up and onward to other Senate offices, committees, or the private sector, Senator Clinton's office saw significant staff turnover. During her eight years in office, she had almost two hundred paid employees. She also put together what biographers Jeff Gerth and Don Van Natta Jr. described as a "shadow staff" of a "few dozen" congressional fellows, whose hiring appeared to violate Senate ethics rules.[15] These "fellows" would perform work for Clinton's Senate offices without costing her a dime, and served to significantly expand the size of her staff. "[Hillary's] practices in running her Senate office have sometimes demonstrated a cavalier attitude toward the rules and a proclivity toward secrecy," the authors wrote in 2007. "[I]n the case of some of her shadow employees, she has failed to ensure that they agree, in writing, to abide by the same Senate rules that apply to permanent staff."

Senator Clinton also permitted some staff members to work several jobs. Abedin, for one, at one point received a $27,000 salary in the Senate.

Senator Clinton, however, also allowed her to join the payroll of her campaign reelection committee and her political action committee simultaneously. Such activities, which Clinton permitted for dozens of aides, blurred the lines between government work and political work. Though this was permissible under ethics guidelines, and other senators have performed similar feats, the authors noted that Hillary's use of multiple salaries from multiple organizations for her staffs was exceptional and might well have skirted the spirit, if not the letter, of ethics requirements.

In addition to official and unofficial staff, Senator Clinton maintained close friendships with people who would prove influential to her when she chose to seek the presidency. These included the journalist Sidney Blumenthal, who found work as Washington bureau chief of the influential *Salon* online magazine and wrote fawning books about the Clintons. A *New York Times* review of his book *The Clinton Wars* was scathing: "Barely mentioning others close to the Clintons, and illustrating this memoir with smiling, convivial photographs of himself in their company (though much of the book is about others, like the less lovable Kenneth W. Starr), Mr. Blumenthal sends a clear message to his administration colleagues: Mom liked me best."[16] He proved a tireless defender and promoter of the Clintons' interests, which all but certainly influenced his journalistic integrity. "His most often repeated assertion, throughout an 800-plus-page memoir and political treatise," the *Times* noted in its book review, "is this: 'The charge was, of course, completely false.'"

Exhibiting her paranoid tendencies, Senator Clinton focused quickly on the need to counter what she infamously called "the vast right-wing conspiracy."[17] "We do have to do a better job to compete in the arena with the ideas we already have," Clinton told the *New York Times* in 2003. "But it's also clear to me that we need some new intellectual capital. There has to be some thought given as to how we build the 21st-century policies that reflect the Democratic Party's values."[18] So Clinton would also lend a hand to forming two organizations that would serve as liberal policy advocates and, not incidentally, sharp defenders of the Clintons. One of them was the Center for American Progress. "CAP was founded," one founder would later say, "on the idea that, when you fight on equal footing, progressive ideas come out on top."[19]

The organization would be staffed by loyalists like former aide Neera Tanden, who would later become CAP's president, and who would keep Hillary's aspirations in mind. It also would include as members John Podesta, a chief of staff in the Clinton White House, along with Gene Sperling, Clinton's former economic advisor, and Robert Rubin, Clinton's Treasury secretary.

"There's no escaping the imprint of the Clintons. It's not completely wrong to see it as a shadow government, a kind of Clinton White-House-in-exile—or a White House staff in readiness for President Hillary Clinton," wrote Robert Dreyfuss, a writer for the liberal *Nation* magazine.[20] It was all part of the shadow organization meant in part to serve as a sort of holding ground for policy makers to rethink liberal policy, reframe that policy, fight against conservatives who might see the world differently, and ultimately be ready for when (they hoped) Hillary would retake the White House.

There's another element of CAP, however. It's a Clinton legacy organization. It's founded by Clintonites, for Clintonites. It's this sort of organization that in part helps define the time between President Bill Clinton's time in office and the expected entrance of Hillary Rodham Clinton into office.

Of course, other former presidents in the modern era have presidential libraries—and foundations and other organizations established to preserve and in some way shape the legacy of the president they are named after. No other former president, though, has established organizations such as CAP that take such an active role in *current* politics and policy debates. And no other president has created such a legacy organization that is always present in Washington—and always doing what it can to help prepare for the return of the Family back to town—just blocks away from the White House.

Of equal import was another Clinton-backed creation, Media Matters for America, which bills itself as "a Web-based, not-for-profit, 501(c)(3) progressive research and information center dedicated to comprehensively monitoring, analyzing, and correcting conservative misinformation in the U.S. media."[21] The organization was founded by journalist David Brock, a former Hillary Clinton critic who once wrote for the conservative *American Spectator*. It was Brock who first reported that state troopers assigned to Governor Clinton in Arkansas had arranged trysts for the philandering politician and helped cover his tracks. In that article a woman named "Paula" was identified by first name only—and would later be fully identified as Paula Jones.[22] Jones would later allege that she had been sexually harassed by Bill Clinton—and the whole thing would lead to the Monica Lewinsky scandal and of course the president's impeachment.

Brock would famously break with conservatives a couple of years later and eventually become close to Hillary Clinton. As the head of Media Matters, he had helped it become an influential left-wing hit group that focuses on going after the conservative media and receives enormous credibility and attention. Brock's goal is to keep the media in line for Democrats, a generally easy task made simpler by his hard-hitting maneuvers, which cast all who see the world differently from him as dishonest and evil.

As Hillary Clinton once noted to a liberal audience of activist bloggers, "We are righting that balance—or left-ing that balance—not sure which, and we are certainly better prepared and more focused on taking our arguments and making them effective and disseminating them widely and really putting together a network in the blogosphere in a lot of the new progressive infrastructure—institutions that I helped to start and support like Media Matters and Center for American Progress. We're beginning to match what I had said for years was the advantage of the other side. You know, when I made that comment about the vast right wing conspiracy, I wasn't kidding. What I never could've predicted is that it wasn't a conspiracy—it was wide open for everybody to see and unfortunately they elected a president and a vice president with whom we've had to contend for the last six and a half years. But the fact is, they were better organized, more mission driven, and better prepared to take on the political balance of the last part of the 20th century and the beginning of the 21st century."[23]

An important aspect of her time as U.S. senator was her learning the ability to fund-raise—and to reward friends. She had played a supporting role for years, helping her husband raise money—and helping pay back the donors. But now it was her turn—and within years she earned the nickname, from the media outlet Bloomberg, the "Queen of Federal Pork."[24]

According to documents obtained from an organization that has been doing opposition research on Hillary Clinton and that is combing through her full record, between 2001 to 2007 Mrs. Clinton was able to secure earmarks totaling $536 million for companies that combined to contribute $514,700 to her various campaign organizations. For these companies, for every thousand dollars given to Mrs. Clinton, a million dollars was returned in the form of a federal earmark. BAE Systems got earmarks totaling $9,700,000 in defense appropriations; PACs and individuals associated with the company gave Hillary $10,000. Likewise, Corning, Inc. got $6,700,000 and contributed $95,850 to Hillary; Day-Star Technologies got $1,000,000 and gave $1,000; Delphi Corporation got $3,000,000 and gave $2,000; DRS Technologies got $16,500,000 and gave $14,600; EDO Corporation got $1,800,000 and gave $4,500; General Motors got $10,550,000 and gave $206,000. The list goes on.

In one four-year stretch, from 2002 to 2006, Hillary Clinton was able to secure more than $2 billion in earmarks—an eye-popping sum. The Associated Press reported, "The beneficiaries have ranged from defense giant Northrop Grumman Corp. to New York–based Telephonics, which won $5 million for helicopter equipment."[25]

Just as the Clintons' alleged involvement with crooked donors was the subject of congressional inquiries while they were in the White House, the same allegation was made once Hillary began her own political career. She allegedly deployed a fugitive, Norman Hsu, as a fund-raiser, and there were reports that a New York developer named Robert Congel had made a $100,000 donation to Bill Clinton's foundation in exchange for millions of dollars in federal assistance for a mall project by Congel. The *New York Times* reported that around the time of the donation, "Mrs. Clinton helped enact legislation allowing the developer, Robert J.

Congel, to use tax-exempt bonds to help finance the construction of the Destiny USA entertainment and shopping complex," and nine months after the donation, Clinton "also helped secure a provision in a highway bill that set aside $5 million for Destiny USA roadway construction."[26]

Of course, the Clinton camp—and for that matter the Congel camp—denied any quid pro quo. "Mr. Congel and Philippe Reines, a spokesman for Mrs. Clinton, both said there was no connection between his donation and her legislative work on his project's behalf. Mr. Reines said Mrs. Clinton supported the expansion of Carousel mall 'purely as part of her unwavering commitment to improving upstate New York's struggling economy, and nothing more.'"[27]

Taking on the right—via CAP and Media Matters—and finding future money streams to help achieve future political aspirations was only part of Hillary's planned offensive. She would also spend a considerable amount of time trying to seduce people on the right. In that, she took lessons from the master charmer himself, her husband, Bill Clinton, who in the first years after his presidency was building his own entourage and set of institutions.

As he worked to establish his postpresidential gravitas, Clinton could count on the usual hangers-on. One was longtime advisor Paul Begala, who would use his perch on various cable news channels to defend his former boss. And of course James Carville, the bald, serpent-eyed Cajun with a reputation for acidic barbs against Clinton enemies. A man who, like Clinton, was born poor and has used his political connections to become a multimillionaire.

Carville's memoir about Clinton's 1992 election victory, called *All's Fair*, was coauthored with his wife, Mary Matalin, who was the political director for the George Bush reelection campaign. The book came with a $700,000–800,000 advance, and along with Carville's $15,000 speaking fee—today it's at least twice that amount—it was an early indication after the 1992 election that Carville would never need to run another political campaign. He could instead become a millionaire by, in his words, "being me."[28] With a net worth now estimated at around $5 million, Carville has been known to give more than a hundred speeches a year, has published ten books (most of them bestsellers), appeared in more than a dozen movies, sitcoms, and TV dramas (often playing himself), and made a host of commercials with Matalin for everything from Maker's Mark to Alka-Seltzer. He was a cohost of CNN's *Crossfire*, is now a cohost with Tim Russert's son Luke of a sports show on XM satellite radio called *60/20* (a reference to the hosts' respective ages), and is a Fox News contributor. He also, having once flunked fifty-six hours' worth of college classes, teaches political science at Tulane. As the *New York Times* put it, "Carville, largely by dint of energy and personality, has blended politics, entertainment and celebrity into a lucrative empire with a single product to sell: James Carville."[29] Carville had also benefited handsomely from Bill Clinton's financial largesse—Clinton has, according to someone knowledgeable of both Clinton's and Carville's dealings and of the field, helped Carville secure lucrative contracts to serve as a "political consultant" to foreign political leaders who Clinton warns really could use Carville's help.

The Clinton entourage also included various Hollywood celebrities, with the assorted rumors and gossip that seemed to follow him. It wasn't exactly new—and almost everyone who had any real access to Bill Clinton knew about his reckless, Kennedyesque attachments to women. Even in the White House he all but flaunted his assignations in front of Hillary and everyone else around him, seeming to get a thrill by what would be forgiven or excused.

Then, of course, there was Lencola Sullivan, the first African American Miss Arkansas, whose name first arose during the Lewinsky investigation as another alleged Clinton mistress.[30] The relationship began in 1978, when Clinton was attorney general of Arkansas, and Sullivan's job, as the beauty pageant winner, was to take dignitaries around.

In a recent phone call, Sullivan tells me she's still good friends with Bill Clinton and the rest of his family. "My friendship with the entire family

ns. She refers me to Bill's and Hillary's memoirs for "powerful" accounts of their history. (For the record: she's not mentioned in them.)

In 2002, Clinton held an engagement party for her at his Harlem office. Her future husband, Roel P. Verseveldt, was a Danish citizen, a former actor and model, and had a degree in business economics, as well as being a graduate of the Special Branch of the Danish Police Academy. The prospective groom was also co-owner of a security agency and risk management firm.[32]

The party was attended by friends from Arkansas, New York City, and, perhaps most pleasing to the former president, by other former Miss America contestants. Of course, the question on everyone's mind, according to attendees, was an obvious one: Did the man she was about to marry know about her purported relationship with Bill Clinton? No one knew the answer.

But Sullivan answered it in her phone call with me. "I keep no secrets from my husband at all," she insists.

And even today, Lencola Sullivan makes an effort to see her dear friend President Clinton.

"If he's anywhere around where I am, of course, I do my best to try to see him. Of course he has an extremely busy schedule. So that can be very challenging, of course." Sullivan says she's "very self-sufficient" in contacting organizers of European conferences or meetings where the former president will be speaking—and that's how she gets in touch with him these days.

Clinton's involvement with various celebrities also had long been rumored—Eleanor Mondale, daughter of the former vice president; actresses Gina Gershon and Elizabeth Hurley; and even the singer Barbra Streisand.

A close Clinton friend, who's hit the links with him and worked for him, met me in a low-key and secluded Washington, D.C., eatery and spoke only on background. He offers a sympathetic defense. I rattle off names and ask about the various stories, from the more outlandish rumors that almost certainly have been exaggerated to the multiple affairs

extends over thirty years and I don't have any desire whats⸻
part of any publication—because there's been so many negativ⸻
have been talked about and written about the entire family,⸻
both Hillary and Bill, that I wouldn't want to be a part and ⸻
through something more negative because that doesn't serve any⸻

When I make the point to Sullivan that President Clinton i⸻
torical figure—and that, therefore, his relationships with any⸻
worth exploring, she responds with snark. "I'm keenly aware of h⸻
name has kind of been dragged around with this historical figure.⸻

And when I remind Sullivan that there have been previous re⸻
linking her "romantically" with Clinton, she says, "You read the pap⸻
and laughs heartily. "That's what they say. No one has talked to m⸻
have not talked to anyone."

"Right," I say, "so I'm talking to you now."

Sullivan declines numerous attempts to confirm or deny a "romantic⸻
relationship, often objecting to the line of questioning. (Yet she confirms⸻
to me another previously reported on fact: that she dated singer Stevie⸻
Wonder. "We're very good friends," she says of that former boyfriend.)[31]

"I'm not going to be involved in any kind of negative press regarding [the Clintons]—because I don't see where this is relevant. The line
of questioning where you're going—I don't see how that is relevant to
what's going on today. Right now. I mean, because this whole interview
is supposedly based on the fact that Mrs. Clinton may possibly run for
president. Is that correct or not?"

It's not, and after explaining my idea for this book, Sullivan says she
likes that it's about how the Clintons came back and overcame "adver-
sity." But dredging up the past is not something she wants to be a part
of. They've come back, she maintains, because "they're sincere people. I
mean, they're honest and sincere. They care about their relationships."
That's how they went from the low of leaving the White House to the
relative high where they are today.

"I think it's more important to talk about where they're going," rather
than talk about the scandals or relationships of the past, Sullivan main-

confirmed to me by those in the Clinton inner circle. "Everybody you think he fucked, he did—and the more dangerous the better," he says, mentioning various celebrities. "All genius is flawed. The great artists are addicted, whether to alcohol or they're drug addicts or whatever. His addiction is pussy."

Former president Gerald Ford, whose wife, Betty, had become an expert on addiction through the Betty Ford Center, once reached the same conclusion. "Betty and I have talked about this a lot," Ford told biographer Thomas DeFrank in 1998 (DeFrank published a collection of his conversations with the deceased president in a 2007 book titled *Write It When I'm Gone*). "He's sick—he's got an addiction. He needs treatment."[33]

Clinton also found a new friendship that would have an outsized role in his postpresidential life. At least for a while. Ronald Burkle was a billionaire in the supermarket industry who got his start as a bag boy at one of his father's grocery stores. Labeled the "billionaire party boy" in the tabloids, he formed a close relationship with Bill Clinton in Clinton's postpresidential life. (They first had met in 1992.) Each used the other—Burkle showed Clinton how to make money and put him on his payroll as a paid advisor to Burkle's group of investment funds. Meanwhile, Clinton gave Burkle access to Clinton's network of A-list celebrities, CEOs, and politicos. Clinton was happy to make connections for Burkle while giving himself, as the *New York Times* put it in 2006, "the potential to make tens of millions of dollars without great effort and at virtually no risk."[34]

The two flew around the world together in Burkle's private plane—a Boeing 757 that, according to an exposé on Clinton in the July 2008 issue of *Vanity Fair,* was privately labeled "Air Fuck One" by aides for its reputation of being close to a flying brothel. The magazine reported one scene in Paris involving Clinton and Burkle, whom the magazine described as "Clinton's bachelor buddy, fund-raiser, and business partner." Burkle, the magazine noted, had come to an event "with an attractive blonde, described by a fellow guest as 'not much older than 19, if she was that.'" Burkle was devoted to Clinton, according to a wide variety of sources.

While the duo had many surface similarities—they were of the same generation, from modest beginnings, and of course enjoyed reputations as womanizers—the Burkle-Clinton friendship, like many others in Clinton's life, was not destined to last.

Burkle aside, no one person was more important to Clinton's post-presidential life than Doug Band, water-carrier, fixer-upper, and all around consigliere. In the third episode of *The West Wing*, Charlie Young learns that he's being considered for a job as the president's body man. It's "traditionally a young guy, twenty to twenty-five years old," Josh Lyman tells Charlie during an interview, "excels academically, strong in personal responsibility and discretion, presentable appearance."

When the actor who played Charlie Young, Dulé Hill, was researching his role, he asked for advice from Doug Band, who had recently become President Bill Clinton's body man. Band had arrived at the White House in 1995 as an unpaid intern straight out of college, where the fratty English major—with, in what might later be seen as an irony, a minor in ethics—had been president of the University of Florida's council of fraternities. Unlike many starry-eyed twenty-somethings, Band arrived in Washington without any appearance of an ideology or agenda, other than an ambition to be around powerful people. When his fellow intern Monica Lewinsky invited Band to the White House Congressional Ball, he accepted the invitation. He wasn't so much interested in Lewinsky as in the chance to be around so many movers and shakers in one place.

After Band's internship, the tall, dark-haired, and friendly-faced Floridian was hired by the White House counsel's office. He started taking night classes at Georgetown's law school, and his colleagues assumed he'd aim for a job as a lawyer after graduation. But Band had his eyes on backrooms, not courtrooms. He turned heads when he applied for a job on the White House advance team—which came with an office in the West Wing, not in the Old Executive Office Building, like the counsel's office—and by 2000, he was Clinton's body man.

Band was finally where he wanted to be: at Bill Clinton's side. When the administration ended and Goldman Sachs offered him a high-paying job in New York, Band turned it down. Clinton was establishing the William J. Clinton Foundation, and Band had big ideas about what it could do for Clinton—and for Band.

They hit the road together. For the next decade, Clinton and Band were almost inseparable. He certainly saw his young male aide far more often than his wife. Those most familiar with Clinton's activities estimate that since leaving office, the former president spends around 320 nights a year on the road—a number so staggeringly high, it's really hard to say that he even has a place he can call home. It's hotel room after hotel room. Fund-raiser after fund-raiser. One global awareness event (for AIDS or climate change or any liberal cause) after another.

He and Band traveled together to approximately 125 countries and two thousand cities. They met with titans of industry and heads of state. They played cards late into the night and flew around together on Ron Burkle's plane. Clinton once said he "wouldn't be able to get through the day" without Band,[35] and he seemed to confirm his trust and dependence on Band in 2004 when the Clinton Foundation's chief of staff, Maggie Williams, tried to fire Band for evading her authority. She was tired of Band acting like he was in charge of Clinton's schedule, the foundation's employees, and its multibillion-dollar agenda, but with Clinton's support, Band stayed at the foundation. Williams didn't. "That's when I realized," a Clinton associate told the *New Republic*, "this guy has got it figured out—he's never going to go away."[36]

Band came to know more about Clinton than Band knew about anyone else in the world—and probably more about Clinton than anyone else has ever known. "In some part of his mind, he melded them into being one person," says the Clinton associate. "You thought that if he said something, it was coming from the top. . . . If he called and said, 'We need tulips for the apartment,' you assumed it was the president who needed tulips for the apartment."[37]

To his enemies within ClintonWorld, Band came to see himself as

Clinton's "equal"—entitled to eat at the most exclusive restaurants, sleep in the ritziest hotels, and carry around rolls of hundred-dollar bills.

Even before he exited the White House, Clinton examined various models to follow in postpresidential life. Unless his life's ambition was to play golf or paint pictures of birds, there weren't many great examples among modern presidents. George H. W. Bush understood his time in the spotlight was done and was happy to live a quiet life of luxury with his wife and family. Ronald Reagan gave a couple of speeches when he was out of office but his health left him in bad enough shape that he didn't have much of a choice but to retire from the spotlight. Gerald Ford moved to the golf course and successfully stayed out of the news.

Clinton read books about former presidents with more active postpresidential lives, most notably John Quincy Adams and Jimmy Carter. Adams had remained in politics: He's the only ex-president to really have a political life, serving nearly twenty years in the House of Representatives *after* the White House. Though both Clintons publicly mused that Bill might run for another office someday, that wasn't really practical. For one, there was Hillary's career to consider now. Bill's campaign would just dilute the brand, taking money, attention, and support away from her.

As much as he hated to admit it, the most relevant example came from a man he despised: James Earl Carter Jr.

"Bill Clinton found the prospect of looking to Jimmy Carter totally unattractive," writes *Clinton in Exile* author Carol Felsenthal. "How galling it was to Clinton to give even a moment's thought to Carter, whom he genuinely disliked—Carter and Clinton had a long, unpleasant history, and the ever-pious Carter made no attempt to keep private his disgust at Clinton's trysts with Monica Lewinsky."[38]

Yet Carter's case was perhaps the most relevant, since he, like Clinton, was a young ex-president and a Democrat in the modern era. The peanut farmer from Plains, Georgia, was just fifty-six when he left office; Clinton was fifty-four. Like Clinton, Carter also believed he had much work yet to do and would carry it out as only an ex-president could. So Clinton studied the Carter Center, the do-gooder organization in Carter's home state of Georgia established to promote human rights, mainly abroad. Clinton also studied the diplomacy and humanitarian work that his fellow former southern Democratic governor had done since leaving the White House.

"It was a brilliant strategic model," says former Speaker of the House Newt Gingrich, a Republican, in an interview. Clinton has managed "to create a cloak of invisibility based on his sincerity and goodness, so whatever he does must be moral and justified."

"Postpresidencies are wonderful because they get to avoid the big red-button, hot-button controversies," Ari Fleischer told me. "The Clinton Foundation can focus on feel-good activities, all of which has helped bring President Clinton back."

One person familiar with Clinton's postpresidential agenda did not hide the element of cynicism within it. "Look at what a big deal the [Bill & Melinda] Gates Foundation is today," he says by way of example. "But you also have to take into account why and how it started, right. I mean the Gates Foundation started as an antidote to the bad press he was getting by what he did as it relates to the antitrust stuff [involving Microsoft]. . . . Carter was largely the same in a way—to counterbalance what he did as a lackluster president."

There were a few differences between the Carter and Clinton approaches, however. As one associate familiar with the projects put it to me, "President Carter does five hundred different things, but the Clinton model was to be more effective in a few things, more narrowly." Those issues included a focus on global development and HIV/AIDS.

Also unlike Carter, Clinton had another primary motivating factor besides rebuilding his reputation: money. Lots and lots of it. Not having money wasn't new for Clinton. He was always a poor man. He was born to a single mother in Hope, Arkansas, mere months after his father drowned in a ditch after losing control of his car. Clinton's mother did her best to raise him by herself, but would often rely on his grandparents to watch him and raise him. Clinton's grandfather worked two jobs: running a grocery store and, at night, being a watchman at a local sawmill, according to Clinton's retelling of his family history.

Clinton "grew up feeling" the Depression, and with it came a sense of poverty and unease about money.[39] It was a feeling that would follow him the rest of his life, and was particularly present when he left the White House. At that time, Clinton is believed to have had about $12 million in unpaid legal fees as a result of the various investigations into his affair with Monica Lewinsky, sexual harassment charges from Paula Jones, the White-water investigation, and other scandals that had embroiled him. Getting impeached had taken a financial toll on the president and his family.

It was his duty, he believed, to repay these debts and to ensure that he'd never be in such a financial situation again. And, because he was so unsure of his health even in the immediate years after leaving the White House, he wanted to provide for his family—more than enough to live on, just in case his health failed him and he unexpectedly died.

He'd do what he had done to get him this far in life already: a combination of joining his gift of gab with his ability to bring important people together into the same room to work toward a similar goal. But instead of making laws and political deals, now the primary focus would be to make money.

"No matter how much money he has, it's never gonna be enough, because he was so poor at one point," says a former aide. Filling his coffers with money is his way to make up for a childhood where he felt deprived, the aide reflects, and Clinton will embroil himself in all sorts of questionable deals in the pursuit of wealth. Money is the latest of Bill Clinton's many addictions.

In 1989, after President Ronald Reagan left office, he received scathing criticism in the press for his decision to receive a $2 million speaking fee during a visit to Japan. The *Los Angeles Times* was among many in offering the opinion that "the main impression to be overcome is that he has been inappropriately cashing in on his eight-year presidency."[40] His postpresidential approval ratings tumbled. Reagan had nothing on Bill Clinton, who has cashed in on his time in public service to build a financial and political empire. Leaving office, Clinton would once again lower the bar for what was considered acceptable behavior, with only occasional scrutiny from the press.

The former president has earned well over $100 million in speaking fees, according to some estimates, including $17 million in one year alone. (A typical fee for a speaking appearance is $250,000.) He received a $15 million advance for his 2004 autobiography, *My Life*, which, reflecting its author, was largely considered a bulky, self-absorbed tome with moments of sparkle and brilliance.

Following Carter's lead, Clinton established a number of do-gooder foundations. The first was the William J. Clinton Foundation, a nonprofit established in 2001 and dedicated to issues including "health security; economic empowerment; leadership development and citizen service; and racial, ethnic and religious reconciliation." The second was the Clinton Global Initiative, established in 2005 with the mission of "conven[ing] global leaders to create and implement innovative solutions to the world's most pressing problems."

Clinton was also nurturing a political organization and assembling a coalition that would be ready for Hillary. In contrast to most former presidents, who were known to campaign on occasion for various big-name candidates, Bill Clinton stayed involved in a "huge number of political campaigns," a former high-level Clinton aide tells me. "He'll go out and do fund-raisers for people running for state senate and Congress and Senate and other things. They've kept their network very much alive that they cultivated when he was running for president the first time, even before he was running for president. If you look at some of the fund-raising he's done for state and local candidates and even getting involved in races from time to time, that you wouldn't necessarily think he'd get involved in, it's pretty extraordinary."

The aide added, "He knows every congressional district in the country. Clinton could go toe-to-toe with that guy around each district and what the dynamics are. It's something he's spent a lifetime thinking about and living. I think it's just a passion, for lack of a better word."

Maintaining this network had dual purposes for Bill Clinton. For one, Clinton is a natural barnstormer who loves making an argument before a cheering crowd of supporters. But the other reason was of course more personal. As one senior aide to the outgoing president told me, "he felt he owed Hillary the presidency." This and Chelsea were what really held them together. The duo always kept their options open for a return to the White House, an opportunity that might present itself in 2004, when George W. Bush would likely seek a second term. But first there was a problem that the Clintons needed to overcome.

3

CHARM OFFENSIVES

"When Clinton was president, the common media portrayal from relatively hostile media was that Clinton was this lovable Bubba who was charming and a rascally rogue who just could manipulate people, but not very bright kind of people. But Hillary was this unpleasant grind . . . If anything, the exact opposite is true."

—Michael Medved

Hillary Clinton's advocacy of groups such as the Center for American Progress and Media Matters, her vocal opposition to Bush administration policies, and her continued belief in the need to counter the "vast right-wing conspiracy" were not feints. She remained a committed liberal throughout her Senate tenure, voting to raise taxes more than 232 times, opposing conservative judges nominated by President Bush to the bench, including Supreme Court justices John Roberts (the chief justice) and Samuel Alito, and eventually opposing the Iraq War, despite first supporting it. Her poll numbers reflected this. In the Gallup polls, her numbers were disastrous for anyone seeking to win the White House by appealing to independent voters. Her unfavorables were consistently in the mid- to upper 40s. Among independents she fared only slightly better. Among Republicans she was easily one of the most unpopular politicians in America. Gallup recorded her unfavorable ratings among that group consistently in the 70s and 80s. If Hillary had any hope of seeking higher office, she needed to do something to at least soften her image as a brittle, harsh leftist radical and win over a few center-right votes.

What has been little understood in the past decade, from 2001 to the present, is how successfully the Clintons undertook a systematic, comprehensive, and sustained effort to win over leaders in the GOP, especially figures who were once their biggest critics. In return, both Clintons were able to develop a bipartisan, statesmanlike image that had eluded them through eight years in the White House.

Hillary's difficulties with the right were well earned. Not only had she famously raged against a "vast right-wing conspiracy," but she led efforts to wage a counteroffensive against them. As was revealed during the impeachment investigations, the Clintons hired private investigators to look into the personal lives of their political enemies. At one point, their dishonesty about these efforts won the ire of press secretary Mike McCurry. "On several occasions, McCurry threatened to quit if they kept deceiving him—once, early in the year when they misled him about whether they were using private investigators to research Clinton enemies and, more recently, when [White House counsel Chuck] Ruff refused to tell him whether Starr had issued a subpoena for the president's testimony," the *Washington Post*'s Peter Baker reported.[1]

The Clintons also got lucky in who their enemies were. For the most prominent congressional Republicans during the Clinton administration— who tried to find out just how many laws the Clintons had broken, or who voted to impeach or convict the president of his crimes—decline, defeat, or disgrace awaited them. The aging and once widely respected Henry Hyde, who chaired the House Judiciary Committee, was outed as an adulterer, his sterling reputation tarnished. Also exposed were affairs by Speaker of the House Newt Gingrich, who resigned; by Louisiana congressman Bob Livingston, who would have replaced him; and by Dan Burton, the Indiana congressman who exhibited an almost Javert-like determination to uncover Clintonian duplicity and dirty dealings.

Thus what Hillary Clinton pulled off with her Republican Senate colleagues was nothing short of masterful. I spoke to many, if not all, of Senator Clinton's biggest opponents within the Republican Party during her time as First Lady. On or off the record, no matter how much they were coaxed, not one of them would say a negative thing about Hillary Clinton as a person—other than observing that her Democratic allies sometimes didn't like her. Their love affair with Hillary—at least in their private conversations—probably says more about their susceptibility to flattery and praise than it does about her personality. But it also demonstrates the difficulty her likely 2016 Republican challengers will face in trying to build a coalition against her. Hillary Clinton has built a virtual dossier of praise and support from Republican colleagues who might publicly denounce her for political purposes but in private seem to downright like her. That work began in the United States Senate.

To the surprise of many observers, Hillary Clinton seemed to work hardest to ingratiate herself to those who only recently had voted to throw her husband out of office during impeachment proceedings. She threw a baby shower for Republican senator Kay Bailey Hutchison of Texas, who had adopted a child.[2] She attended prayer breakfasts with a mostly evangelical crowd of right-wing Republicans, including Sam Brownback of Kansas, who memorably confessed to hating her and asked for her forgiveness. (She gave it gladly.)[3]

One of the managers of the Clinton impeachment, Republican congressman Asa Hutchinson of Arkansas, was nominated by George W. Bush as administrator of the Drug Enforcement Administration. To his evident surprise, Senator Clinton voted in favor of his confirmation. Working with her, Hutchinson told me, was "always a joy. On the homeland security issue she was very supportive of what I was trying to do. And we had a very good working relationship."

"I was very critical of [Bill] Clinton during the impeachment," says another Republican Senate colleague, who requested to speak on background so that he could be more honest. "I didn't go over the top, but I was critical. She didn't seem to hold a grudge about that."

"From a personal standpoint—as far as personality is concerned—I think she's highly regarded by a lot of leaders around the world," former Republican Indiana congressman Dan Burton, one of the fiercest champions of impeachment, told me recently in an interview. "That doesn't mean that I think that the decisions that have been made are the right ones."

"She was a very active member of the Senate and reached out across party lines, for obvious reasons of trying to get bipartisan support but also in a thoughtful way," Georgia Republican senator Johnny Isakson said during an interview in his Senate office. "I remember, in particular, when we were doing TARP and some of the other things during the depth of the financial crisis, because of my background in housing and the tax credit that we had passed earlier on, she sought me out on a number of occasions, asked some very insightful questions that I could answer because of my experience. She was a very engaged member of the Senate and was a good senator."

Other Republicans remembered her as sharp and occasionally playful. Jim Nicholson, the former Republican National Committee chairman during the Clinton administration, who was then serving as secretary of the Department of Veterans Affairs for George W. Bush, recalls his department's effort to shutter a veterans hospital in Canandaigua, New York. The facility was in an area of the state Hillary frequented when she was first campaigning for the Senate, and Senator Clinton was determined to lobby him to keep it open.

The duo met on a small love seat just outside the Senate chamber, where Clinton could plead her case between Senate votes. At one point the Senate clock buzzed, indicating an imminent vote, and members began streaming toward the chamber. Many passed the tiny couch, glancing with surprise at the cozy closeness between the Democrat and the Republican publicly known as one of the Clinton administration's biggest opponents while party chairman.

"She's sitting here, and I'm sitting here," Nicholson says, pointing to tiny spaces very close together. "Cheek to cheek," he says, "cheek to jowl."

As startled Republican senators walked by, some stopped and gawked. Hillary thought it was funny. "I'm really going to get you in a lot of trouble," she said. Nicholson laughed. She also made a dogged case to the veterans secretary that proved to be forceful and data driven. And in the end she won.

"There was not enough political will to close the hospital, so we came up with a plan to make it a center of excellence for some . . . I think traumatic brain injury research," Nicholson says years later. "So, it's still open. It's underutilized, and very expensive, but it's a lovely facility."

Other Senate staff members recalled an instance when Senator Jon Kyl, a staunch conservative from Arizona, hosted a press conference for an immigration bill he was sponsoring. The bill sought federal funds to help cover the costs of emergency-room care for illegal immigrants. A number of Democrats had signed on to the bill, including Clinton. None, however, was expected to attend the press conference, particularly since it was being held in the office of the Republican Policy Committee. Populated by brainy conservatives and with a mission to undermine efforts of Democrats, the RPC was one of the more partisan operations in the Senate.

Staff members stood agape therefore when Hillary Clinton walked right through the front door. "She was walking into the Death Star, basically," one Senate aide recalls. "The ground zero of Hillary hating. People had their mouths open." Clinton had come to support Kyl's legislation and say a few words for the cameras. Not a single person in the room had expected her. Nearly all of them had considered Hillary Clinton as Public Enemy No. 1 of the Democratic caucus. And yet there she was.

One senator with whom Clinton became particularly close was the hawkish John McCain. "Hillary and I developed a very friendly relationship," McCain acknowledges in a conversation in his Senate office.

"She's a very smart person, extremely smart person, and she immediately joined the Armed Services Committee, because that was what was not in her resume, and she went out of her way to have a relationship with me."

"He respects her," says longtime McCain advisor Mike Murphy, a Republican consultant and another erstwhile Republican opponent of the Clintons. "And McCain and Hillary like each other. They get along. He respects her. She's tough. She's everything that McCain likes. She's funny. She's smart. And she respects McCain."

Almost by necessity, Senator Clinton also befriended another of her husband's impeachment managers, Lindsey Graham, so close to John McCain that the two are the Senate equivalent of Bert and Ernie. One Republican colleague remembers Graham acting almost fanatical about his latest celebrity friend. "I remember he'd always say, 'Well, Hillary said this,' or 'Hillary said that.'"

To McCain's delight, Clinton also developed a reputation as practical and hawkish, which played well among the entire Republican delegation. She voted for the war in Afghanistan and the war in Iraq. She even resisted calls in late 2005 for an immediate withdrawal of U.S. troops from Iraq, prompting the director of the liberal organization MoveOn.org to accuse her of "cowardice in the face of the right-wing noise machine." But Hillary's war views appear to have been ones of political calculation, rather than belief. Her colleague in the Obama administration, Defense Secretary Robert Gates, now retired from government service, made headlines in 2014 by revealing that Hillary had confided to him that her opposition to the surge of forces into Iraq in 2007 had been motivated by her presidential aspirations. Gates wrote, "Hillary told the president that her opposition to the surge in Iraq had been political because she was facing him in the Iowa primary."[4]

In her ingratiation efforts, Senator Clinton benefited from her stiff and unapproachable public image. Republicans expected the Cruella de Vil of Chappaqua. She startled them instead by appearing knowledgeable, quick-witted, and mischievous. Her personal qualities do not tend to come across in public settings—such as speeches and press conferences—but they are an underestimated strength in one-on-one encounters.

Michael Medved, the conservative talk radio host and a fellow student at Yale Law School with Bill and Hillary Clinton, offered similar notes in an interview for this book. "When Clinton was president, the common media portrayal from relatively hostile media was that Clinton was this lovable Bubba who was charming and a rascally rogue who just could manipulate people, but not very bright kind of people. But Hillary was this unpleasant grind, who was absolutely brilliant, with this kind of mega-mind and she was the brains behind the outfit, the ideological commitment behind the outfit. That was the conventional portrayal. . . . If anything, the exact opposite is true," he told me. "And I think anyone who knew them in law school will tell you that. That Bill was much less likable than Hillary; Hillary was intensely likable," Medved says. "In fact, to this day I don't know anyone, literally not anyone, who didn't like her, find her warm, sympathetic, a manifestly good person, well-meaning person, not full of herself, not puffed up at all, down-to-earth, and a good friend."

Though neither would welcome the comparison, Medved likened Hillary to Rush Limbaugh. "She is one of those people, the two people that I have been privileged to know where it's most striking that they are in person much, much nicer than their critics think, are Hillary Clinton and Rush Limbaugh. Rush is also an intensely nice guy and a good guy and somebody who is trustworthy and loyal to his friends."

Echoing her "listening tour" when she ran for Senate, Hillary made an effort to appear to be trying to hear and understand the views of her political opponents. Michael Novak, a conservative Democrat and well-regarded Catholic writer, recalled for me his appearance at Renaissance Weekend, an annual event that the Clintons attended in Hilton Head, South Carolina, at which gathered policy wonks to debate the issues of the day. Mrs. Clinton, Novak recalled, made a point of putting him and another conservative Democratic colleague, the former speechwriter Ben Wattenberg, right beside her at her table. "I thought it was quite remarkable that out of all the people in the crowd she put two of perhaps the most conservative Democrats in the room [beside her]," he said. "Ben and I both formed the judgment she was much more to the left in her thinking—if not her acting—than either of us thought wise there for the Democratic Party or for her."

To some observers of the Clintons, there was a psychological element to Hillary's unusual outreach. As former California congressman Jim Rogan, a Republican who was one of the managers of Bill Clinton's impeachment, put it during our interview, "They seem to miss their enemies more than they miss their friends." That was doubly true for Bill Clinton, who in his years out of office set out on a charm offensive of his own.

Upon the death of Nelson Mandela in 2013, Clinton claimed that the former South African president provided the inspiration for forgiving his enemies.[5] Just as Mandela forgave those who had oppressed and imprisoned him during apartheid, so too could Clinton forgive his enemies. Left largely unnoticed was that Clinton was comparing himself favorably to the famed African hero and Republicans to white racists.

Whether Mandela really had anything to do with Clinton's overtures—or whether the former president was just looking for a convenient and timely anecdote—is unknowable. What is known is that Clinton, by many accounts a classic narcissist, craves approval and praise.

A former senior aide recalls Clinton's time as a young Senate intern, probably around the time he worked for Senator Fulbright. "He used to take three or four showers in the morning because he wanted to run into as many [other interns] as he possibly could," the aide tells me. It was his way of meeting all the other pages in the prestigious program, because he was certain he would go on to do great things. A former Clinton roommate at Georgetown recalls that Clinton used to attend two or three different church services on a Sunday morning in order to meet more people. "I don't know what your college experience was like," the former Clinton aide tells me. "That's *crazy*."

The need for attention, love, and approval seems especially keen with Clinton's enemies. As one Clinton confidant told me, "If you want Clinton to pay attention to you, act like you don't love him anymore."

Former Democratic senator Joe Lieberman told me about his "fascinating" experience with Clinton shortly after he was chosen to be Al Gore's vice presidential running mate in 2000. Lieberman had publicly chastised Clinton for his behavior with Monica Lewinsky, winning widespread coverage as he blasted the president for "willfully deceiving the nation." Lieberman was unsparing, noting that "The president apparently had extramarital relations with an employee half his age and did so in the workplace in the vicinity of the Oval Office. Such behavior is not just inappropriate. It is immoral. And it is harmful, for it sends a message of what is acceptable behavior to the larger American family—particularly to our children—which is as influential as the negative messages communicated by the entertainment culture."

Shortly after the speech, the Connecticut senator received a call from Bill Clinton himself. Clinton, known to have a volcanic temper, was instead contrite. "'Joe, I can't say that I disagree with a single word you said,'" Lieberman quoted Clinton as saying.

"It was kind of an apology," Lieberman told me. "He talked about how he was seeing not one minister but two for counseling."

A Clinton confidant tells the story of a senior deputy in the administration who left to pursue other interests. A few months later, when a more senior job opened up, Clinton approached his former aide to get him to come back. The aide politely refused, telling the president that he was enjoying his new work. As the confidant tells it, "Clinton pursues, and pursues, and pursues, and pursues, and pursues, and finally gets him. And the guy comes back and Clinton ignores him. It's like you're in college and you're pursuing this girl and you gotta have her, gotta have her, gotta have her, and you finally get her and you're like, 'Yeah, didn't need that. Did I really want her after all?' But Clinton's like that with *everybody*."

Psychology aside, it is hard to ignore the fact that Clinton's outreach to Republicans had a component of naked self-interest. If his harshest critics could say nice things about Clinton, an obsessive poll watcher, then the public would likely feel the same. In his postpresidential life, by the accounts of many people I spoke to, Clinton has used that charm to advance a single aim: to win over, and ultimately neutralize, his and Hillary's most potent enemies. This is the less well known aspect of Clinton's obsessive legacy building. And in that effort, absolutely no Republican is off-limits.

His rapprochement with Richard Mellon Scaife is just one remarkable example. Scaife, a billionaire, had financed most of the anti-Clinton attacks during his administration. With Scaife's support, the conservative magazine the *American Spectator* launched a years-long effort to take down President Clinton. It was the *Spectator* that uncovered Paula Jones, the woman who was allegedly sexually harassed by the then-governor of Arkansas. Jones's allegations, because of the Violence Against Women Act, which Clinton himself signed into law in 1993, made Clinton's other sexual dalliances relevant—which of course led to Monica Lewinsky, which in turn led to the president's historic impeachment.

Scaife was the main moneyman behind these devastating attacks. And yet, when Scaife fell ill, a source close to Scaife tells me, Clinton made amends through phone calls, conversations, and letters, like this one, which I obtained, on letterhead with the presidential seal and his name, William Jefferson Clinton. The former president wrote:

Richard M. Scaife
One Oxford Centre
Suite 3900
301 Grant Street
Pittsburgh, Pennsylvania 15219

Dear Dick:
I'm so sorry to hear that you've been going through such a difficult time.
I want you to know that I'll be praying for your strength and comfort.
    Hang in there—I'm pulling for you.

Sincerely,
Bill

Scaife was touched, a friend of his says. Whether this effectively moderates any 2016 activity for the Republican moneyman is yet to be known. But it's safe to say that Scaife feels much warmer to Clinton now than he did in the 1990s. And that is only going to be a help for the Clintons.

"I talk to him once a year," Newt Gingrich confirmed over a year ago about his former nemesis. "Whatever's on his mind. Last time he called me to talk about the 'fiscal cliff' and how we could solve it and all that stuff." Gingrich's view of both Clintons has also softened—or been softened up—over the years, to the point that even he offers praise for their abilities, in tones he did not use when he went to battle against them early in his speakership. President Clinton is even said to have called Gingrich, according to an aide to the former Speaker, the night his mother died in 2003 to offer his condolences and to let him know that he was thinking of him in his time of mourning.

Gingrich once labeled the Clinton White House the "rough equivalent of the *Jerry Springer Show*"[6] and called Clinton's impeachment effort "very simply about the rule of law, and the survival of the American system of justice. This is what the Constitution demands, and what Richard Nixon had to resign over."[7] As Speaker of the House he once vowed, "I will never again, as long as I am Speaker, make a speech without commenting on this topic," referring to the Lewinsky scandal.[8] Today the former Speaker comes close to offering a defense of the Clintons and their tawdry behavior. "First of all, you have no idea what their lives are like," he says. "None of us do. They kept their marriage together. They seem to have a good relationship with their daughter."

Gingrich goes so far as to leave open the possibility that Hillary Clinton might be a good president. "Who knows?" he responds, when I ask him that question. "Compared to what? She would be a methodical, an intelligent, an extraordinarily experienced, very tough-minded liberal. She would be marginally more conservative than Obama. And dramatically more liberal than any Republican. That's who she is. That's who she's been for her whole life." He also suggests that she would be an effective president. "I mean partly because she just knows so much, she's been around so long, she's done so many favors. She would be instinctively more bipartisan than Obama because she's been here so long."

As a U.S. senator from Texas, Phil Gramm was one of the Clinton administration's most vigorous opponents. The staunch conservative almost single-handedly halted Hillary Clinton's health-care reform plan by vowing it would pass the Senate over "my cold, dead political body."[9] He excoriated Bill Clinton over his various scandals and voted without reservation for his impeachment. In fact, Gramm was ranked by his former colleagues as one of the most enthusiastic and effective antagonists the Clinton administration had ever known.

But that was then. Now Phil Gramm is all smiles when it comes to the Clintons. Labeling the former president "a great communicator" on par with Ronald Reagan, Gramm says, "I think he is a people person. I think he's capable of having warm feelings toward people that don't necessarily agree with him." In our interview, the former senator gushes, "I always was impressed by how prepared he was, how quick he was."

What accounts for the change of attitude? Bill Clinton has spent years working his former political enemies by using what he uses best—ingratiation and flattery. He knows well the benefits that come from small, cost-free gestures. Gramm is a Clinton fan for life, apparently, and for one primary reason: "Any time we are on a program together or if he sees me in the audience," Gramm, who now works in finance in New York City, tells me, "[Clinton] goes out of his way to say nice things about me."

Clinton has also maintained a close and personal relationship with Trent Lott, the former senator and Senate majority leader from Mississippi. "He and I still talk," Lott admitted a few years ago at a public Hudson Union Society event. "You know, when he had a heart attack, I really got worried about it. I was afraid he was going to kill himself. I called him and told him so."

Lott continued, "You know, I had my little disaster—I was talking before I put my mind in gear one time and I wound up having to leave the majority leader's position. Unceremoniously, you know, a lot of my friends—including the president at the time, George Bush—pulled the rug out from under me. But it was a rug that I should have had pulled out from under me. But I didn't go away and pout and sulk about it, I stayed. I hung in there and kept doing my job, I kept doing my job, and four years later, back in the leadership. Again as majority whip. And what was one of the first calls I got? Bill Clinton. He said, 'Well, I guess I'm going to have to give you my moniker as the Comeback Kid.'"

Lott's comments that got him in trouble—the ones that didn't seem to hurt his relationship with President Clinton—were about his support for Strom Thurmond, the Democratic senator from South Carolina who had run for president in 1948 on a "Dixiecrat" segregationist platform. "When Strom Thurmond ran for president, we voted for him. We're proud of it. And if the rest of the country had followed our lead, we wouldn't have had all these problems over the years, either," Lott said. It would result in his fall from Senate leadership.

Lott's audience laughed at the anecdote of Clinton calling him the "Comeback Kid."[10] And then he launched into only a semi-defense of impeachment, saying that the votes were "never there" to remove Clinton from office, suggesting his role was only to marshal the will of people but without getting too hostile and too acrimonious.

"I thought we got through it pretty well," he said. "And I talked to Bill Clinton, not much during the proceedings, of course, but as soon as they were over," he says, shrugging his shoulders, "we went right back to work. And did some more things for our country."

A similar tone is offered by Mike Huckabee, who, as governor of Arkansas, worked frequently with Clinton during his presidency. "Clinton was extraordinarily attentive to governors in general, and to me in particular, and if I were to call and request a conversation with him about something, I'd generally get a call back within half an hour," Huckabee tells me in an interview. "You couldn't get that kind of attention from the Bush White House."

Huckabee, like Gramm, was susceptible to Clinton's small gestures. He tells me of a visit that he and his wife made to Toronto. Mrs.

Huckabee noticed that Bill Clinton was in town for a book signing and suggested that they go and see him. "Well, of course, there was a huge line and they said no photos, you can't say anything, just get your book signed and move on," Huckabee says. "So she just got in the line, went through, and when he saw her he looked up and stood up from his seat and said, 'Janet, what are you doing here?' Well, it disrupted the whole thing and he gave her a big hug and they talked a minute. You could tell that all the people looking were just aghast, you know, 'Who is this person who's disrupting the whole thing?' I'm sure they'd have a fit to find out it was the wife of a Republican governor, but that's Bill Clinton. That's just who he is."

As with Hillary, the men who led the effort to impeach Clinton weren't off-limits, either. Clinton has exchanged warm letters with Jim Rogan, the former impeachment manager. In our conversation, Rogan declined to release the letters, but acknowledged that "[w]e've corresponded back and forth over the years. It's been very friendly."

"Did he ever try to win me over?" Asa Hutchinson asks. "Every time we met. I mean that was the level of his engagement. He was always trying to make those connections and he generally did."

"President Clinton tends to hold you in a man grip that's just a little too close for comfort and he doesn't let go," Utah Republican congressman Jason Chaffetz says with a laugh. He met the former president at a wedding reception for Huma Abedin and Anthony Weiner. (The event was hosted at the Clintons' Washington residence.)

"I think the thing that I admire really about President Clinton is he's mature enough not to hold against somebody like Ray LaHood," says LaHood in an interview for this book. LaHood, a Republican congressman from Illinois who later served as Obama's secretary of transportation, noted that he voted for four articles of impeachment while in the U.S. House. "It would be very easy for [Bill Clinton] to turn and have a cold shoulder toward me as a Republican who served during the time of his impeachment. He's a mature enough individual that we had a good relationship."

Clinton has even gone so far as to entertain a reconciliation of sorts with the chief bogeyman of the Clinton years, at least as Bill and Hillary saw it: former special prosecutor Kenneth Starr.

Starr, a soft-spoken but thoughtful man, has had his motives impugned by Clinton himself, who told a Fox News reporter that the investigation into him led by Starr was not done with integrity. "There were things done in Arkansas . . . under Mr. Starr's direction that were unforgivable, lots of them. And so no, I [do] not agree that it was done with honor and integrity," Clinton said publicly in 2010. "I trusted the justice system and I trusted the press to cover it right, and I didn't realize what the real game was. It was my fault as much as anything else for agreeing to be investigated, but I knew I hadn't done anything wrong. And so they just kept it going on and on and on. It was a nightmare. And I think, as a result of it, we'll never have it again. The only good thing to come out of it was, it killed this whole system. I don't think there'll ever be another one like this again."[11] Clinton loathed Starr, as he made clear to aides and occasionally to reporters.

Starr, who is now the president of Baylor University in Texas, said that while he hasn't met with President Clinton since his investigation into him, he would. Gladly. "Would you be willing to have a smoke?" Starr, with a laugh, says he was asked. "A smoke with the peace pipe. I'm from the West. I have Indian blood. I have been taught to talk that way—to have a time of possible reconciliation," he explains. Starr, who wouldn't name the Clinton associate who asked him, said he responded, "Of course. Anytime." It hasn't happened yet, but it's likely one day soon it will.

Starr says he's not surprised by the Clintons' comeback in public esteem. "We . . . have short memories, and he's lovable," Starr now says of his former nemesis. "If he weren't lovable, I mean then he would have an enormous problem." If Clinton could charm Starr, even though he's eviscerated him and his motives in public, one might wonder if anyone is safe from his charms.

"Listen," Georgia Republican senator Johnny Isakson tells me. "If they ever write a book on charming initiatives, he ought to be on the book cover. He can charm anybody."

Indeed, most people who have met him call Bill Clinton the most charming person they have ever met. "Clinton was the most talented politician I ever met, certainly the most charming man I ever saw," says Brit Hume, who covered the Clinton White House for ABC News. "He was easygoing, seemingly, and he had an amiable way about him. All politicians have it to some extent, but he had it in spades. It was interesting to cover him because he could talk at incredible lengths, and would wield detailed knowledge on all sides of issues."

"To a one-on-one, when you're with him then, your whole world just kind of disappears—I don't know if other people have said this—but he just kind of locks you in," says one former longtime aide.

It's a line I indeed heard from nearly everyone who interacted with President Clinton—usually from those who do not know him well. His eyes connect with yours and for that moment, you become the most important person in the world—to a person who is, or at least at one point was, the most important person in the world. People describe it as an exhilarating experience. Even people who once reviled Bill Clinton.

"He really does have some of the most remarkable eyes," says Michael Medved. "Even though you know you're being conned, when he looks at you, you have the impression that you're the only person in the world, and that he is listening and hearing."

Jim Nicholson recalls a time shortly after he began serving as chairman of the Republican National Committee when Father Andrew Greeley, one of the most well-known Catholics in America, went on television to express his opposition to the Bush-led war on Iraq. The priest went even further, announcing that it was a "mortal sin" for a good Catholic also to be a Republican. The pronouncement led to a predictable outcry, especially among the GOP faithful, who flooded RNC headquarters with irate calls and faxes demanding a response.

As Nicholson told the story and his reaction to it, the Bushes appeared largely uninterested. "They didn't know Greeley from Schmeeley," Nicholson says, laughing. "They don't connect to the story at all. But Bill Clinton does." (In short, Nicholson basically decided to do nothing, lest he engage in a "pissing contest" with the media-loving Catholic.)

Clinton not only knew who Father Greeley was, but also was well aware of his dozens of novels. So much so that he was conversant about various titles and characters. Many of those novels, Nicholson notes, have a "prurient" flavor. (Greeley was once dubbed "the dirtiest mind ever ordained.") The principal characters, usually men of cloth, are involved in heavily sexual storylines. One character, for example, was a cardinal who'd broken the vow of celibacy with a mistress. Clinton appeared to have read them all. "Every one of them!" Nicholson exclaims in amazement.

"I was absolutely astonished," Nicholson recalls. He also was clearly impressed. "When did he ever have time? And not only had he read them, but he remembered everything about them. I think he remembers everything he's ever done; it seems like he remembers everybody he's ever met."

What Nicholson notices, Michael Medved tells me, is the true secret to the Clinton "charm": the former president's "freakish, phenomenal off-the-chart memory for people, faces, details about people."

Medved relates the story of a woman named Winnie Lewellen, who managed a bed-and-breakfast called Wensley House in Chautauqua, New York. Many years ago, when Clinton was governor of Arkansas, he came up to the western New York town to deliver a speech. And he stayed at Winnie's guesthouse. Clinton was never known as a great orator, and this speech too proved disappointingly long-winded and self-indulgent. Returning to the guesthouse after watching the speech, Winnie found a room in a shambles. "The room had very clear evidence of partying," says a source familiar with the story. "There was broken glass. There was stuff spilled all over the place. There were papers strewn everywhere, and ashes and tobacco. The governor had clearly not spent the night alone."

Winnie had never seen a room in such a state of disrepair. Disgusted, she hoped she'd never lay eyes on the man again. That very afternoon, however, she received a phone call.

"Hey, Winnie, it's Governor Clinton," said the voice on the other line. "I made a little mistake, and I'm hoping you can do a big favor for me." Winnie assumed Clinton was planning to apologize for his rock-star antics. Instead he said, "I left some papers in there, and they're really, really important."

"You left more than papers in there, Governor," Winnie replied, "and I cleaned everything up."

Again without an apology or sense of shame, Clinton pressed, "Well, could you go to the Dumpster and get those papers because they're a bunch of fund-raising calls I have to make?"

So Winnie went to the Dumpster, retrieved the papers, and returned to the phone. "Okay, I have the numbers," she said. "Do you want me to send this to you?"

"No, no," Clinton replied. "Just read me the phone numbers and the information."

"Are you writing this down?"

"I don't need to write it down. I'll remember."

She read him about twenty numbers, and he remembered everything. Every digit. "Thank you, Winnie," he said in the hoarse singsong voice. "That's just so wonderful. I love you, and I'll never forget you." Then he hung up.

Many years after Bill Clinton first stayed in Winnie Lewellen's Chautauqua guesthouse, he returned to town as president to deliver another speech. Remembering how Clinton had unapologetically trashed his room and then called to ask *her* for a favor, Winnie was still simmering. However, she was too curious to resist attending Clinton's latest speech in her small town.

After the speech, Clinton worked the rope line, where Winnie was standing, maybe four or five rows back. And then he saw her.

"Hey, Winnie! Winnie!" he cried out, his eyes locking on hers. "Boy, it's great to see you. I told you I would never forget you."

And that in essence is Bill Clinton. Self-indulgent, shameless, brilliant, capable, scandalous, and, for want of a less overused phrase, a con-

summate charmer. Like Winnie Lewellen, not everyone in Washington
has fallen for Bill Clinton's reported charms. Where some see a warm-
hearted, lovable sincerity, many others see pure calculation, even ruthlessness.

"When I first met him, there was no real charm," recalls a veteran
network reporter, who requested anonymity to speak more freely. "All I
saw in his eyes was ice."

Bill Richardson, stinging from the deterioration of his relationship
with the former president, tells me his belief is "that every relationship
that he has is mainly about him and not about the other person." Richardson himself calls Clinton a megalomaniac who "presumes the world
revolves around him."[12]

Indeed, it is easy to overestimate Bill Clinton's legendary powers of
charm and persuasion, against which Hillary long has suffered in comparison. But Bill was not always so flawless in currying favor. To some he
comes across as selfish, sad, and needy.

As a young man, for example, Clinton famously worshipped J. William Fulbright, the powerful United States senator from Arkansas. So
much so that law school classmates still remember young Clinton's obsession. "I don't know anyone else who talked openly about his political
plans like Bill Clinton," one fellow student at Yale Law School recalls.
"He was going to take over for J. William Fulbright, and he was already
planning campaigns, and clearly, he had ambitions as a candidate, and
that was considered kind of unusual and gross."

Fulbright is mentioned fifty times in Clinton's memoir, *My Life*, and
the former president took great pride in working as a driver for Fulbright
in 1968. "When we were driving from town to town on those hot country
roads," Clinton reflected in his memoir, "I would try to get Fulbright to
talk. The conversations left me with great memories."

But not, however, for Bill Fulbright, who viewed the young Clinton
as selfish and transparent. It "sharply curtailed my career as his driver,"
Clinton recalls. And as Fulbright later told family members, "We'd go
somewhere, and I'd be in the car with him, and by the time I was out of

the car he was already out of the car introducing himself to people all the time, never mentioning me."

"The guy was unbelievable," Fulbright would say to relatives. When Fulbright died in 1995, then-President Clinton spoke at his funeral and, according to observers, would not leave the scene, even as aides pressed him to go. Eventually the crowd of mourners diminished to Fulbright family members—and Bill Clinton. When the family decided to take a group picture after the funeral, Clinton still wouldn't get the hint. "You have to look really carefully at the photo," says a source connected to the Fulbright family, "but there's Bill Clinton in the back with his face between the shoulders of two people."

"Hillary has friends that go back to high school and Bill not so much. In fact, I would say not at all," Michael Medved says. "Apparently the most emotional relationship in Bill's life was Buddy the dog."

Beneath Clinton's smiles, a darker side constantly lingers, characterized by purple-faced tirades and a hair-trigger temper. "Look, you read the accounts from his administration inside the White House, and his temper is an occasional explosion," says Brit Hume. "They are a part of his personality. I think he's emotionally stunted in some ways. His feelings of guilt and shame, I think, are limited. I think his physical appetites are strong and shall we say dominant, but he does have the capacity to get mad briefly."

A former mainstream news correspondent tells me that the oft-cited reports of the Clintons screaming at each other and throwing lamps while living in the White House "really did happen."

"He is cranky and yelling half the time," says one former aide in our interview. "People don't really talk about that, which is interesting, but he does."

These aspects of his behavior seem to have created something of a distance between the former president and other people. Bill Clinton is largely a person for public consumption, not private. The charm works best on those who know him least.

His life is largely about politics, giving speeches that put him in the public spotlight and collecting chits for the future. "He's done a lot of fund-raising, visiting, almost like the way the chair of the [Democratic Congressional Campaign Committee] would be going running around to races so much," says a former Clinton press secretary.

Within the first few years of his postpresidential life, Clinton established the Clinton Global Initiative, a group that brought together private and public leaders to talk about ways to combat major problems, such as development in the Third World or poverty. CGI, as it was more commonly known, was started, according to a source, out of Bill Clinton's frustration with the ponderous meetings of various global elites in Davos, Switzerland. He believed he could do the same thing with the Global Initiative, except more effectively.

Clinton used his celebrity to bring together people like Bill Gates, Warren Buffett, and the leaders of Rwanda at forums where he could charm them, flatter them, and have a bull session about whatever crossed his mind. The former president hosts events that gather CEOs and major hedge-fund investors. He is said to have been particularly successful at wooing Muhtar Kent, the CEO of the Coca-Cola Company, and Andrew Liveris of Dow Chemical. "He's also developed an extraordinary network in the corporate and business community," says a former Clinton official. Of course, that's the right word. *Network*. Not *friendships*.

As some aides talk about their former boss, it's hard not to see it as rather sad in its way. Just another way to try to satisfy an unfillable void in Bill Clinton's life, with attention. "It's a big event. A lot of people around," says the former aide. "They talk about this, that, and the other thing. But there's nothing to it, other than chatting."

Contrary to the general impression of Clinton as the flawless charmer, his seemingly endless need for attention and approval, particularly from those who don't like him, can sometimes backfire in dramatic fashion.

"These two old Jews are walking down the street." The former president, always eager to please, was grinning as he retold a favorite joke to a group, which included some prominent Republicans, in 2003. Clinton was at the Turf Club at Baltimore's Pimlico Race Course on Preakness Day with Doug Band, Jon Bon Jovi, Maryland governor Robert Ehrlich, other well-heeled celebrities, and his host for the day, Frank Stronach, an auto parts billionaire.[13]

Clinton, who couldn't resist knowing everything about everything, offered reporters his prediction for the race—the New York–bred Funny Cide. He made the choice, he said, "In deference to the junior senator from New York."

As he made his way to a table of Republicans, which included Tucker Carlson and his father, former U.S. ambassador Richard Carlson, Clinton could not help trying to ingratiate himself. How to do it? Well, his audience being Republicans, Clinton apparently assumed that anti-Semitic jokes were totally appropriate and welcome.

As the joke begins, everyone around the table looks dubious. *Where is he going with this?* Surely the former president of the United States is not about to tell an anti-Semitic story in front of people he hardly knows. This, of course, is exactly what he does, according to a number of the people present.

Clinton's story about "two old Jews" takes them to a Catholic church, where they encounter a big sign reading, "Be a Catholic. We'll pay you a hundred bucks." One of the Jews, whom Clinton names Abe, says, "Well, that sounds like a pretty good deal. For a hundred bucks I'll do anything." He tells his friend to wait outside. If he does, the friend gets half of the money.

Clinton describes Abe going into the church, meeting with priests, and learning the traditions of the Church. "Son, you're now a Catholic," the priest tells him.

Abe collects the hundred dollars and walks back outside, where his friend is waiting. "Hey! Look at the new Catholic here," the friend declares. "You got my money?"

Abe shakes his head. "You fucking Jews," he says. "It's all about the money, isn't it?"

As the former president laughs, the others offer weak smiles. No one wants to offend him. So Clinton goes on to tell a complicated anti-gay joke, involving a hermit living in a cabin in Arkansas. "The joke was really weird," says one of the attendees, who couldn't recall the details with any specificity. The former president has long seemed visibly uncomfortable about gays, according to acquaintances. Once the president spotted a male acquaintance and complimented him facetiously about wearing a pink tie. The acquaintance replied, "Thank you, Mr. President, I wore it just for you." Clinton was silent for a long moment. He looked frazzled, then furious. The gay-tinged repartee "made Clinton nervous," a participant in the conversation recalls.

Doug Band was no better at making strangers feel comfortable that afternoon at the racetrack. "You know there's this model," he said. "The press is saying Clinton's fucking her." He looked offended. "I'm the one who's fucking her." (The model Band was bragging about was Naomi Campbell, whom the *Washington Post* would tie the aide to a few years later.)

As Band holds forth, Clinton walks back to the table with another awkward recollection.

"You'll remember I had that trouble with Gennifer Flowers," Clinton tells the stunned guests. Of course, they all remember. "The day the scandal broke, we were having a meeting and James Carville came running in and told us that Gennifer Flowers is holding a news conference, right now to say all these things about me."

Clinton continued, "Carville comes in. He says, 'She's saying all these bad things, all these terrible things about you. And claiming that she had an affair with you and so forth.'" The tableful of people listening to Clinton had no idea where he was going with the story. "Well, Stephanopoulos fell on the ground," said Clinton, referring to his former aide and now ABC News personality George Stephanopoulos. "George fell on the floor. And he curled into the fetal position and he started crying. 'It's over. It's over. We're done, you know. You're going to destroy us and all that.' So Carville kicked him."

As the guests looked on amazed, Clinton lapsed into a pretty good imitation of Carville's well-known Cajun drawl. "Carville said, 'Get up, bastard, stop doing that. What's the matter with you, you stupid motherfucker?'"

In Clinton's version of the story, Stephanopoulos then gets up. "And he's sniffling and he's all upset," Clinton told the group. "And Carville says, 'We'll weather this, we'll take this on, we'll do whatever.'"

Clinton finished the story with a smile. The group of strangers was stunned that Clinton would go out of his way to trash his former aide in such a manner. Some, however, had their theories for his motivation—that Clinton was still feeling vengeful over the memoir Stephanopoulos wrote about his tenure with the Clintons.

"He laid George Stephanopoulos out," one participant recalls. "It made him look like a little girl. Clinton used that phrase, saying he was even crying like a little girl."

The recklessness of Clinton's jokes and comments was perhaps rivaled by his behavior that day. At least two participants at the event confirmed a story involving Clinton and a woman often linked to him in newspapers and magazines over the years—Canadian politician Belinda Stronach, the daughter of Clinton's host that afternoon, Frank Stronach.

In June 2003, the *Vancouver Sun* reported that "Stronach, [then] 36, and Clinton, [then] 57, have been spotted together on at least three other occasions, including a private dinner last July when he was in Toronto to honour rock and roll legend Ronnie Hawkins. Over the past six months, the two have dined together at the Democratic governors' conference in Baltimore as well as a Democratic fund raiser in California." The newspaper noted that spokesmen for both Clinton and Stronach insisted the relationship was not romantic.[14]

In 2008, as Hillary made a bid for the White House, *Vanity Fair* also alluded to Clinton's questionable relationships with women, naming specifically the actress Gina Gershon and Stronach. The propriety of the Clinton-Stronach relationship was also alluded to in the

New York Times in 2006 under the headline "For Clintons, Delicate Dance of Married and Public Lives," which stopped short of accusing the former president of adultery. "Several prominent New York Democrats, in interviews, volunteered that they became concerned last year over a tabloid photograph showing Mr. Clinton leaving B.L.T. Steak in Midtown Manhattan late one night after dining with a group that included Belinda Stronach, a Canadian politician," the *Times* reported.[15]

Clinton insiders date their first meeting to 2002, when Stronach was married to a Norwegian speed skater named Johann Olav Koss. With rumors of the Clinton-Stronach relationship already making the rounds in elite social circles, what Clinton did next, in the view of witnesses, seemed ill-considered at best. According to former ambassador Carlson, Clinton drove off with Stronach, described as an attractive woman wearing a tight, short skirt and displaying what an attendee called "a ton of cleavage."

Belinda didn't bother to tell her father that she was leaving with Clinton, and according to Carlson, "her father was freaked out. He was running around, upset she wasn't there."

The two returned just before the first race.

Such behavior was anything but charming. Indeed, it demonstrated, as the *Times* warned, Clinton's penchant for interfering with his wife's political ambitions: "Just as it is difficult to predict how voters would feel about Mrs. Clinton as a presidential candidate, Clinton advisors say, it is hard to foresee how they would judge the Clintons' baggage in the context of their third White House bid."[16]

"Mr. Clinton is rarely without company in public," the *Times* went on to note, "yet the company he keeps rarely includes his wife."[17] At around that same time, ironically enough, Hillary Clinton was on the Senate floor defending the institution of marriage during debates over gay marriage legislation.

"I believe that marriage is not just a bond but a sacred bond between a man and a woman. I have had occasion in my life to defend marriage, to stand up for marriage, to believe in the hard work and challenge of marriage," Hillary said on the floor of the Senate on July 13, 2004, discussing a constitutional amendment regarding marriage and her support for the Defense of Marriage Act.

"So I take umbrage at anyone who might suggest that those of us who worry about amending the Constitution are less committed to the sanctity of marriage."

As the 2004 election dawned, Bill Clinton was still making every effort to ingratiate himself with Republicans, so much so that he had taken to comparing his administration to that of the business-friendly Dwight D. Eisenhower. Many liberal Democrats bought that argument, too, and the backlash gave rise to a progressive movement that saw a primary reason for existence in countering the Clintons' studied moderation and chumminess with big business and Wall Street.

Running as a candidate of the left, Vermont governor Howard Dean criticized the Clintons, though in veiled terms, as "the Republican wing of the Democratic party."[18] The attacks were said to have infuriated Bill Clinton, newspapers reported at the time. Though Dean did not win the Democratic nomination that year, his liberal supporters yearned for another candidate to challenge what increasingly came to be seen as the Clinton Democratic establishment.

Still suffering from middling approval ratings, Hillary took a pass on the 2004 race against the incumbent Bush. In truth, it wasn't her move entirely. Clinton pleaded with John Kerry to select Hillary Clinton as his running mate. But he was rebuffed.

"I think she looked at it," a former Clinton aide tells me in an interview, "and saw that it wasn't a really good shot. They saw that they didn't really want to take on an incumbent, you know. Because taking on an incumbent is harder."

The deciding vote appeared to have come from Chelsea Clinton. According to published reports, the former first daughter urged her mother to keep her promise to New York State voters that she would serve a full Senate term if they elected her. At that point, Hillary, if she was seriously entertaining it at all, firmly closed the door on a run.[19]

Besides, Bill was already working on an important side project in the Clintons' charm offensive—one that promised to offer heavy dividends. He sought to make the Bush family, perhaps his most notorious political enemies, his new allies. And he succeeded in a historic fashion, changing the Clintons' political fortunes dramatically.

4

SEDUCING THE BUSHES

*"For their own reasons, the Bush people thought having
Clinton with his father would be clever. They're right.
The consequence may be a Hillary Clinton presidency."*

—Newt Gingrich

If Clinton hoped to rehabilitate his image, and by implication Hillary's, an improbable bonhomie with his most well-known adversaries would be an excellent beginning.

Just before 1 a.m. on December 26, 2004, tsunamis six stories tall crashed into the coasts of Indonesia, Sri Lanka, Thailand, and about a dozen other nations. The tsunamis' cause was an oceanic earthquake registering magnitude 9.0, and its effect was massive devastation and death. More than two hundred thousand people died, and millions more were left homeless. Survivors needed medical care in the short term and an almost unimaginably costly rebuilding effort in the long term. In between, something needed to be done to stave off famine and the spread of disease.

Governments and private citizens across the globe were quick to promise tremendous amounts of aid—including a pledge of $350 million from the United States. But how to channel it all? How to minimize waste and make sure the money found its way to the people who could do the most good? And, since it would take about $10 billion to rebuild what the tsunamis had destroyed, how to raise enough?

The answer, President George W. Bush decided, was to put his father and his predecessor in charge. They had the gravitas. They excelled at fund-raising. And neither would be distracted by a day job. Both men immediately agreed to W.'s request to head the relief mission, and in February 2005 they spent four days in Thailand, Indonesia, Sri Lanka, and the Maldives—an island nation that had lost 62 percent of its gross domestic product. Clinton saw in the trip an opportunity to help not just the wrecked region, but his family's political fortunes as well.

"Being next to Herbert Walker Bush was good for Clinton," says John McCain, who has observed both men up close for decades. "Bush 41 always had an unimpeachable reputation. I mean service in World War II; you know all the things that he did." Clinton could only benefit from the proximity.

The psychology of the elder Bush is not complicated. Despite his later efforts to model himself a Texan, the elder Bush grew up an aristocratic Connecticut Yankee, in a land of country clubs, prep schools, and noblesse oblige. Bush's maternal grandfather founded golf's Walker Cup, and his father, Prescott, was a United States senator. Their country-club set prizes graciousness, good manners, and kind gestures, even small ones.

The old man "is the last of the great gentlemen," an admiring former aide to the senior Bush tells me.

"We all love Bush 41," John McCain says fondly. "He and Gerald Ford, both losers, were viewed in my life as two of the nicest people that inhabited the White House."

Trained by his mother to demonstrate modesty and embrace service, Bush the elder is susceptible to graciousness as well as flattery. Greenwich, Connecticut, was a world where such messy things as ideologies were nuisances. A place where big ideas were dwarfed by small kindnesses and the proper showing of deference.

Bill Clinton's wooing of the senior Bush thus began with the friendliest of arguments. As the former opponents flew together on an Air Force Boeing 757 toward South Asia, they argued over which ex-president would get to sleep in the lone bed. Bush, whose patrician politeness was the closest thing he had to an ideology, insisted Clinton should take it. Clinton wouldn't hear of it. Touched by this act of selflessness, Bush would later say, "That meant a lot to me."[1]

In truth, it wasn't that big of a sacrifice. As an aide later told me, Clinton ended up playing cards all night with Bush's chief of staff.

Clinton's "good son" act continued at every stop, when Clinton would respectfully wait at the bottom of the plane's steps while the octogenarian Bush slowly descended. Clinton knew and at every opportunity abided by the code of chivalry Bush followed—the unwritten rules of small gestures, tactful words, and signs of respect passed down from Prescott Bush and his wife, Dorothy Walker Bush, to the heirs of their dynasty.

The senior Bush was smitten. As he would later gush to presidential chronicler Hugh Sidey, "I thought I knew him; but until this trip I did not really know him. . . . He has been very considerate of me."[2]

To be sure, on the tsunami trip Clinton wasn't always on his best behavior. He talked too much for Bush's tastes, and he was always running late—a true taboo in BushWorld. He also hit on Lani Miller, the redheaded White House aide whom Clinton couldn't resist telling, "You remind me of my first girlfriend." It was interpreted as a pickup line, not a literal comparison. Before Bill Clinton's trip to South Asia with George H. W. Bush, he was held in unreserved contempt by many—perhaps most—Republicans, but after the trip and the many pictures and footage of the two former enemies hand in hand amid carnage and disaster, Clinton's approval rating climbed.

In 2005, Clinton and the man who once called him a bozo[3] went to the Super Bowl together. The former rivals went golfing together. Bush's chief of staff told a visitor to Bush's Houston office that when Clinton underwent a follow-up heart surgery in March of that year, Bush was "deeply, deeply, personally disturbed by it." The visitor, who did not know Bill Clinton well, insisted, "That wasn't for show. I mean, the old man was just pacing, and it was like a family member had gone under the knife."

Like a true member of the Bush family, Clinton spent part of his summer vacation that year with his new friend at Bush's compound in Kennebunkport, Maine. He even took up Bush's habit of letter writing—at least in his own way. Ever the ribald, Clinton sent Bush a cartoon depicting the younger Bush making a statement opposing gay marriage. The next frame showed Clinton and Bush 41 sitting on a couch holding hands. In the cartoon, Clinton says, "George, maybe we'd better cool it."[4]

Pope John Paul II, eighty-four, was nearing the twilight of his historic papacy, one that hastened the end of the Cold War and left him a reputation as one of the most influential figures of the twentieth century. He had survived two assassination attempts, battles with cancer, and other illnesses, and time was finally taking its toll. He had slowly been dying for years.

It was early 2005, and Jim Nicholson, a trim, mustachioed Coloradan, was ending his stint as the U.S. ambassador to the Vatican, a position to which he had been appointed by George W. Bush in 2001. The low-key ambassador, a West Point graduate and highly decorated Vietnam veteran, had been recalled to Washington to serve as Bush's secretary of veterans affairs.

But before his departure, Nicholson made a final visit to the frail pontiff at the Apostolic Palace, which housed the pope's luxurious private apartments in the Vatican. The palace, construction of which began in 1589, consists of a series of buildings that house the pope and his offices, as well as other administrative staff.

"It was a really personal visit," Nicholson tells me, clearly moved. "To thank me for the work I'd done there." As they met in a sitting room adorned with soft green high-back chairs, the Holy Father experienced trouble breathing. Suffering from Parkinson's disease, he barely spoke above a whisper. Nicholson would be the last U.S. ambassador to be acquainted with the legendary pontiff.

On April 2, 2005, in that very apartment where he met with Nicholson, the Holy Father died. Ever cognizant of the Catholic vote—an obsession among Bush political advisors like Karl Rove—as well as deeply respectful of the pontiff's contributions in the Cold War, the president himself decided to attend the pope's state funeral. As the most recent U.S. ambassador, Nicholson was an obvious choice to accompany Bush, and he boarded the flight along with the First Lady, the prolific Catholic writer Michael Novak, and Bush's two immediate predecessors: Bill Clinton and George H. W. Bush. Jimmy Carter chose not to accompany the delegation aboard Air Force One. This was all for the best, since both Bushes and Clinton had little personal regard for the Georgian.

For Nicholson, a devout Catholic, the trip undoubtedly conjured a wealth of emotions. It was almost incidental that the flight also offered Nicholson his first encounter with his onetime nemesis, Bill Clinton.

From 1997 to 2001, the entirety of Clinton's tumultuous second term, Nicholson had served as the Republican National Committee chairman. In that time, on radio and television, the Colorado lawyer was the chief Republican spokesman against the Clinton administration. And the mild-mannered westerner had taken to his job with relish. With the 2000 election approaching, Nicholson took memorable aim not only at Clinton, but also his would-be successor, Vice President Al Gore.

One of the more famous encounters occurred after Nicholson authorized advertising on a massive billboard situated across the street from Gore-Lieberman campaign headquarters in Nashville, Tennessee. The billboard displayed a giant photograph of Gore embracing Clinton beneath a Gore quote that had labeled Clinton "the greatest president ever!" In 2000, at the nadir of Clinton's personal popularity and as the

Monica Lewinsky scandal continued to be a drag on Gore's fortunes, the billboard proved a major irritant to Gore campaign staffers, who were greeted with it every time they drove into work. It also outraged the famously petulant vice president, who was offended and embarrassed by Clinton's private behavior and longed to keep his distance. "[Gore] was just so upset about the Lewinsky matter and angry about it," Joe Lieberman tells me in an interview, "not just because he disagreed with it, but because I think he felt that it was going to hurt him in the campaign." The billboard was just another reminder of the scandal and the toll it might have on Gore's personal fortunes.

"[Gore] tried to use the muscle he had in Tennessee to have it taken down," a grayer Nicholson remembers, when I visited recently with him in his law office in downtown Washington, D.C. "The outdoor advertising company said they were getting a tremendous amount of pressure." Nicholson finally relented, knowing that the removal of the sign would lead to another burst of publicity, and more fury from the Gore campaign. In addition to harassing Gore, Nicholson had at one point or another accused Clinton of dishonesty, corruption, shamelessness, pursuing "a legacy of vengeance," and of "practicing the politics of personal destruction."

Now, in the spring of 2005, aboard Air Force One as it jetted toward Rome, Nicholson and Clinton met eye to eye. To those who haven't been on the presidential plane, it might seem like a vast fortress in the sky. Large it is, but not so large that VIPs don't cross paths rather easily. This was exactly what happened with Clinton and Nicholson as they made their way down the narrow, tan-carpeted corridor.

"Ah, Nicholson, I've been looking forward to meeting you," said the former president. He looked trimmer than he did during his time in office. His hair, overdue for a cut, was almost completely white.

"Hello, Mr. President," Nicholson replied.

"For four years you did nothing but beat me up," Clinton said, with a chuckle. He remembered specifically a vacation with Hillary in the summer of 1999. "Every time we turned on the TV or the radio, I had to hear you beating up on me."

Nicholson is not a visibly emotional man, and he took Clinton's ribbing in stride. "That was my job, Mr. President."

"I know," Clinton replied with a smile, as if to say, *That's politics. All
part of the game.* Always eager to forge a connection, Clinton referred to
a close mutual friend who lived in Denver. "[Jim] Lyons is always telling
me you're a good guy."

"Good to know," Nicholson replied.

"Anyway," Clinton added, leaning in toward the former ambassador,
"you can make all this up to me by telling me who the next pope's going
to be."

"Oh, Mr. President," Nicholson said, with a slight turn of his head,
"the Holy Spirit's not talking to me about that." Which, in fact, was not
wholly accurate.

Nicholson did have thoughts on the matter, detailed ones. As part of
their duties, every ambassador regularly assesses candidates who might
replace the current head of state. And Nicholson, a seasoned political
operative and a committed Catholic, had a keen sense of the politics and
intrigues behind a papal succession. But he saw no need to share any of
this with Bill Clinton.

"Aw, come on," Clinton pressed.

"Sorry," Nicholson replied. Shortly thereafter, the two parted company. At least for the moment.

A few hours later, Nicholson found himself in a senior officials' compartment aboard the plane with Clinton, both the current and the former
Presidents Bush, and a few other very senior aides.

Clinton and the Bushes were chatting amiably when seemingly out of
the blue, Clinton turned to his successor. "George, make Nicholson tell
us who the next pope's going to be."

George W. Bush, in his usual blunt, to-the-point way, quickly put
his former envoy on the spot. "Do you have anything on that?" he asked
Nicholson.

"Yes, I do, Mr. President," he replied, addressing his boss and now
giving a straight and forthcoming answer.

"Well, what do you think?"

"I think it's going to be Cardinal Joseph Ratzinger."

"Really?" Clinton interjected. His tone betrayed surprise—and skepticism. "It won't be Ratzinger; he's a German. They'll never elect a German pope."

The ambassador doubled down, insisting it was his best guess from what he'd been hearing.

"No," Clinton said, although he seemed to be dwelling on the possibility in his head. "Why do you think so?"

"Because he is the dean of the College of Cardinals. He is a very highly respected, well-known theologian. He's been in the job as the keeper of the faith, in the Dicastery for the Propagation of the Faith in the Curia. He's known worldwide. He is very respected. He doesn't want the job, he wants to go to Bavaria and play the piano and read and take walks and pray. He's also going to preside over all these ceremonies that we're flying to this morning."

Clinton maintained a look of skepticism. But as the conversation in the room turned to other matters, the former president disappeared.

"I didn't think anything of it at the time," Nicholson recalls now, though he soon learned where Clinton went.

The former president wandered down the corridor of the presidential plane and, as if by happenstance, soon found himself in the small compartment in the back of the plane reserved for the press corps. The reporters aboard Air Force One pay for these cramped quarters, where the communication equipment is poor and actual news rare—but they do it for quality time with high-ranking officials. And on this trip, they were lucky. Clinton was happy to glad-hand them, stroke their egos (and his), and take part in his favorite pastime: political gossip. When the conversation turned to the successor for Pope John Paul II, Clinton held forth with a knowledgeable gaze.

"I think it's going to be Ratzinger," Clinton predicted, making it seem like all along his own thoughtful analysis had led him to what would be a prophetic conclusion. "A German. He's got a lot of momentum."

Reporters started scribbling. Many undoubtedly were dazzled once again by Bill Clinton's legendary political acumen. And they would be even more impressed when the prediction soon turned out to be correct.

Nicholson shakes his head as he recounts this. "Typical Clinton," he says. And soon he and others among the delegation would get other glimpses of the former president, with whom they'd spend the next two and a half days.

First, of course, was the talking. "He talks all the time," said one of the passengers aboard that flight. "He just wears you out."

"He tells a lot of stories," a Clinton intimate tells me. "Some of them I've heard four hundred, five hundred times, but it is what it is. I think that's why people cycle through. It's kind of enjoyable for the first six months and then, you know . . ."

"He would dominate the conversation on all sorts of topics," Nicholson says. "Sometimes we'd be in a conversation that would trigger a thought of his, and he would start talking about something that was related to that, either related to an experience of his, or somebody that he knew, or something . . . and he would just go on with that, even though the other conversation might continue as well. It was odd to me. It was like he was sitting over there, and you and I were having a chat about the Nationals, and if there was something else on his mind, he'd be talking about it."

Clinton talked so much, one Bush official said, that he'd exhaust the attention of both of the Bushes. "You could see Dubya's mind drifting off," the official said.

Clinton's now-famous bond with the Bush family—and the larger BushWorld in general—was a key element in the rebuilding of the Clinton "brand." Indeed, it may well rank as one of Bill Clinton's most ambitious and personally rewarding achievements, one that not only had been a decade in the making, but was in effect a master class in Clinton's ability to win friends and influence people. Despite the glossy spin now put on the relationship, the Arkansan had had a steep hill to climb.

On November 3, 1992, after an economic recession and a hard-fought three-way race for the presidency, Arkansas governor Bill Clinton defeated incumbent George H. W. Bush by a margin of 43 percent to 37 percent (with 19 percent for third-party candidate H. Ross Perot). The defeat was seen as an embarrassing rebuke to the sitting president, who had earned acclaim only a year earlier for the liberation of Kuwait from Iraqi dictator Saddam Hussein. At the time, it also seemed to place a period on the Bush family's political fortunes. Looking back on his father's defeat years later, George Walker Bush remembers no ill will. "Dad had been raised to be a good sport," Bush wrote in his bestselling memoir, *Decision Points*. "He blamed no one; he was not bitter."[5] As Bush writes, his father called Clinton that evening to offer a gracious concession—which began, as George W. Bush put it, "one of the more unlikely friendships in American political history."[6]

"What a lot of people don't realize is we've never really been hostile," the elder George Bush once said to an interviewer. "You get into a campaign and there's understandable hostility. But I've always had a rather pleasant personal relationship with him. . . . So it's not surprising to us. But it is surprising to everybody else."[7]

Although there is significant evidence today that the senior George Bush and Bill Clinton have moved beyond their 1992 election and become close friends, the sunny version of that pairing—that the two grew to appreciate each other almost as soon as the smoke cleared in 1992—is not consistent with the facts. The real story is more complicated, more interesting, and far more revealing.

The 1992 loss was understandably painful for the hypercompetitive Bush family. Indeed, it was so painful that it might well have altered history.

For much of the next decade, family members lashed out in very personal terms at the man who had vanquished their beloved patriarch. George W. Bush, in particular, was said to be furious over his father's defeat—"the better man lost," he seethed on election night—and lashed out at the media for its bias. He was not alone. His mother, Barbara, recalled writing in her diary "over and over again that Bill Clinton did not have a chance." She was sure that "The American people would never vote for him."[8]

In Houston on election night in 1992, while most of the Bush clan received news of election returns together, Mrs. Bush spent much of the time reading a romance novel in another room, as if refusing to consider the possibility of defeat.[9]

"We saw a good man, and a great leader, brought down by distortion, innuendo, and fabrication," said Bush's daughter, Dorothy (Doro), who went on to compare Clinton to Richard Nixon.

George H. W. Bush apparently agreed. He considered Clinton a "sleazeball" who "dodged" the draft, as one Bush biographer put it.[10] "I remember many conversations with President Bush when he was incredulous about Clinton's lead," the Republican Party chairman Rich Bond recalled. "He'd say, 'How can voters support someone of so little integrity?'"

At Camp David, the presidential retreat in Maryland, a depressed Bush reached out to a visiting Colin Powell, then serving as chairman of the Joint Chiefs of Staff.

"Colin, it hurts," Bush told him. "It really hurts. I never thought they'd pick him."

"I know it does," Powell replied. "It has to."[11]

George W. Bush, who could be peevish and petty, made a point of saying at the opening of his father's presidential library in 1997 that his father "left [office] with his integrity intact."[12] It was meant to be a poke at Bill Clinton, who was in attendance and did not miss any of the implications of Bush's reference to integrity. "Of course," Clinton later said, "he's never forgiven me for beating his father."[13]

The animus toward the Clintons extended all the way through George W. Bush's successful 2000 presidential campaign. At one point, when Clinton mocked then-governor Bush's qualifications for the job—"How bad could I be? I've been governor of Texas. My daddy was president. I own a baseball team. . . . Their fraternity had it for eight years, give it to ours for eight years"—the Bushes unleashed their not-well-contained fury.[14] The elder Bush, for example, warned reporters that the attacks on his son might prompt him to tell Americans what he really thinks about Clinton "as a human being and a person."[15]

A former high-level Clinton aide scoffs at the revisionism of the Bush-Clinton relationship. "George Bush Senior—he *hated* us," he tells me. "The reason W. ran [for president] was to avenge the loss of his father to that trailer trash, Bill Clinton."

There is, in fact, significant support for that assertion, and from Bush's fellow Republicans. In 1999, for example, as George W. Bush mounted his campaign for the White House, California congressman James Rogan faced a tough reelection in his swing district, in part because of Rogan's prominent and controversial role as one of the managers of Bill Clinton's impeachment.

Knowing that then-Texas governor Bush was considering a White House bid, Rogan joined a small number of his colleagues to endorse him. Throughout 1999, Bush made a few visits to Washington, meeting with various advisors and fund-raisers—a group that included Rogan and some of the other early boosters.

Rogan recalled for me an unusual encounter with Bush while visiting with him in a private meeting room at the Library of Congress. "We had a whole bunch of congressmen in there—and, you know, I'm just one of four hundred and thirty-five members of the House," Rogan, now a judge in California, tells me by telephone. "But [Bush] grabbed me by the arm and he was calling me 'Jimmy,' and he said in that Texas twang, 'You know, Jimmy. I know your district. Glendale, Pasadena, Burbank.' He named the cities in my district."

"I know they're coming after you," Bush told the embattled congressman. "I want you to know something: I'm going to be there for you. I'm going to be there campaigning with you. I'm going to be there helping you raise money."

Rogan was taken aback. "You know, here's this presidential candidate, or he's about to become one, who's taking the time to actually research my district to know that I'm in trouble," he says. "I said something like, 'I'm really impressed.'"

In response Bush offered a "steely" look. Grabbing the congressman and pulling him in close, he whispered, "You avenged my father."

Equating a vote for the impeachment of Bill Clinton with avenging George H. W. Bush's political defeat "never dawned on me," Rogan says. "I never connected any dots until Bush said it to me and then I thought, 'Oh, yeah, okay, sure, well, that's why he knows about my district. I mean something to him. He was watching these guys taking cannon fire, stand up in a very unpopular process to the guy that beat his dad.'" In the end, Bush wouldn't actually be there for Rogan. During a swing before the November election, Bush's campaign would view impeachment too warily to allow him to stand next to Rogan. Days later the incumbent congressman would be defeated by Democrat Adam Schiff.

By the time the Bushes returned to the White House, they felt a greater generosity of spirit toward those who'd vanquished them, and the relationship between the two famously feuding families found new contours. It was a relationship that Bill Clinton seemed determined to improve. The outgoing president—at the time a hated figure to Republicans and a source of exhaustion to many on the left—sensed the bonanza such a pairing offered.

The thaw began slowly, but immediately, in December 2000, only days after the U.S. Supreme Court ended a recount in Florida and in effect handed the presidential election to Bush. Heading to Washington to meet with his transition team, President-elect Bush paid a "courtesy call" visit to Clinton as well as the man he'd just so narrowly defeated.

"Al Gore was terrible to him," a senior Bush aide recalls, as the Bushes arrived at the vice president's residence on Massachusetts Avenue. For the Gores, the residence on the grounds of the U.S. Naval Observatory was a mere two and a half miles—and Florida's twenty-five electoral votes—away from the White House. It had also, until a day or two earlier, been the site of round-the-clock protests by Bush supporters, who wore "Sore-Loserman" T-shirts (a play on the Gore-Lieberman ticket) and chanted through the gates and into the Gores' bedroom, "Get out of Cheney's house!"

This was the first presidential motorcade for the incoming Bush administration. One of the new members of Bush's detail opened the door for Bush and watched the president-elect and his wife, Laura, exit the car and walk up the steps, across the covered white porch, and into the Gores' residence. Soon—much sooner than Bush's aides expected—Bush reemerged from the mansion, grim-faced and irritated.

"Okay, let's go," he said.

"They'd only been in there for like thirty seconds," an aide reflects with amazement. (The awkward meeting, which Karl Rove later described as "tense and cold," was actually closer to fifteen minutes.)[16]

"Gore's a prick," a senior Bush press aide says. "He's not the kind of person that has the ability to lead at that level, I believe, because he's a jerk."

Due to the unique circumstances, the Bush-Gore meeting was all but fated to be tense and perfunctory. But in any event it stood in sharp contrast to the reception the Bushes received minutes later at the White House from Bill and Hillary Clinton.

"They were just warmly welcomed," a Bush aide later reflects. A "relaxed, even funny" Clinton, as described by Karl Rove, treated Bush to a steak while Hillary showed Laura the family quarters. Clinton oozed with ingratiation, even complimenting the tie worn by one of Bush's aides. The current and future president dined together for ninety minutes, while Clinton held forth on the economy, advised on North Korea, and, at Bush's request, offered his successor pointers on giving speeches. (The key, he said, was timing.)

That Gore and Clinton by that point all but hated each other probably made Clinton's overture even more palatable. As a former senator puts it, "You get the feeling that Clinton acts like he likes Bush a lot better than he ever liked Al Gore." The not-so-secret truth was that the Clintons weren't heartbroken by Gore's loss. Not only did Gore not quite fit the mold of a president in their eyes: A Republican in the White House also offered Hillary the chance for a potential run for the White House in 2004.

By the time Hillary made clear she would not challenge the Bushes, the Clinton-Bush relationship had really begun to flower.

Perhaps the first recorded defrost in the Clinton-Bush relationship occurred, of all places, at the White House itself. It was June 14, 2004, and hundreds were gathered at 1600 Pennsylvania Avenue for the ceremonial unveiling of the official portrait of President Clinton.

It was an election year. Bush would be squaring off against John Kerry later that year in November, and Democrats had turned against Bush on myriad issues, especially the Iraq War. Indeed, it could've been either a quick, ceremonial, and formal affair, or worse: It could've been nasty. Bush could've brought up President Clinton's impeachment. Clinton, ever the politician, could've turned the knife and embarrassed the somewhat unpopular Bush.

Lanny Davis, a longtime friend of Hillary Clinton, has explained.[17] "So it's the spring of 2004 and the hatred—H-word, horrible word—toward George W. Bush for going into Iraq, for his tax cuts, and for a lot of other policies that offended liberal Democrats, policies that I did not agree with, was in such a fever that it reminded me of the worst days of the hate machine against Bill Clinton, except this time it was my side against George Bush." In fact, neither of those things happened. What the aides, families of Presidents Bush and Clinton, and friends witnessed was something else entirely. "President Clinton and Senator Clinton, welcome home," Bush began, exuding genuine warmth as he pointed his remarks directly at the guests of honor.[18] Clinton appeared touched as he mouthed thanks and lowered his head with a slight nod.

Bush would thank the appropriate parties for attending and then, in essence, welcome Clinton to his family—the Bush family and the family of ex-presidents. "As you might know, my father and I have decided to call each other by numbers," Bush said. "He's Forty-One, I'm Forty-Three. . . . It's a great pleasure to honor number Forty-Two. We're glad you're here, Forty-Two."

The compliments in the East Room would continue to be exchanged. "Over eight years it was clear that Bill Clinton loved the job of the presidency. He filled this house with energy and joy. He's a man of enthusiasm and warmth, who could make a compelling case and effectively advance the causes that drew him to public service."

It was perhaps an understated gesture, but a meaningful one. "Bill Clinton was moved. I could see him right in front of me. And the entire audience, when President Bush was done, stood up and gave President Bush a standing ovation," says Davis, who served in the Clinton White House and considers George W. Bush a close friend, too.

"Oh my God," Davis thought as he watched the scene unfold. "George Bush has proven what I've always known about him and maybe about politics: that when you transcend the hate and the polarization, there's humanity there that people were recognizing, the graciousness of President Bush."[19]

Bill Clinton would return the favor when he took the stage after unveiling the massive painting. The portrait is on canvas, about forty-six by fifty-eight inches, and captures former president Clinton "standing in the Oval Office, behind his desk," according to the painter, Simmie Knox, the first African American to get the privilege and honor of creating a presidential portrait. "He's a wonderful man," Knox told National Public Radio.[20] It captures, as the artist explained, eye-to-eye contact between the painted president and the viewer—a telling trait, perhaps the charisma and ability to connect with just about anyone that Clinton has shown throughout the course of his lifetime.

"Mr. President, I had mixed feelings coming here today, and they were only confirmed by all those kind and generous things you said. Made me feel like I was a pickle stepping into history," Forty-Two said to Forty-Three.[21]

Clinton's next big opportunity to cement the public image of a Bush-Clinton alliance arose after a category 4 hurricane with 145 mph winds crashed into the Gulf Coast on August 29, 2005. George W. Bush asked his father and Clinton to do for New Orleans and the Gulf what they'd done for South Asia.

No natural disaster in seven decades had killed more Americans than Hurricane Katrina. To be in the Gulf region was to lose, in many instances, all of the little you owned. To be in parts of New Orleans, especially the Superdome, was to be subject to disgusting conditions and estranged from many of the trappings of civilization. And to be in the rest of the country was to be inundated with images of our fellow Americans looting abandoned shops, waiting for rescue on the rooftops of flooded homes, or pleading for water from reporters who had found a convention center of refugees that the Federal Emergency Management Agency apparently couldn't.

Katrina was the costliest natural disaster in American history, and it was the beginning of the end of George W. Bush's presidency. After a start that was slow—glacierlike would be more precise—Bush vowed to spend whatever it took to rebuild New Orleans and the rest of the Gulf. And one of the first things he did was ask his two predecessors to tour the region, raise money, and spend it wisely.

Clinton and the elder Bush taped public service announcements, sat for joint interviews, and started calling donors. Checks were sent—by everyone from Girl Scouts to billionaires—to Bush's and Clinton's offices in Houston and Harlem. Most were addressed to the nonprofit foundation the ex-presidents had set up for Katrina relief, but some of the checks were simply addressed to them personally. The two presidents whose two most famous quotes were untrue—"Read my lips" and "I did not have sexual relations with that woman"—were now so trusted that Americans who wanted to help hurricane victims were simply sending Bush and Clinton cash. They raised $130 million.

Bill Clinton's new best friend also worked his own family hard on his successor's behalf. By all accounts, the highest reverence within the Bush family is reserved for their aging patriarch. That Clinton seemed to be genuinely interested in the Old Man counted for a lot. The effect on the Bush family was in keeping with the old man's status as patriarch, hero, and idol.

Clinton's charm offensive extended not only to the Bushes, but to key aides as well. In his memoir, Karl Rove recalls Clinton going out of his way to profusely praise the phrase "compassionate conservative"—an indirect way of praising Rove himself. And when Rove was under fire for masterminding the loss of Congress to the Democrats in 2006, Rove remembered Clinton telling him, "no one's ever going to give you credit, but it was sheer genius what you and [RNC chairman Ken] Mehlman did with the seventy-two-hour task force. We should have won twice as many seats, but we didn't because of what you all did to get out your vote."[22]

"He's very engaging, very personable, wants to know the latest gossip, has lots of interesting insights and opinions," Rove tells me in an interview. The Bush strategist then lapses into an uncanny imitation of Clinton: " 'You just ran an incredible campaign. It was just, what you did to John Kerry it was unbelievable. You're a genius. I just tell you, you're remarkable. It's really something what you did.' "

The controversial Bush defense secretary Donald Rumsfeld wasn't off-limits, either. After the Iraq War and the Abu Ghraib prison abuse scandal plagued the Bush administration, Bill Clinton went so far as to offer words of support to Rumsfeld, the Democrats' top target. In his memoir, Rumsfeld tells of a visit to the World War II memorial in Washington on May 29, 2004, when he encountered Bill Clinton. "Mr. Secretary," the former president said. "No one with an ounce of sense thinks you had any way in the world to know about the abuse taking place that night in Iraq." Rumsfeld was touched by the gesture, even though Senator Clinton, the administration's Democratic opponents, and probably Bill Clinton himself were advancing an entirely different narrative to the press.

Deputy assistant to President Bush Pete Wehner says, "My sense is that there was an admiration" of W. by Clinton, which mattered in a White House that placed a high priority on loyalty to the president. It's hard for many critics of the Bush administration to believe that Bill Clinton actually admired George W. Bush, but what really matters is that the Bushes—and the president—thought he did.

By the end of Bush's presidency, Bill Clinton was a frequent lunch guest in the White House, trading war stories, gossip, and grievances. It was never disclosed on the public schedules, but when Clinton came to Washington, D.C., to visit Hillary, for business, or to give a speech, the world's most famous Democrat made time for the world's most famous Republican. It was far more often than has previously been reported, and indeed so few people know of the frequent lunches between Bush and Clinton that getting an exact number is hard to do.

One former top press aide tells me, "They got along really well and liked to share ideas and talk things through."

They also shared a mutual frustration with the press, which Bush believed was hostile to him and which Clinton believed was biased toward Obama and against Hillary. "That cat isn't remotely qualified," Bush raged at one point.

"President Bush really thought that the media gave Hillary Clinton a raw deal during the campaign," one senior aide says, "and certainly the Clinton campaign thought that as well. So I think [Clinton] would call him just to talk about politics. They shared a frustration with the media."

Today, the former rival families appear to be as thick as thieves. They pose for photos together, deliver speeches with each other, and offer each other bountiful praise. A few years ago, when a Bush family picture was taken at the Kennedy Center after ceremonies celebrating the life of the forty-first president, there were twenty-seven Bushes in the photograph—and Bill Clinton. (There again was Clinton, without much of an extended family of his own, inserting himself into another family's photo.)

To many close Bill Clinton observers, the elder Bush was the replacement father he never had. (Clinton's biological father, William Blythe Sr., died in a car accident shortly before his son was born. His stepfather, Roger Clinton Sr., was an abusive alcoholic.)

Clinton is a "little bit vulnerable," says a former Bush administration press aide who has observed the Bush-Clinton interaction up close. "Like he might sit down across the table from you and just say, 'God, am I a flawed character.' . . . I do think that if you're looking into this relationship, one thing that's worth considering is how the Bush family tends to pick up orphans along the way, meaning that because it's such a big and strong, vibrant family, and a lot of us don't have that in our life, but we long for it."

There are signs, however, that the Bush-Clinton love affair is a rather shallow one behind the scenes. George H. W. Bush's affection for Clinton is said by almost all accounts to be genuine, but no one is sure that holds true for Clinton, or for the other Bushes. Many suggest this is more PR than reality.

Consider John McCain, long acquainted with the Bush family, as among the skeptics. "I'm not sure that they're close," he opines, as he reflects on the relationship in his Washington office in 2013.

"The relationship's been overstated a lot, which I always find interesting," says a source close to Bill Clinton. "I mean, they see each other and they talk to each other, you know, maybe three times a year kind of thing. It's not like they're hanging out all the time, but yeah, I think it's certainly been hugely beneficial to them both. No doubt about that."

Of course, the real source of power in the Bush household is not the gentlemanly George H. W. Bush, but his wife, Barbara. The toughest and perhaps shrewdest member of the family, Barbara Bush is a hardened New Englander born to wealth, a woman of strong opinions and sharp edges. A notorious grudge holder, she famously despised Nancy Reagan for "snubbing" the Bushes during the Reagan administration, and when

she became First Lady went out of her way to mock Mrs. Reagan's designer clothes before an approving press corps. In 2001, still steaming
over her husband's loss to a "lesser man," Barbara threw Monica Lewinsky in the former president's face. "Clinton lied," she told a reporter with
her usual, blunt style. "A man might forget where he parks or where he
lives, but he never forgets oral sex, no matter how bad it is."[23]

For public consumption, at least, Mrs. Bush is on board with the
Clinton-Bush lovefest. She's told interviewers that she likes Clinton and
humors his claim that he is the Bush family's "adopted son." Sitting for
an interview with *Parade* in 2012, Barbara Bush offered what the *New
York Daily News* called a gushing review of Mr. Clinton. "He's very nice,"
Mrs. Bush said. "Thoughtful . . . a good fellow."[24]

"I was surprised by the fact that I liked him, truthfully," Barbara
Bush added. "And I do like him a lot."

Privately, others have heard a different view. "I expect she didn't
fall for him for one second," a Bush family observer says. According
to sources, a former Clinton aide and a person with high-level connections to the Bush family, Barbara Bush not only dislikes Bill Clinton, she
despises him. "What's Clinton call Barbara Bush?" a source asks. "His
second mother? It's so crazy. The funny thing is she hates him."

Mrs. Bush was overheard telling a close friend in Washington of her
firmly held belief that Clinton was simply beneath them. "She still thinks
of him as not of the same class."

But Bill and Hillary often seemed to be operating at cross-purposes,
perhaps as part of a sort of clever good cop/bad cop strategy. Because
while Bill was working so hard to appease the Bushes, his wife, over in
the Senate, was operating in a totally different fashion. Throughout her
Senate tenure, she demonstrated a penchant for criticizing the Bush administration in strident, even hyperbolic, terms. "There has never been
an administration," she declared in a typical critique, "more intent upon
consolidating and abusing power to further their own agenda." She said
in her speeches that the administration has "no shame," "[has] never
been acquainted with the truth," and "play[s] politics with national se-

curity."[25] Her constant attacks led a fuming George W. Bush to bark to aides in 2008, "Wait till she gets her fat ass in that chair."

The effect was something of a twofer for the Clintons—Bill would be the nice guy who would improve his own image with the help of the Bush family, while Hillary would bolster her bona fides with the liberal base by attacking their chief villains.

There is evidence that even today Hillary Clinton's attacks on Bush have hardly ingratiated her with the Bush family, as her husband has done so successfully. (In a 2012 interview, Barbara Bush would say, coolly, "We really have spent no time with her.")

Barbara Bush's skepticism extends to her brainy son, Jeb, the one she hoped would have been elected to the presidency.

"[Bill]'s been incredibly gracious to our dad," the former president once said, "and if somebody is gracious to our father, he ingratiates himself to us."[26] Suggesting a self-interested motivation to Clinton's outreach, the former Florida governor said, "President Clinton's advisors have figured out that, in terms of character and integrity, a rising tide lifts all boats. So I could see President Clinton's motivation."[27]

In an email to family members that was leaked to the public in 2013, Jeb wrote that his father "helped restore [Clinton's] sordid reputation" and "probably helped Bill Clinton [more] than anything [Clinton] himself has done." It's not clear whether Jeb thought that was a good thing.[28]

Many other Republicans certainly don't. One former Republican officeholder says, "They legitimized him. They moved him from the left to the center. And from that point on, he hasn't looked back."

Superficial or not, the Bush-Clinton pairing has now won the praise and approval of the mainstream media. Which means the relationship has proven so beneficial to both the Bush and Clinton "brands" that it is not likely to end anytime soon, even as the 2016 election approaches. Indeed, George W. Bush and Bill Clinton have begun delivering speeches together across the country (for a reported hefty sum).

In the fall of 2013, Hillary Clinton joined her fellow honorary co-chair of the U.S.-Afghan Women's Council: former first lady Laura Bush, whose own political ideology has always fit more comfortably with the Democratic Party. The event was hosted by the Georgetown Institute for Women, Peace and Security, whose honorary cochair is Hillary Clinton herself—and the executive director is Melanne Verveer, who was the debut U.S. ambassador for global women's issues.[29]

"The most single damaging thing the Bush family has done to politics was to resuscitate Bill and Hillary Clinton and give them a bipartisan veneer," says Newt Gingrich in our interview. Given the fact that Bush was as radioactive to the left as the Clintons were to the right, the very public demonstration of bipartisanship between the country's two most famous political families would only help them. "For their own reasons, the Bush people thought having Clinton with his father would be clever," the former Speaker noted. "They're right. The consequence may be a Hillary Clinton presidency." That might have happened by now, had the Clintons not underestimated a young African American senator with a short résumé but long ambitions.

5

DEATH DEFIERS

"I don't get it. Can you tell me what it is about this guy?"

—Hillary Clinton, 2008

Destiny beckoned Hillary Rodham Clinton. She had waited her turn. She had stood by her husband for the best and especially the worst—those most abhorrently humiliating moments. She had been the political spouse, a largely ceremonial role that she tried (and largely failed) to parlay into something greater. She had served for one full term as a senator from New York and handily won reelection for a second. Now was her time.

The timing suited the most well-known Democrat in the nation. The two-party system in the United States tends to swing like a pendulum, giving power to Republicans, then Democrats, and back and forth. It didn't take high-paid political consultants—though she had plenty of them on her payroll—to determine that after two terms of the unpopular George W. Bush, a Democrat would have to be favored right off the bat to win the 2008 presidential election. And the Democrats needed her, of course—or at least that was clearly what she believed. They had lost the last presidential elections with wooden liberal elitists, Al Gore and John Kerry. Now they had a chance to make history with a woman.

According to the political punditry, as thick in Washington as corn-fields are in Iowa, a Clinton nomination was inevitable. As one "promi-nent Democratic operative" told the *New York Times* in May 2006, "I do think she's inevitable as the nominee, or pretty close to it. Put it this way: she's as strong a front-runner as any non-incumbent presidential candi-date has been in modern history."[1] Columnist Bob Herbert, who quoted that operative, would write, "Many of [the political] strategists and party bigwigs—not all, but many—speak as though there is something inevi-table about Mrs. Clinton ascending to the nomination."[2]

Few in the know gave any of Senator Clinton's potential rivals much of a chance. There was Joe Biden, a creature of the Senate, who came from the tiny state of Delaware, a bumbler who'd immediately begin the election by apologizing for racially insensitive comments toward another rival, Barack Obama. There was Chris Dodd, the senator from liberal and small Connecticut, who didn't have much of any notoriety outside the halls of Congress. There was John Edwards, the vice presidential can-didate for Kerry's run, who was considered a lightweight pretty boy who had probably run for president one time too many. There was Dennis Kucinich, who knew full well he wouldn't be elected but who wanted to drag the race leftward and make sure the most liberal parts of the Dem-ocratic Party had a voice. There was Bill Richardson, who modeled him-self after Bill Clinton but lacked the former president's intelligence and charm while having similar baggage when it came to womanizing. And there was Barack Obama, the well-spoken senator from Illinois, who had served only a couple of years on the national stage and whose most famous moment to date was a speech he had given at the 2004 Demo-cratic convention. He was running, the conventional wisdom went, to bolster his credibility for a more serious presidential bid in the future.

None of these people posed a threat, at least in the collective mind

of Hillaryland. They were blind to the Democratic Party's deep-seated resentment toward her and her husband, ignoring shots across their bow by people like Howard Dean. And while Hillary had been busy making friends with the Republicans in the Senate, the resentment from those most ideologically aligned with her only grew. All of which would soon become apparent to the president-in-waiting.

She announced on January 20, 2007, two years to the day before she expected to be sworn into office. Speaking on her campaign website from a gold-colored sofa in her adopted hometown of Washington, D.C., Hillary sat alone. Talking into the cameras, the multimillionaire portrayed herself as a champion of the middle class, telling viewers, "I grew up in a middle-class family in the middle of America, and we believed in that promise. I still do. I've spent my entire life trying to make good on it, whether it was fighting for women's basic rights or children's basic health care, protecting our social security or protecting our soldiers."

In her remarks she followed the guidelines set up by Mark Penn, a moderate Democrat who had served as Bill Clinton's pollster for six years while he was in the White House. During that time, he became one of the president's most prominent and influential advisors. In 2000, the *Washington Post* concluded in a news analysis that no pollster had ever become "so thoroughly integrated into the policymaking operation" of a presidential administration as had Penn.[3] From 2000 on, Penn transferred his services from one CEO of Clinton, Inc. to the other, serving as Hillary's chief pollster in both of her successful runs for the Senate. Few people were as close to both Clintons as he was, and he was said to have bragged about his access, "a source of jealousy and suspicion among other senior staff," reported *Vanity Fair*.[4]

Penn believed Clinton's campaign should rally a coalition of voters he called "Invisible Americans," a group that included women and the middle class.[5] She ran as the candidate of experience. A tough and policy-minded Democratic Margaret Thatcher. That strategy appeared to be successful, at least at the outset. For most of 2007 she led all polls by double-digit margins. One Gallup poll released in October, for exam-

ple, had her ahead of Obama, 50 percent to his 21.[6] In an accompanying release, Gallup's chief pollsters noted that "Clinton holds a commanding lead among nearly every major subgroup of potential Democratic primary voters. Some of her strongest showings are among women, nonwhites, those in lower-income households, those with less formal education, and Southerners."

What the polls didn't detect was the deep underlying resentment toward her among the Democratic base. The first to break free from the Clinton chokehold were the millionaires of Hollywood—which was logical, since they more than anyone had the power and financial means to separate from the Clintons with little repercussion. David Geffen, the Hollywood mega-mogul and former Clinton donor, was among the early defectors, lashing out at the Clintons in personal terms in a dishy interview published by Clinton nemesis Maureen Dowd, the snarky *New York Times* columnist. He labeled Hillary's campaign "overproduced and overscripted," in Dowd's words. The years of Clintonian mendacity had not been forgotten. "Everybody in politics lies," he said, "but they do it with such ease, it's troubling."[7]

As one high-dollar Democratic donor explained to me, again under condition of anonymity, she and her friends felt betrayed by President Clinton. They felt like he had the perfect opportunity: It was a time between the end of the Cold War and before September 11, 2001. It was, for the first time in years, a period of relative peace. And markets were booming—the Internet was taking off, job growth was explosive, and there was much hope. It was Bill Clinton who was president over all this, a talented and impressive smooth-talking Southerner, and his liberal allies hoped that he could use the moment to accomplish big things— universal health care and a lasting liberalism. They were hoping that he'd be to Democrats what Ronald Reagan had become to Republicans. And instead he squandered it. Because he couldn't keep his pants on— and got caught with the intern. Because he couldn't run a White House without persistent and crippling chaos. And because in reality he never lived up to the potential so many of his supporters saw in him. Hillary,

when she finally hit the trail, wouldn't live up to the billing, either. Those willing to toss her overboard just needed to find another captain to steer their ship. They found him in the bitter cold of Iowa.

For whatever reason, the prim midwesterners of Iowa had never really warmed to the Clintons. Lingering memories of the Lewinsky scandal and the Clintons' other personal foibles did little to help. Unlike nationwide polls, where Clinton still enjoyed a wide lead, she was in a dogfight in the state with John Edwards, who had been working Iowa for years, and a surprisingly confident Barack Obama. In mid-2007 some polls had her behind both men. Worrying about the potential for a surprise loss for the "inevitable" nominee, a senior Clinton campaign aide, Mike Henry, suggested she bypass the state altogether. The memo suggesting that Clinton turn her back on Iowans, which was leaked to the *New York Times* by a rival campaign, only made Clinton's prospects in the state that much shakier.[8]

On January 3, 2008, a state that was over 90 percent white propelled Barack Obama to a shocking victory, demonstrating nationwide that the country was ready to elect an African American to the White House. (As polls had been predicting, Clinton found herself with a humiliating third-place finish.)

The Iowa victory made the prospect of the first African American president more of a reality than ever—and those eager to shuck themselves of the Clintons climbed aboard the Obama bandwagon almost instantly. Suddenly Hillary was facing a totally different race. Her once-strong lead in New Hampshire, which was to hold the next contest, crumbled. On the eve of the balloting, she was behind Obama in some polls by as many as 10 points. As CNN reported, "That's a dramatic reversal from the last CNN/WMUR New Hampshire poll taken after Christmas and just before the Iowa caucuses, when Clinton beat Obama in electability by a two to one margin."[9] Just like that, Hillary Clinton was inches—or to be precise, one more election—from her political grave.

Her advisors knew she would never recover from a second consecutive defeat by a political novice. If Obama won both early contests, along with the likelihood of a third victory in the African-American-vote-rich South Carolina, which was the next primary on the calendar, then the race would be all but over. She would almost certainly be out of the race within days—her money would dry up, her endorsements would disappear. She would be what her husband never was, even in his (many) embarrassing moments on the national stage: a loser. And to make the sting worse, the final blow would be struck by the people of New Hampshire, the same voters who had revived her husband's political fortunes during his 1992 campaign for the presidency, when he battled charges of adultery and draft dodging. Worse for Clinton, CNN's pollsters reported that Obama had polled even with Clinton among female voters, "a voting bloc that she once dominated in the polls."[10]

So she did what a woman is never supposed to do in national politics. She cried before dozens of television cameras. Intended or not, the moment touched the shriveled hearts of the Democratic voters who were abandoning her. The frosty shrew, as she was characterized in focus groups, showed she had a heart after all.

Up until that point, Mrs. Clinton ran as the Queen of the Democratic Establishment. She was programmed, protected, and robotic. Which is to say her campaign was almost from the outset on the wrong footing.

Her performance in 2008 won bipartisan scorn from veteran political pundits. "She's always been a problematic candidate," Republican strategist Mike Murphy tells me. "Her 2008 race was not very impressive. She kind of blew the lead to Obama."

"I actually thought that when she was off the script, she was much better than when she was on the script," says Bob Shrum. "Now, part of that was because the script was entirely wrong. She ran as a candidate of restoration in a period of change. . . . The day before the New Hampshire primary, when she cried, and people said, 'Oh my God, she cried. It's a disaster,' I think voters liked it, and said, 'I've seen a glimpse of who she really is.'"

Defying the polls and defeating Barack Obama by 2.5 percentage points in the New Hampshire primary, the Clintons also had defied death. Again. The most remarkable political comeback in American history journeyed forward, onward, upward, the presidency still in Hillary's reach. The key to her comeback, which startled most Washington reporters, was women, who at the last minute switched back to Clinton by a margin of 13 points over Obama. "Over the last week, I listened to you, and in the process I found my own voice," Hillary proclaimed to an enthusiastic crowd in Manchester. "I felt like we all spoke from our hearts, and I'm so glad that you responded. Now together let's give America the kind of comeback that New Hampshire has just given me."

For the first time since entering the race, Hillary Clinton was back on track. But first she had to get past Barack Obama—the guy she credited herself with helping get elected to the U.S. Senate only three years earlier.

Never one with a keen political antenna, Hillary was more confused than angry by Obama's improbable rise. At a private dinner in Los Angeles shortly after her come-from-behind New Hampshire victory, she put it bluntly. "I don't get it," she said. She managed a passable imitation of Obama's speaking style—hitting just the right notes of haughtiness passing for sincerity, and mocking his content-free happy talk—"We're the change we've been waiting for." That was the kind of speech a graduating college student might make—not a serious candidate for the highest office in the land. In fact it sounded a lot like a young Hillary Rodham at Wellesley College in 1969. She grimaced at the insanity of it all.

For Hillary Clinton's supporters knew something about her colleague that many other Democrats seemed to (or wanted to) miss: As a politician, Obama was overrated to a perhaps unprecedented degree. As a person, he was a bloodless bore. In fact, Hillary's own public caricature—arrogant, ponderous, chilly—was not really how she came across to her friends. Those adjectives did, however, describe the private just-above-room-temperature Obama. Perfectly.

Voters got a glimpse of the real Obama in the days before the New Hampshire primary. When Mrs. Clinton was bluntly asked by a moderator why voters didn't seem to like her as much as Obama, her rival was given an opportunity to say something cheerful and gracious. Instead Obama responded with faint, seemingly mean-spirited praise. "You're likable enough, Hillary," he said coldly. It was another Rick Lazio moment—another man patronizing her, and the Clinton campaign made the most of it in New Hampshire.

In general, however, the woman angle seemed to fail her, too. Hillary had based her campaign on the belief that the country would rally to the First Woman President—a modern-day Eleanor Roosevelt finally making it to the Oval Office. Instead they chose to make a different kind of history.

"I don't get it," she said again, really pressing for the logic. "Can you tell me what it is about this guy?"

"With all due respect, ma'am," a friend at the dinner replied, "a lot of it is that he's not you."

This infuriated the senator even more, probably because it was true. Obama was the beneficiary of the long if subterranean sense of grievance that Democrats felt toward both Clintons, her husband in particular. A grievance that did not dissipate during her years in the Senate or his time out on the hustings, campaigning for Democrat after Democrat. Many senior Democrats had felt used, lied to, embarrassed, and resentful from the first Clinton era. They were tired of the intimidation tactics of hatchet men like James Carville and Terry McAuliffe, who would cut them in public or in private if they ever violated the Clinton omertà. They resented the cavalier treatment toward allies who were no longer of use to them. Stephanopoulos, for example, was now a nonperson to the Clintons. As was Al Gore, who'd served Bill Clinton loyally for eight years, but who'd challenged him over the Lewinsky scandal and his ethics in an explosive fight that, according to multiple aides and published reporting, left both fuming.

Most members of the political press were tired of the Clintons, too. They long had been victims of rough treatment and sharp elbows from the First Family's media handlers—and the ever-looming threat of being frozen out by the Clintons, and their careers stunted, if they deviated too far from what the Clintonistas felt was fair game. A prime example of this tendency involved the commentator David Shuster, who dared to raise questions about the crown jewel of the Clinton family—their beloved and sheltered daughter, Chelsea. Shuster's brush with the Clintons has never before been fully reported, but the story offers a textbook example of the Clintons' willingness to manipulate and punish disfavored reporters.

As the 2008 campaign turned into a delegate-by-delegate dogfight all the way to the Denver convention, the Clinton campaign had pulled out a secret weapon to try to kick things back into gear: the heretofore reclusive Chelsea Clinton. She of course had grown up in the White House, but had long been sheltered by an off-limits rule to which the press and other Washington fixtures by and large strictly adhered. Few forgot the kerfuffle that resulted when John McCain, in one of his famously acerbic moments, joked at a private fund-raiser, "Why is Chelsea Clinton so ugly? Her father is Janet Reno."[11] The senator quickly apologized.

The hands-off policy had now been managed to such an extreme that most reporters even extended it to a time when a now-grown-up Chelsea inserted herself into the political spotlight. In 2008, for example, her mission was to pressure so-called superdelegates—unpledged delegates to the Democratic convention who could, in theory, sway the outcome of the nominating process—of primary states into supporting her mother.

"Hey, don't commit yet, we want you to wait," Chelsea would tell the superdelegates, who were surprised and startled to hear from the former first child.

Shuster was a fill-in host and political commentator for MSNBC. A telegenic forty-one-year-old, he'd been in broadcasting for nearly two decades. Shuster wanted to do a story for the liberal cable news network on Chelsea's involvement in the campaign. It was novel, after all, and more than anything he just thought there was news value in figuring out what exactly she was telling these superdelegates in these phone calls.

So he asked her himself. At a South Carolina campaign event, Shuster got his moment and pulled Chelsea aside.

"Hey, do you want to chat?" Shuster asked her. "Can I ask you a couple of questions about what you're doing with the superdelegates?"

Unsurprisingly, Chelsea declined. "Nah, I really don't want to talk about it." This was the kind of rejection a veteran reporter like Shuster is used to—news subjects, especially political ones, prefer to manage the press by bringing them the story. They don't usually like being asked cold what they themselves are up to.

The encounter was seconds-long, perfunctory, and otherwise meaningless. At least to Shuster. But the next day, Shuster received a phone call from the Clinton campaign.

"Stay away from Chelsea," warned a gruff Howard Wolfson, Hillary Clinton's communications director.

"What?" Shuster asked.

"She is off-limits," Wolfson replied. "She is not, you know—you are not allowed to just go up and talk to her."

By now most reporters covering the Clinton campaign were prepared for Wolfson, a tough Clinton loyalist who could play hardball. Having worked on Hillary Clinton's 2000 election to the U.S. Senate and her 2006 reelection, Wolfson returned in 2008 to direct communications on her White House campaign. For the first part of the election, Wolfson played a fairly conventional role in a fairly conventional campaign. But as Clinton's losses to Obama started to pile up in early 2008, Wolfson's style appeared increasingly desperate. In April, he raised questions about Obama's relationship with the American terrorist Bill Ayers. He was ferocious in his defense of Chelsea Clinton.

"Look," Shuster recalls telling Wolfson, "she's perfectly capable of defending herself and saying, 'No,' politely, as she did. And that's fine. If she didn't want to comment that's fine, but you guys are sort of jumping down my throat. . . . She's twenty-seven years old."

"Well, she's the president's daughter. You need to be respectful," Wolfson said, ending the call as quickly and bizarrely as it began.

Looking back on the encounter years later, Shuster still remembers what he thought: "Wow!" Never before had he been warned so harshly to steer clear of a campaign surrogate—of someone who was on the campaign trail publicly making the case for a candidate.

But Shuster was a busy guy, and campaigns are busy times, so he carried on. The importance of that phone call and the implicit warning not to talk about Chelsea was missed.

A couple of days later, February 7, 2008, Shuster found himself filling in for host Tucker Carlson's short-lived show, *Tucker*. Before the program, as Shuster was going over some segments, an MSNBC executive nonchalantly asked, "Well, how was your trip? What's going on?"

"Oh, the trip was fine," Shuster responded. "But I got the most bizarre reaction from the Clinton campaign when I tried to talk to Chelsea, just to see if she would be willing to talk about her phone calls to superdelegates."

"What do you mean?" replied the MSNBC suit.

"Well, you know, Chelsea said calmly 'No,' she wasn't going to talk and the next day I got this irate Clinton campaign staffer telling me to get the hell away from her. She's off-limits."

The executive offered a quick retort, "Oh, so it's like they're pimping her out."

"That's a great way to explain it," Shuster said. They put her out there, making those phone calls, making her almost impenetrable in terms of media access. And by doing so they don't have to explain anything that's going on—it's all upside, with nothing on the downside. The phrase stuck in his head.

That night, Shuster's guests included radio talk show host Bill Press and the former CNN reporter Bob Franken. Shuster opened a segment about Chelsea's efforts to woo the superdelegates and, addressing Press, said, "Bill, there's just something a little bit unseemly to me that Chelsea's out there calling up celebrities, saying support my mom, and apparently she's also calling these superdelegates."

"Hey, she's working for her mom," Press said. "What's unseemly about that? During the last campaign, the Bush twins were out working for their dad. I think it's great. I think she's grown up in a political family, she's got politics in her blood, she loves her mom, she thinks she'd make a great president—"

"But doesn't it seem like Chelsea's sort of being pimped out in some weird sort of way?" Shuster asked, stealing the line the MSNBC suit had offered up earlier.

Press said no and defended Chelsea's choice. Off camera, Bob Franken could be heard loudly laughing.

It was, in short, a typical cable TV news show: Nonsense uttered, nonsense replied. Except to the Clinton campaign. Throughout the evening, Shuster started to receive emails from Clinton campaign officials. "Did you really accuse Chelsea Clinton of being pimped out?" some of the emails asked. Shuster engaged in quick and rough email exchanges with Wolfson and Philippe Reines, Hillary's spokesman and personal bulldog.

Chuck Todd, the ever-savvy NBC political analyst, observed the back-and-forth and offered a friendly warning. Like every other D.C. reporter, he knew the Clintons' media operation well. He knew the stories and had felt the occasional sharp elbow. "Be careful," he advised, "because they're going to use this against you."

The next morning, preparing for a previously scheduled appearance on the morning show on MSNBC, *Morning Joe*, Shuster was greeted by the president of the network. The visit, needless to say, was unusual.

"I'm starting to get a lot of these, you know, a lot of rumble about something you said about Chelsea," Phil Griffin told Shuster.

Shuster couldn't believe it. Sure, maybe the phrase "pimped out" sounded a little coarse to an older generation, but no one—at least no one under forty—could possibly think he was saying that Chelsea Clinton's parents had literally pushed her into prostitution. Shuster was sure they knew exactly what he was saying.

"Can you just do an apology on *Morning Joe*?" asked Griffin, referring to the cable network's morning talk program. It wasn't really a question. "Just do an apology now to take care of it."

At the end of Shuster's appearance on *Morning Joe*, Shuster had his moment. "Can I take care of a housekeeping matter?" Shuster asked. "So you know how yesterday we ran this clip of women from *The View*. Chelsea Clinton had called them. Well, last night on Tucker's show we ran the same clip, and then out of that I said a lot of wonderful things about Chelsea."

It was a lead-up to an apology, and the lead-up took some time. He noted that the previous night he had said that we should all be "proud" of Chelsea, that Mike Huckabee praised the way the Clintons raised her, and that "everybody, all of us, love Chelsea Clinton."

At this point, *Morning Joe*'s viewers could have been forgiven for wondering why David Shuster was going to such lengths to sing the praises of Chelsea Clinton. If they hadn't heard his "pimped out" comment the night before, they surely would have thought Shuster's morning tribute to the Clintons' daughter was completely out of the blue. But then, finally, Shuster got to the point.

"But we also talked about the fact that Chelsea Clinton, as the campaign has acknowledged, she's making calls to these superdelegates." Still inclined to defend the substance of his comments from the night before, Shuster added that Chelsea's calls "can be the unseemly side of politics."

Finally, the apology came. Sort of. "Well, last night, I used a phrase, some slang about her efforts. I didn't think that people would take it literally, but some people have, and to the extent that people feel I was being pejorative about the actions of Chelsea Clinton making these phone calls, to the extent that people feel I was being pejorative, I apologize for that. I should have seen people would, might, view it that way. And for that, I'm sorry."

As apologies went, it was not exactly full-throated. Shuster put his "pimped out" comment in the context of his prior praise of Chelsea. He defended the substance of his underlying criticism. And then he finally got around to a sorry-if-anyone's-been-offended-by-my-comments type of apology.

It was shortly after the appearance that Shuster received a memorable call from a friend on the Clinton campaign. "I'm going to give you a heads-up. The Clinton campaign is about to roll you." Far too late, Shuster was being warned that this was a fight the Clinton campaign wanted—indeed, they believed this was a fight they needed.

Throughout the campaign, the problem the Clinton campaign kept coming up against was simple: The liberal base was more excited about Barack Obama than Hillary Clinton. The new guy showed more promise, showed more ability to carry out the liberal dream than the old-timer—Hillary Clinton. And the deep-seated liberal disappointment was given a powerful voice at the liberal network, MSNBC. "The Clinton campaign was pissed-off at MSNBC over coverage that they had thought had been unfair," says someone who worked at MSNBC at that time. A prime source of ire was directed toward Chris Matthews, the loquacious host of *Hardball*, who'd been known to wax eloquent over Barack Obama on-air and make sexist comments about Hillary Clinton—"she-devil," "Nurse Ratched," "Madame Defarge," "witchy," "anti-male," and "uppity" were just a few of the choice phrases Matthews used to assail her.

An MSNBC employee believed the Clinton team went so far as to orchestrate a letter-writing campaign against Matthews, especially after he said what many people long believed: "The reason she's a U.S. senator, the reason she's a candidate for president, the reason she may be a front-runner, is that her husband messed around." But Matthews was a little harder to roll because he was a far more entrenched figure, one of the low-rated network's only marquee names.

"Chris got in some trouble internally," a former employee says, "but I think MSNBC wouldn't dare to take away Chris's show."

The morning of the Shuster apology, the Clinton campaign sent a nasty letter to Steve Capus, the president of NBC News. There was a presidential primary debate scheduled for February 26. MSNBC, part of the NBC News group, was the sponsor. And according to the letter Capus received, Hillary was considering pulling out of the next debate in protest over Shuster's comment.

The entire network began to panic. "Keep in mind the financial situation," says a source close to the situation at the time. MSNBC struggles for ratings, and it's almost always a losing struggle—except on debate nights. "Debates make millions for the networks," says the source. "They boost their ratings in a huge way." If Hillary pulled out of the debate, there would be no debate. And "MSNBC couldn't afford financially to lose a debate."

Moments later, Shuster got called into a meeting with Phil Griffin, Steve Capus, and several other people, including the vice president for communications at MSNBC, Jeremy Gaines. The consensus from the corporate executives was "We've got to do something about this." As one MSNBC employee puts it, people were "going apeshit."

Shuster tried to push back. "Don't you guys get the politics in this?" he asked the corporate bigwigs. "The Clinton campaign is trying to appeal to women, and trying to make Hillary a sympathetic figure." They wanted to make it look like men, such as David Shuster, were beating up on the woman who could be the first female president of the United States.

Griffin, Capus, and company may have understood the politics of the situation, but it was irrelevant. This wasn't a fight being waged on the merits. All that mattered was the February 26 debate.

So Shuster tried again, this time explaining to his bosses that Hillary was bluffing. "They need this debate more than Barack Obama does," he pleaded. Obama was the front-runner and weaker debater, and Hillary's debate performances were her best chance at snatching the momentum from him. "There's no way Hillary is pulling out of this debate."

"It doesn't matter," one executive responded. "I mean, we can't even afford the possibility that they are not going to participate in this debate."

Shuster disagreed, but by then he knew he was alone. Looking for a way out, he asked, "What do you want me to do? Do you want me to apologize directly to Hillary? To Chelsea?"

"Yeah, why don't you do that," one MSNBC suit said. "That would be a good start."

Shuster got right on it. "Howard," he said in a phone call to Howard Wolfson, "sorry about all the confusion over everything. I'd like to apologize directly to Hillary Clinton. Can you patch me through to Huma, on the campaign trail, so I can call and apologize directly to Mrs. Clinton?" Huma—the wife of then-congressman Anthony Weiner—was Hillary's personal aide, a constant presence at the presidential candidate's side.

"We're not going to let you do that," Wolfson replied.

"Okay. Um, all right," Shuster said. "Can I send a note of apology?"

Wolfson relented, but only slightly. "If you want to email Huma, here's her email."

Moments later Shuster sent Huma an apology, hoping it would get directly to Hillary, who had supposedly cried, according to her aides, when she heard Shuster's remarks about Chelsea. Shuster was hoping the direct apology would be the beginning of his rehabilitation.

It wasn't.

In fact, it wasn't even acknowledged. An hour later, Howard Wolfson held a press call with reporters. "The worst part of this," he said, misleadingly, is that Shuster "has not apologized to Hillary and Chelsea Clinton."

"Fucker!" Shuster thought when he got wind of Wolfson's call. "He wouldn't let me apologize!"

Shuster wasn't on the call, but he found out about it when the Associated Press called him up for a reaction. "Howard Wolfson just went off on you for not apologizing," the AP reporter told Shuster.

"This is crazy!" said Shuster. Wolfson's statement on the press call was of course technically true, but only because Wolfson had personally blocked all attempts at a direct apology. Like a laundry list of Clinton targets and scapegoats, from Paula Jones to Ken Starr, Shuster was seeing the lengths to which the Clintons have always gone to destroy inconvenient obstacles to their power, and he felt like a helpless pedestrian watching a speeding bus (driven by the Clintons) plow straight at him.

Meanwhile, as someone who worked at MSNBC at the time explains, "NBC is freaked out. The Clinton campaign is, like, ratcheting this up." According to a source close to the situation, the Clintons called people on the board of NBC's parent company, General Electric, to say, "Well, this is outrageous, how NBC News and MSNBC are handling this, and we need to do something about it." Before long, GE's chairman, Jeffrey Immelt, was on the phone with Jeff Zucker, the president and CEO of NBC Universal at the time, and Steve Capus asking, "What the hell is going on over there? Why are my board members talking about the reporter, and why is your reporter referring to Chelsea as a prostitute?"

Since Shuster, though a liberal, had once been on the wrong team from the Clintons' perspective—he had worked at Fox, reported there on the Whitewater and Lewinsky scandals, and had at the time maintained deep contacts in Ken Starr's office—the Clintons, Shuster believed, took a special joy in trying to destroy him. Their decision to turn against him was a little like Paddy O'Neill's decision in *Patriot Games* to turn against a female fellow member of the Irish Republican Army. "Paddy O'Neill can sleep at night," says Harrison Ford's Jack Ryan. "In fact he probably enjoys the irony. She's not Irish; she's English."

By that Friday afternoon, Steve Capus, Phil Griffin, and Jeremy Gaines told Shuster he'd have to accept a two-week suspension. "We need this debate," said Capus, who was then president of NBC News. "You're going to be the one who is going to have to jump on the grenade," added Gaines.

"If NBC buckles on this," asked Shuster, once he realized the time had passed for defending himself on the merits, "what kind of message does that send?"

The response was dismissive: "That's not your job to worry about." They weren't there for a debate. The decision to make Shuster a sacrificial lamb on the altar of Clinton, Inc. had been made before Shuster walked into the room. The best they could do for their reporter was to promise to pay him during the suspension—so long as he kept it a secret.

Shuster's colleagues tried to comfort him. Tucker Carlson, Pat Buchanan, Joe Scarborough, and even Clinton confidant Lanny Davis came to his defense—in private. (Davis would call several times to ensure that, regardless of what happened with the Clintons, he'd still have a relationship with Shuster.) And Tim Russert, the most respected reporter in the

NBC News empire, candidly told Shuster. "I know what's going on." Russert had been through the same sort of games before he grew too powerful for politicos to play games with, and he assured Shuster, "Someday we're going to have a beer and laugh about this." (Russert would suddenly pass away before the two ever had a chance to laugh about it over beers.)

The Clintons, however, weren't finished. As Chuck Todd had warned, sure enough the exchange of emails between the Clinton campaign and Shuster was leaked by the Clinton campaign to *Politico*, and organizations like Media Matters, run by Clinton ally David Brock, whipped up liberal fear. The story took a long time to die, because the Clintons didn't want it to die.

After two weeks, David Shuster returned to the airwaves, but he felt he never fully recovered from the harm to his standing at the network. Shuster believed he had once been "seen as some sort of straight-shooter, take-no-prisoners" political commentator, but that was before the fights with management and the bad-mouthing by someone of Hillary Clinton's prestige. After the "pimped out" affair, Shuster believed his bosses thought he "was some kind of a hothead."

Whether Shuster could have handled the situation better is debatable. Should he have apologized more enthusiastically on *Morning Joe*? Probably. Should he have tried harder to more quickly apologize directly to Hillary and Chelsea? Maybe. There was, after all, nothing stopping him from offering his regrets to them over the air. It's unclear, however, whether anything Shuster could have done would have made a difference, because with the Clintons, one couldn't be sure whether their outrage was sincere or feigned for political purposes. What *is* clear is that the Clintons saw a political opportunity and seized it with the desperate tenacity they'd shown countless times when their backs were against the wall. Consider what their character assassination of David Shuster accomplished. In a matter of days, they silenced any criticism of Chelsea's refusal to answer questions about her role in lobbying superdelegates. More important, they appealed to female voters by making Hillary and Chelsea look like persecuted victims of men. Finally, they sent a message to the media: You may like Obama more than Hillary, but you'd better watch what you say, because we have the power the destroy you.

To deliver their message, a popular ex-president, the nation's most famous senator, and their powerful friends bullied a relatively obscure reporter with powerless friends and spineless bosses. While they were at it, the press and public were misled about his attempts to apologize. And Chelsea was used not just to lobby superdelegates, but also to portray themselves as victims of a malicious media and score political points with the public.

Of course, the biggest way to hit Shuster and MSNBC would have been to actually boycott the MSNBC debate. That would have been, in *Godfather* terms, the equivalent of "going to the mattresses." But punishing Shuster wasn't really the Clintons' goal. He was just the collateral damage of their opportunism, and because Hillary needed the debates more than her front-running opponent did—and was better at them than he was—a boycott of the debate would have hurt Hillary more than it would help, just as Shuster had told his bosses. As someone who worked at MSNBC at the time says, "Their strategy was so transparent and weak that I think calling it a mafia tactic does a disservice to mafia families."

After Shuster's gaffe, his subsequent apology, and the announcement of his suspension, Hillary Clinton went through eleven state elections and almost a month before she won another state primary. If her attempt had been to win votes at David Shuster's expense, she had failed.

As the 2006 midterm election neared, Josh Green, an enterprising reporter who was then with the *Atlantic* magazine, began to consider 2008. Green pitched his editors a story on the Clintons, and when given approval, he turned to Clinton's Senate office with the pitch: He was going to study her entire Senate career up to that point (nearly one full term served) and dive in deeper and more comprehensively than any reporter had done until that point.

The piece was going to be written regardless, and the Clinton team figured that if they cooperated with the story, they would be able to shape it. Besides, politically, Green fits the mold of a liberal journalist, dating back to his time as an editor at left-of-center publication *Washington Monthly* and as a staff writer at the devoutly liberal *American Prospect*, where he wrote about "frustrating Republican talking points" and the "nauseating roller coaster ride" of the Bush presidency. It helped, too, that he approached Senator Clinton's office from the *Atlantic*, which might not have been as overtly liberal as the other places Green worked but would on its face suggest friendly coverage.

So Hillary's Senate staff let Green in. For the most part, they weren't wrong: It was overall a flattering piece that detailed how Hillary had won over skeptical Republicans and Democrats alike in the Senate and became, against all odds going into the job, pretty well liked among her colleagues.

Clinton, Green uncovered, enthusiastically attended the Senate prayer group, which was dominated by Republican senators who had pretty much all over the years spoken out staunchly against her husband when he was president. Some had even a history of speaking out against Hillary. The piece was filled with great tidbits like that, giving a full picture of how Clinton had been spending her time in the Senate.[12]

But not all of it was completely flattering. "Today Clinton offers no big ideas, no crusading causes—by her own tacit admission, no evidence of bravery in the service of a larger ideal. Instead, her Senate record is an assemblage of many, many small gains. Her real accomplishment in the Senate has been to rehabilitate the image and political career of Hillary Rodham Clinton. Impressive though that has been in its particulars, it makes for a rather thin claim on the presidency. Senator Clinton has plenty to talk about, but she doesn't have much to say," Green concluded.

It was this conclusion that infuriated the Clinton camp, and in a retaliatory mode, they'd move to kill his next Clinton story.

"Early this summer, Sen. Hillary Rodham Clinton's campaign for president learned that the men's magazine *GQ* was working on a story the campaign was sure to hate: an account of infighting in Hillaryland," the Virginia-based trade publication *Politico* would report a few months later. "So Clinton's aides pulled a page from the book of Hollywood publicists and offered *GQ* a stark choice: Kill the piece, or lose access to planned celebrity coverboy Bill Clinton.

"Despite internal protests, *GQ* editor Jim Nelson met the Clinton campaign's demands, which had been delivered by Bill Clinton's spokesman, Jay Carson, several sources familiar with the conversations said," reported Ben Smith of *Politico*.[13]

That killed *GQ* story was written by Josh Green, the same reporter who had cast doubt on Hillary's tenure in the Senate. It is how the Clintons operate with the media, controlling the narrative and dictating the story.

Some Clinton apparatchiks did come to the senator's defense and advocated her candidacy—the always reliable James Carville and the supposedly unaligned website Media Matters for America, among the most prominent.

One of Carville's broadsides—"If she gave [Obama] one of her cojones, they'd both have two"—led Obama to rebut the former Clinton spokesman turned CNN commentator directly. "Well, you know, James Carville is well known for spouting off his mouth without always knowing what he's talking about," Obama replied. "I intend to stay focused on fighting for the American people because what they don't need is 20 more years of performance art on television."

By law, Media Matters for America is a tax-exempt organization that cannot back political candidates. Nonetheless, the David Brock–run operation became an all-but-official supporter of the Clinton campaign, there to "expose" Obama supporters in the press and defend her against controversies of all kinds.

In December 2007, for example, Media Matters went after MSNBC's Chris Matthews, as they would throughout the election season, for his apparent preference for Obama over Clinton. So determined was the organization that it examined "every evaluative remark Matthews made on MSNBC's *Hardball* during the months of September, October, and

November" and concluded that Matthews was "extremely hostile toward Hillary Clinton." On January 4, 2008, the organization defended Clinton against a panelist's assertion on Fox News that her "nagging voice" was turning off men. Again, on March 11, 2008, it defended her against accusations that she had implied Obama was a Muslim. (She had denied he was a Muslim during a television interview while slyly adding, "as far as I know.") "When people suggest that the press employs a separate standard for covering Clinton, this is the kind of episode they're talking about," the website complained. "There simply is no other candidate, from either party, who has had their comments, their *fragments*, dissected so dishonestly the way Clinton's have been."

The conservative-leaning website the *Daily Caller* would later report that "[f]ormer employees of the liberal messaging organization have told [the *Daily Caller*] that Brock, a well-known supporter of the former first lady, was often in communication with her presidential campaign during 2008 and was in regular email contact with longtime Clinton advisor Sidney Blumenthal as recently as 2010. . . . Indeed, from the time that Obama announced his candidacy on February 10, 2007, until Edwards dropped out on January 30, 2008, Media Matters ran 1199 posts for Clinton and only 700 for Obama. 378 posts mentioned Edwards."

These were the exceptions, however. Much of the media, enamored with Obama's candidacy and (momentarily) relieved at the prospect of paying back the Clintons for a decade of bullying and rough treatment by their media team, seemed only delighted to pile on. The defections of the media and Senate Democrats hurt the Clintons. But Hillary also had another surprising weakness or, more accurately, the same old vulnerability that had dogged her for more than a decade: a renegade husband.

6

OUT OF CONTROL

"If she becomes president, Clinton's fucked.
He's gonna be the guy that got a blow job and was impeached."

—senior aide on Bill Clinton's 2008 "sabotage"

While Hillary struggled against a surprisingly resilient foe, Bill Clinton was making more disastrous headlines. For one, his complex and largely mysterious financial relationship with Ron Burkle came to a bitter and well-publicized end—news that broke right in the middle of Hillary's primary fight. The former president was said to be demanding a $20 million payout from Burkle in exchange for ending the relationship. Meanwhile, his ties with Burkle were raising questions about conflicts of interest between the Clintons and scores of foreign entities with which Burkle's fund did business, such as the government of Dubai.[1]

Hillary was having money troubles of her own. She had raised over $100 million for the 2008 race and had spent it all by January, due to a top-heavy campaign organization and an unexpectedly tough Obama challenge.[2] By February, she was in the embarrassing position of having to loan her campaign $5 million while Obama continued to rake in record sums from donors.[3] Fortunately, her husband had improved their financial standing in the time between leaving the White House and Hillary running for president—for once, she was able to pull from her own coffers.

Clinton's narrow, death-defying New Hampshire victory meant a long primary fight against Obama—one that Hillary was certain she had the team and experience to win. Only days later, however, her hopes crashed again. In the most unlikely of places. Wrecked by the most unlikely of people. The smooth-talking Bubba who had improbably been labeled America's "first black president," William Jefferson Clinton, suddenly seemed to make it his mission to alienate black voters. In South Carolina, of all places, a state in which as much as half the Democratic electorate was African American.

As the *Los Angeles Times* among others reported at the time, the former president had overruled Hillary's campaign advisors such as Mark Penn, who believed that Obama was almost certain to win South Carolina and who wanted to cede the state to him.[4] The *New York Times*, for one, paraphrased Clinton advisors as saying that Senator Clinton was "pursuing a national campaign strategy that includes South Carolina but that does not elevate the state to the level of critical importance that it usually has in the presidential nominating contest. This reflects the Clinton team's view that it does not expect to beat Mr. Obama in South Carolina, where he enjoys strong support from black voters, and that it wants to lower expectations there."[5] Never lacking confidence in his own campaign skills, Clinton decided to head there himself, launching what one pundit would describe as "a not-very-charming charm offensive" and what the pundit would describe, quoting an unnamed campaign aide, as "a quixotic 'one-man mission' in territory that had already turned fallow."[6] And he didn't care much if Hillary's campaign aides liked it.

Indeed, Bill Clinton, according to aides, thought his wife's campaign was hopelessly disorganized, run by unworthy cronies who lacked any street smarts. This wasn't an unorthodox view. Hillary 2008 was, as the *Washington Post* put it, "a campaign that is universally acknowledged to have been a management catastrophe."[7] Which is why he didn't listen to their suggestions. At all. The hostility between the Bill and Hillary camps during the campaign was legendary.

A later autopsy of the 2008 campaign in *Vanity Fair* discussed the outright war between teams Hillary and Bill—as two rival business partners disagreed on the best way to move their enterprise forward. One Hillary fund-raiser told the magazine that "Bill Clinton was out of control . . . even the night she won in New Hampshire. Even Hillary couldn't control him."[8] Sidestepping his wife, Bill began to offer his advice directly to figures like Penn and Wolfson. He offered to create his own operation within the Hillary campaign headquarters, until members of the campaign talked him out of it.

The *Vanity Fair* piece so infuriated the Clintons that they mounted an effort to identify its sources. One of the "main sources," according to an insider, was an obscure Clintonista, who, by the way, now works for a Clinton rival.

As he headed south, the former president did, however, agree to one request from his wife's campaign team: not to bring along his latest mistress. According to John Heilemann and Mark Halperin's juicy campaign book, *Game Change*, rumors of the former president's affairs involved no fewer than three women—Belinda Stronach, Julie Tauber McMahon, and Gina Gershon.

That the former president was involved romantically with women outside of his marriage while campaigning for his wife's election to the White House was hardly shocking. Nor, to be fair, was it unique to Mr. Clinton in that election cycle. At least Bill and Hillary maintained a cordial relationship; the same could not be said for the leading candidate on the other side of the aisle, John McCain, and his wife, Cindy, who fought unproven infidelity rumors on both sides of their marital equation. Similarly, unproven infidelity rumors long plagued New Mexico governor Bill Richardson, the former UN ambassador and cabinet secretary, who was waging a long-shot campaign against Hillary in 2008. And then there was of course John Edwards, whose affair with a B-list documentary producer while his wife, Elizabeth, was dying of breast cancer made headlines for months.

That Bill Clinton was willing to refrain from flaunting his extracurricular activities in front of reporters during his South Carolina trip was seen by Mrs. Clinton's aides as a (rare) act of discretion. "There were a lot of advisors who told him that was a bad idea," a former Clinton aide tells me, laughing. Unfortunately for Mrs. Clinton, that act of discretion was his only one.

The spiral started when a furious Bill Clinton—whose contempt for Barack Obama was already infamous—seemed to castigate his candidacy as mythic. In the midst of a harangue about Obama's reputation for having good judgment and his positions on the Iraq War, Clinton groused, "Give me a break. This whole thing is the biggest fairy tale I've ever seen." It seemed pretty clear to many reporters that Clinton was referring not just to Obama's Iraq vote, but to his entire candidacy.

In truth, Clinton aides couldn't believe the good fortune that seemed to follow this Obama guy from the outset. In his first Senate race, he lucked out as his most formidable rival, Jack Ryan, a handsome multimillionaire and Harvard grad who'd given up a high-paying job at Goldman Sachs to teach at a parochial school outside Chicago, imploded after his former wife accused him of taking her to sex clubs, including "a bizarre club with cages, whips and other apparatus hanging from the ceiling."[9] The Ryan disaster—involving charges of a kind Bill Clinton would have likely survived—led state Republicans to make the disastrous choice of replacing him with African American iconoclast Alan Keyes, perhaps best known for staging a hunger strike when he was barred from a debate during the 2000 presidential elections. Keyes, who was not even from Illinois, was a gaffe-prone disaster from start to finish, managing only 27 percent of the vote.[10]

Once elected, Obama offered hopeful, if empty, rhetoric that was inexplicably and uncritically embraced by much of the Washington media.

His star, more like a supernova, was so bright, Obama didn't even bother to stand for reelection before seeking out the White House. "Everybody else is waiting in line," one Senate colleague recalls, "and he's like 'fuck it.'" Obama never had to work for it. It all seemed to fall into his lap. And he was winning the adulation within the Democratic Party that had once belonged to Bill. That more than anything pissed Bill Clinton off.

The former president further exacerbated the problem when he dismissed Obama's imminent victory in South Carolina by comparing him to another African American candidate—one who had no hope of winning the nomination. "Jesse Jackson won South Carolina in '84 and '88," he said, adding that "Jackson ran a good campaign. And Obama ran a good campaign here."[11]

Clinton was furious with reporters covering the campaign. His legendary charm was gone. "Shame on you!" he yelled at reporters at one point on the trail, a clip replayed endlessly on television and YouTube. He accused Obama of playing the "race card on me."[12]

The racial controversy Clinton touched off infuriated African American officeholders, who rallied around Obama and sent Mrs. Clinton's numbers even further south. Suddenly the Clintons had a race problem. The campaign seemed snakebit on the question. Even when former Atlanta mayor Andrew Young endorsed Hillary, he unhelpfully noted in a live television interview that "Bill is every bit as black as Barack. He's probably gone with more black women than Barack."[13]

Only Doug Band was there to lend support. Just as he'd always been over much of the past decade. When Clinton was about to go into his heart bypass surgery, Band was beside him. When Clinton met with Kim Jong Il to bring home two American women imprisoned in North Korea, Band was standing behind him. When Clinton and President Obama played golf, Band was in the foursome. And when a finger-wagging Clinton lost his cool with a Nevada television reporter during the 2008 caucuses—"Get on your television station and say, 'I don't care about the home mortgage crisis. All I care about is making sure that some voters have it easier than others, and that when they do vote . . . their vote should count five times as much as others.' That is your position!"—a balding Doug Band was in the camera shot, with a worried look on his aging face, standing behind the only employer he'd ever known.[14] Band was also in South Carolina, where he reportedly was furious over the media's attack on his boss and the implication he was a racist.

In that, Clinton also received sympathy from an unexpected quarter. One senior Bush aide remembers hearing the president say that he made a point of calling Clinton "on the days that nobody else would call him," like the day that he was called a racist by the Obama team in South Carolina. On the phone, Bush apparently told Clinton that he knew he wasn't a racist and that he was still his friend. Bush said, "Those are the days when you need friends to call you, but sometimes they never do."

By the time Bill was finished, the damage sustained by his wife's campaign was mortal. "What killed us was South Carolina," a former Clinton official told *Vanity Fair.*[15] In a CBS News poll, 58 percent of South Carolina voters "said Bill Clinton's involvement was important to their decision and most of them voted for Obama. Seventy percent believed Hillary Clinton had unfairly attacked Obama. As a warning to Clinton, just 77 percent said they would be satisfied with her as the nominee."[16]

From then on, Hillary Clinton's campaign seemed to meander from one controversy to another—some of her making. Many of her misstatements on the trail awakened the image of Hillary the Liar, an image she'd tried to extinguish after a decade of senatorial work. She had, for example, claimed for years to have been named after explorer Sir Edmund Hillary—until it was learned that she wasn't. She claimed to have been opposed to the 2003 Iraq War from the start—like Obama. Only in Obama's case was that true. One prominent TV reporter remembers hearing word that Hillary claimed she once arrived in Bosnia under sniper fire. "That couldn't be the same trip I was on," she thought, but it was. The one in which Hillary was accompanied by Chelsea and was greeted at the airport. There was, of course, no sniper fire at all. Even when she tried to speak the truth and say what was on her mind, Clinton found trouble, such as when she made a reference to the assassination of Robert Kennedy to justify staying in the race against Obama, which led to furious outcries that she was rooting for his death—and to the long-standing wrath of Michelle Obama.

Hillary was not expected to be a flawless stage performer like Bill. Yet many of the bafflingly tone-deaf missteps in 2008 were made by her husband. At one point, Senator Obama, to his obvious delight, noted that he wasn't sure which Clinton he was running against. And yet Bill Clinton's irate harangues continued, stunning veteran reporters and campaign operatives who'd long admired his ability to charm audiences. Months later, he was still angrily defending his comparison of Obama to Jesse Jackson, declaring, "You gotta really go some to play the race card with me. My office is in Harlem, and Harlem voted for Hillary by the way." With his temper rising, he ranted, "I have 1.4 million people around the world, mostly people of color, in Africa, the Caribbean, Asia, and elsewhere on the world's least expensive AIDS drugs," and the quote about Jesse Jackson "was used out of context and twisted for political purposes by the Obama campaign to try to breed resentment elsewhere."[17]

The once sympathetic CBS News website published a column titled "Bill Clinton's Lost Legacy." In it, the author noted that Clinton's former labor secretary, Robert Reich, had accused Clinton of spearheading a "smear campaign against Obama" and quoted former Senate majority leader Tom Daschle describing Bill Clinton as "not presidential."[18]

To close observers, Bill Clinton's lead-footedness seemed increasingly puzzling. It certainly was to his wife. Hillary often marveled about how her future husband managed to talk his way into a closed museum while they were dating at Yale Law School. How he could have handled things so badly now was a subject of speculation and amateur psycho-analysis.

Some aides wondered if Clinton's heart surgeries—in 2004 and 2005— had left him a step off his game. Still others, including close and longtime Clinton associates, thought a more sinister motivation might be at work.

I discussed the subject with one of Clinton's friends, a man who has golfed with him, worked with him in the West Wing, and who, like most former Clinton aides, spoke to me only on condition of anonymity. He knows the penalty for talking out of school—exile, humiliation.

Referring to the South Carolina disaster, he volunteers a thought. "[Hillary] knows better than anybody that whatever [Bill] does is intentional. So part of her has to be, when she's lying in bed at night, going 'was that real, did he make a mistake, or was it on purpose?'"

This clearly was something that had been on the former aide's own mind for a while. "Want to go conspiracy theorist?" he continues. "How does Mark Penn, who's her chief strategist, not know that the [primary] states aren't winner-take-all, but proportionate? How does he, the guy that's been at it forever, he's her chief strategist, doesn't have a brief—and Harold Ickes is there, too—on delegates and how they get amassed? You *have* to. How do these guys from the Obama campaign, they know the delegates and Hillary Clinton doesn't? That doesn't make sense. . . . It's either unbelievable arrogance, or it's sabotage."

Penn, who had built up a share of enemies within the Clinton orbit, was an early scapegoat for Hillary's disaster. "A lot of people would like . . . to see him go," a senior Clinton advisor told reporters. "I think about all camps think it's Mark's fault," a source described as a "Clinton White House veteran close to the campaign" told the *Washington Post*. "I don't think there is a Mark camp." On April 6, 2008, after several more stories pointed the finger at his management, Penn stepped down as chief strategist, and was rewarded with more blind quotes from his many enemies.

"The depth of hostility toward Penn even in a time of triumph illustrates the combustible environment within the Clinton campaign, an operation where internal strife and warring camps have undercut a candidate once seemingly destined for the Democratic nomination," stated reporters Peter Baker and Anne E. Kornblut in the *Washington Post* exposé. Baker and Kornblut cited Howard Wolfson, James Carville, Harold Ickes, Rahm Emanuel, John Podesta, Paul Begala, and advertising consultant Mandy

Grunwald as among Penn's many enemies. They also would be long-term survivors in the Clinton orbit. Penn, however, would not. A 2013 *Washington Post* article still branded him in Clinton circles as the man who "has been tagged as the egocentric villain of the campaign who sowed seeds of dissent." The Clinton team let it be known that Penn would not be back for another Hillary Clinton run.

The same could not be said, obviously, for another person many blamed for Hillary's travails. Speaking about Bill Clinton, Bob Shrum tells me, "I think he's a very, very good strategist for himself. I don't think he's always a good strategist for other people."

One explanation for Bill's 2008 behavior is of course the obvious one. Bill was, and remains, deeply conflicted over the prospect of a Hillary Clinton presidency. The former commander in chief worries about what that would mean to his place in history. "If she becomes president, Clinton's fucked," says a former senior advisor. She'll be the first woman president, and "he's gonna be the guy that got a blow job and was impeached." Other senior Clinton aides, those who know him extremely well, share that view. That secretly the former president "dreaded" the idea of a White House return, where as one aide put it he would be "trapped"—kept out of decision making but also unable to fly around the world and do whatever he wanted. In other words, his bizarre behavior in South Carolina and elsewhere demonstrated an internal conflict between a guilt-ridden need to help his wife and his own self-interest.

Bill wasn't the only person who cost Hillary Clinton dearly. By the time she was to enter the 2008 presidential election, it was not the Republicans who would give her the most trouble. They had been pacified by her well-crafted plan and in some cases even applauded her tough, resolute effort to battle Obama down to the wire in race after race. No, her problem was that the liberal, antiwar wing of her own party mistrusted her. Clinton tried to pacify them in 2007 at a hearing with General David Petraeus, saying the Iraq commander's testimony required a "suspension of disbelief" and in effect calling the man with his generation's most admired military mind a liar. But for Clinton, it was too little, too late.

As potential 2008 candidates emerged, many Democrats took a shine to Barack Obama. Obama wasn't really doing much of anything in the Senate, except giving well-received speeches. But he contrasted well with Hillary.

"He wasn't in the conferences trying to tell them what to do," one senator says. "Hillary may have felt like she had the ability to tell him what political strategy to use, or we should push this legislation, we should agree to this and fight this." Many Democrats were jealous of her, resentful, in a way that for whatever reason they weren't of the far less experienced Obama.

"We all saw Obama as a fresh, clean candidate and not part of the Clinton crowd and mess," one Democratic senator told a Republican colleague in explaining his support. That tension was going to sting Hillary Clinton soon, when she least expected it.

The new controversies emerging from Senator Clinton's office only reminded Democrats again of the trouble-plagued administration of her husband. Says one Republican U.S. senator, "They got tired of defending them."

Shortly after Mrs. Clinton won the New Hampshire primary, her Senate colleagues seemed eager to crush her momentum. The Obama campaign released endorsements from people who knew the Clintons well—Senators Tim Johnson of South Dakota, Ben Nelson of Nebraska, and John Kerry of Massachusetts. (Kerry is said by colleagues to still be afraid of Hillary over his apostasy.) Chuck Schumer, Hillary's New York frenemy, offered private encouragement to Obama, as did Senate Democratic leader Harry Reid of Nevada, despite official pledges of neutrality.

"They were unbelievably jealous," one Clinton aide tells me, in reference to the "treacherous" Democrats. "There were people in the Democratic Party who said, 'Let's get rid of this fuck.' Right now if you poll governors and senators—anyone who's in statewide elected office, eighty percent of them will tell you that they should be president, that they have what it takes to be president. Right? You don't think Kennedy would resent Clinton? All these guys who took a pass [on running for president themselves] did."

By far the most infamous endorsement for Obama that year came from former Clintonite Bill Richardson, who dropped out of the 2008 contest in January.

Richardson had been close to the Clintons for decades, and the former president lobbied him vigorously. The Clintons understood that the endorsement of Obama by someone so well connected to the Clinton inner circle would be a monumental embarrassment, especially with so many Senate Democrats turning against them. Clinton also seemed to consider Richardson an easy get, one susceptible to the former president's charm and attention. Clinton flew to New Mexico to watch the Super Bowl with his former cabinet secretary, pressing him during the game not to endorse Obama or to at least stay neutral.[19] Richardson would not commit—he joked that he would have endorsed Bill Clinton over Obama in an instant, but not Hillary, who he felt was more qualified for the job than Richardson was.

Leaving New Mexico empty-handed, Clinton then sent another former cabinet secretary, Henry Cisneros, a fellow Latino, to press the case.

"He thought I could deliver you," Cisneros told Richardson.

"Why?" Richardson asked.

"I guess he thought we spoke the same language."

"Politics?"

"Spanish."

In the end, Richardson went with Obama. He did so, according to sources close to him, because he shared the views of many prominent Democrats. He believed Obama was special—a once-in-a-lifetime candidate. Second, he didn't want the old Clinton crowd back—a chaotic, backstabbing, drama-filled mess.

A Clinton aide later told the *New York Times* that the former president was "more philosophical than angry" about the endorsement. That, of course, was untrue. Clinton was heard to tell aides and associates that he would never forgive Richardson's betrayal.

Richardson would be spared no invective from the Clinton team, particularly acidic comments in public and private from two of Clinton's primary financial beneficiaries, Terry McAuliffe and James Carville. "Mr. Richardson's endorsement came right around the anniversary of the day when Judas sold out for 30 pieces of silver, so I think the timing is appropriate, if ironic," Carville, in typical bombast, told reporters.[20] Sources sympathetic to Richardson tell me a Clinton loyalist repeatedly bad-mouthed Richardson to reporters and fellow Democrats and spread rumors about his private life. Richardson took such a furious fusillade from the Clinton operation—they wanted their treatment of him to deter other would-be betrayers—that he seems to this day not to have gotten over it.

Despite the fury and invective, Richardson's endorsement was not the biggest blow to the Clintons' efforts. That one came from the heirs to that magical Democratic land called Camelot.

First JFK's daughter, Caroline Kennedy, offered a stirring endorsement of Obama, evoking memories of her father. Then came her uncle. The so-called Lion of the Senate, an ailing Edward M. Kennedy came out for Obama despite a desperate months-long effort by the Clintons to keep him neutral.

Hillary had worked hard in the Senate to court the senior senator from Massachusetts. The families had socialized together on Cape Cod. Bill called Senator Kennedy repeatedly on the phone, pressing for an endorsement or, as a fallback, a pledge of neutrality.[21]

But Bill Clinton's once-vaunted charm offensive somehow failed again. In fact, it backfired. Kennedy would let reporters know that he made his decision to endorse Obama after he took umbrage at a remark Bill Clinton made to him, that "a few years ago, this guy [Obama] would have been carrying our bags."[22] That was only an excuse. The Kennedy family finally had a chance to excise its thinly concealed resentments of the "white trash" Clintons.

In a speech in Washington, D.C., at American University on January 28, Kennedy offered some early, obligatory praise of his colleague Senator Clinton. The rest of his speech, however, was filled with thinly veiled potshots at Obama's rival and her husband.

"I feel change in the air," Kennedy said. "From the beginning, he opposed the war in Iraq. And let no one deny that truth." This was seen, as the Associated Press put it, as "an obvious reference to former President Clinton's statement that Obama's early anti-war stance was a 'fairy tale.'"[23]

Kennedy too offered a poke at the Clintons' long record of scandal and attack-style politics. "With Barack Obama," he said, "we will turn the page on the old politics of misrepresentation and distortion."[24]

Al Gore, who enjoyed his moment to stick it to Bill, waited out the contentious primary contest *without endorsing* Hillary, whom he had come to know very well at the White House, before finally endorsing Obama. "This election matters more than ever because America needs change more than ever," Gore would say at an event announcing his support.[25]

As the nomination slipped further from Hillary's grasp, the Clinton team faced the prospect that she might never be president. A return to the Senate would be a poor consolation prize. The job that she had plotted for, the one a deeply conflicted Bill Clinton (at least in his more magnanimous moments) thought he owed her, seemed to have been taken from them. Perhaps forever. As a result Bill seethed at Obama indiscriminately—to George W. Bush, to reporters, to campaign biographers, to friends, to aides, to strangers on the street. The Clintons were so resentful that Hillary held on to her primary delegates, and her clearly losing campaign, far longer than decorum or reality dictated. Even after Obama received the sufficient delegates to be the nominee, Hillary's campaign chairman, Terry McAuliffe, refused to allow the possibility that his candidate, and financial patron, would drop out of the race.

Once Barack Obama officially received the number of delegates he needed to be nominated on the first ballot at the Democratic convention in Denver, things in ClintonWorld got really weird. At a rally in New York, the losing candidate was introduced by McAuliffe as "the next president of the United States."[26] She walked out with a lip-biting Bill and to the sound of "Ain't No Mountain High Enough."[27] Bill stood at center stage until Chelsea discreetly pulled him aside. Before a crowd in the hundreds, Hillary claimed—falsely, as the Obama campaign pointed out—that she had won a majority of the popular vote in the various Democratic primaries and continued to make the case for a candidacy that was to everyone outside of that room already dead.

Feelings against Obama ran deep, exacerbated by the belief that he'd waged a nasty primary campaign against Hillary and gotten away with it. This was, in fact, true. Obama had portrayed himself as above negative campaigning while successfully affixing that label to Clinton. In reality, he and his team waged a brutal below-the-radar opposition campaign against the onetime front-runner, one that was shielded by cooperative reporters. Obama operatives routinely brought statistics, news stories, and allegations to the attention of campaign reporters, under the strict proviso that none of the dirt be tied to their campaign. This worked for months, until one of their attacks—a memo criticizing Hillary's campaign contributions from the Indian American community and labeling her the senator from Punjab—found its way to a Clinton staffer. Caught red-handed, a furious Barack Obama threw his own staff under the bus, claiming that his team, unbeknownst to him, had made a "dumb mistake."[28]

According to associates, Bill Clinton was convinced the Obama campaign was also fanning the flames on the racial front. His new friend, the current president George W. Bush, was among those privately calling him and offering sympathy over the "unfair" racial attacks. Few recalled that Arkansas was the only state that did not have a civil rights statute when Bill left the governor's mansion. Or how the young governor cavorted with segregationists to win elections. Or how his campaigns used racially coded language.[29] None of that was relevant in 2008. Bill Clinton decided his feelings had been hurt by anyone daring to question his civil rights bona fides. And at the peak of a self-pitying frenzy, he wouldn't be easily sated. "I think that wound . . . the guy who was once called the first black president and had a very strong relationship with the black community, probably ran very deep," said a Democratic strategist.

The Clintons let it be known to reporters that Doug Band was tasked with keeping yet another enemies' list, this time of those who betrayed the Clintons in the 2008 campaign. The existence of the list made head-lines in 2014 in a book called *HRC: State Secrets and the Rebirth of Hillary Clinton*. It claimed that enemies were scored on a scale of one to seven according to the severity of their treachery. In fact, the exis-tence of that list was not news. It was reported by the *New York Times* in 2008. The paper noted that the list included Bill Richardson, South Carolina representative James Clyburn, Obama advisor David Axelrod, Missouri senator Claire McCaskill, "several Kennedys," and many no-name congressmen.

Terry McAuliffe implicitly confirmed the existence of this list to the *New York Times*. "The Clintons get hundreds of requests for favors every week," he said. "Clearly, the people you're going to do stuff for in the future are the people who have been there for you."

There were, according to the reports, media "enemies," too. That list included Matt Drudge, who broke the Lewinsky story, as well as many other torments in the years that followed; Todd Purdum, author of the offending profile in *Vanity Fair*; and Obama "cheerleaders" like Keith Olbermann and Chris Matthews.

The dutiful aide Band would keep the list handy on his BlackBerry, ready to pull it up at a moment's notice in case a congressman or some other favor-seeker called asking for help. And in the coming years it would come in very handy.

When Hillary finally did surrender to the inevitable, at a press event in Washington, D.C., at the National Building Museum on June 7, 2008, Bill was on board in person but not in spirit. He still wanted Hillary to hang in there until the bitter end. When the Obama campaign proved less than effusive in their efforts to unite with Team Hillary, the former president's attitude became somewhat contagious. Their daughter, Chelsea, for example, was filled with contempt for Obama, close associates tell me. "She loathes him," says one.

For weeks the Clintons displayed their penchant for sulking and selfishness. On television, Bill refused to say whether he thought Obama was qualified to be president. In private and public settings, Hillary mused aloud about putting her name in nomination against Obama for a public "catharsis" at the convention.[30] A group called PUMA—People United Means Action—arose in support of Hillary remaining in the race against Obama, which threatened to cause endless trouble for Obama at the Democratic National Convention in Denver.[31] There was an effort to seat the Florida and Michigan delegations, which had been disqualified for violating Democratic National Committee rules and whose votes would all have gone to Hillary.[32] Liberals accused the Clintons of trying to steal the convention and using Nixon-style dirty tricks. Indeed, many of these efforts were spearheaded by Howard Wolfson. Even when defeat appeared certain, Wolfson continued his attacks on Obama, perhaps even increasing them. He even hinted that delegates who were pledged to support Obama could and should break their pledges and jump ship at the convention. There was some truth in Chris Matthews's criticism of Wolfson in the final month of the Clinton campaign that ended in early June: "You're like one of these Japanese soldiers that's still fighting in 1953."[33]

"Some of us can't get over the personal demonization of her by the Obama campaign and the sanctimony," says a high-level Clinton advisor in 2013 (note the present tense). "Every time I see David Axelrod on television, I can't get over that he did the ads that distorted and personally attacked her."

Many demanded the vice presidency for Hillary, which was of course a nonstarter, if only in part because of the two people in charge of the selection process: Caroline Kennedy and Eric Holder. For his part, Barack Obama took every opportunity, in public and in private, to assure people that Hillary Clinton was on his short list for the vice presidency. Which in the byzantine lingo of national politics of course meant she wasn't. The very suggestion met almost uniform opposition within the Obama vetting team, including from the two most powerful voices—Michelle Obama and family friend Valerie Jarrett.

But while an Obama-Clinton ticket was out of the question, Obama did want to do all he could to keep his selection from causing their relationship further angst. It is almost certainly not a coincidence that of all the possible candidates Obama could have chosen, Joe Biden was the one who garnered the most Clintonian enthusiasm.

The other two finalists, Indiana senator Evan Bayh and Virginia governor Tim Kaine, were potentially disastrous—at least for the Clintons. Young and ambitious, they would be able to build a potentially formidable machine by 2016 to challenge Hillary. Biden was almost laughably the opposite. For one, there were questions of his health—he had suffered two cranial aneurysms, resulting in brain surgeons, "literally" taking "the top of my head off," in Biden's telling of the story. Another consideration was his age—he would be seventy-four years old on Inauguration Day 2017. And of course there was his, well, Bidenness. His inability to stay on message and his unbreakable habit of saying dumb things. Often. Senate colleagues viewed him as at worst a well-meaning buffoon or at best an occasionally brainy eccentric. Biden was the kind of guy who couldn't help but undermine himself, such as when he told reporters with a straight face that Hillary would be a better choice for vice president than he was. Even Obama second-guessed the Biden choice almost until the moment he made it. *I can't believe I'm nominating Biden*, he said to himself.

The Clintons received the selection of Biden, a longtime friend, with great enthusiasm. Bill offered an effusive endorsement, saying, "I love Joe Biden, and America will, too." He added, "With Joe Biden's experience and wisdom, supporting Barack Obama's proven understanding, instincts, and insight, America will have the national security leadership we need."

After the Biden announcement, in fact, there was a sudden shift in the Clintons' mood. Though still bitter, depressed, and self-pitying, they now saw a glimmer of hope for a future presidential run. Much of the turmoil of the previous weeks seemed to slip away—there would be no convention floor fight, no real effort to seat Michigan and Florida; Hillary and Bill would both be happy to endorse Obama at the convention and on two separate nights.

Perhaps finally sensing he was going too far in his public performance as a sore loser, and perhaps missing the spotlight, Bill Clinton was now Obama's champion. "Barack Obama is ready to lead America and to restore American leadership in the world," Clinton said to raucous cheers and applause in Denver. "Barack Obama is ready to honor the oath, to preserve, protect, and defend the Constitution of the United States. Barack Obama is ready to be president of the United States." Whether Clinton meant a word of it was irrelevant. "These are two people who hate each other," says one prominent Democrat who insisted he not be named on the record, even though what he was telling me was the worst-kept secret in Washington. "I mean, *hate* each other." But in any event, one of the longest roller-coaster rides in American political history had taken another unexpected, death-defying turn. Clinton embarked on a multistate tour, talking himself hoarse, appearing in TV commercials for Obama, and quickly becoming Obama's best and most persuasive advocate.

In his cooler-headed moments, Bill drew several lessons from Hillary's loss, each of which he was determined to correct the next time around. One was that she did not have enough money to compete over the long run. Two, she had violated one of his most well-known political rules: Campaigns were about the future. Hillary had become identified with the past. Third, Hillary had muddled key relationships with various constituencies—such as blacks, gays, and Latinos. He of course left out the fourth factor—his own contributions, or sabotage, depending on how you wanted to look at it. To the contrary, Bill saw his lack of control of the 2008 operation as the heart of the problem. Next time he was going to be the campaign manager, whether Hillary liked it or not. But that was a fight still to come.

Biden would be a perfect conduit for the Clintons. At some point, it's not exactly clear when, the former president approached Biden about brokering a deal for Hillary to join Team Obama.

"If she comes in, I'll watch out for her in the White House and make sure she's given the power and the autonomy and everything else," Biden reportedly told Clinton, according to sources.

Biden promised that she'd be given free rein and that as secretary of state she would "own foreign policy."

By the time Bill Clinton hit the hustings for his enemy, Barack Obama, it was pretty apparent that Hillary's next candidacy for president was already under way. The Clintons would not be blamed as party poopers or sore losers. In the worst-case scenario, she was a doable eight years away from the White House. Or in the best case, four years if somehow Obama managed to lose the general election.

That tantalizing thought preoccupied Bill Clinton for the rest of the campaign. So much so that he did something no self-respecting politico would do in a presidential race—he flirted, quite obviously, with the enemy. In this case, that was the Republicans' nominee, Hillary's old friend John McCain.

"During the 2008 campaign I talked to President Clinton on several occasions," McCain tells me with a slight smile, as if realizing what he is about to let slip. "We talked about the campaign. We talked about various aspects of it."

McCain shied away from calling Clinton's outreach "advice." "It wasn't 'you should do this, you should do that,'" McCain says.

"It was sort of 'well, here's where I think things are standing and here's the issues I think you should emphasize.'" The conversations continued well into the fall, even after Clinton endorsed Obama at the convention. McCain recalls that Clinton called him to share thoughts about the 2008 financial bailout, which had led McCain to "suspend" his campaign against Obama and urge a legislative solution.

"He's a policy wonk and we would talk," McCain says. "We talked about why the bailout was important and why, who the players were, who you could trust, you know, that kind of thing."

McCain stops just short of saying Clinton had hoped McCain would defeat Obama. "I can't say he favored [my candidacy over Obama's]," McCain says, "but I have to say that he wouldn't be talking to me if he didn't feel that he and I . . . that it would be helpful to have the communications."

McCain's longtime aide Mark Salter confirms the two spoke on occasion during the last stages of the presidential campaign. Salter describes the conversations as Clinton and McCain talking about the state of the race.

As late as September 2008, two months before what promised to be a close election, Bill Clinton was publicly gushing about the Republican. "The American people, for good and sufficient reasons, admire him," Clinton told the women of ABC's *The View*.[34] "He's given something in life the rest of us can't match."

McCain's loss that November left the Clintons with Plan B—a piece of the Obama administration all her own.

The incoming president would give her a department to run, let her fly all over the world, and in the process keep her out of his hair. Hillary was now going into a bubble.

7

THE BUBBLE

"She made, I believe, personal judgment calls that turned out to be the wrong call and it cost people their lives."

—U.S. Representative Jason Chaffetz

On January 21, 2009, Hillary Clinton was confirmed as U.S. secretary of state by an overwhelming majority of senators, 94–2. The only two votes in opposition to her appointment came from two conservative Republican senators: David Vitter of Louisiana and Jim DeMint of South Carolina. Perhaps it was odd that none of the members of the Senate who had voted to convict President Clinton on two articles impeachment opposed Hillary's nomination. But all of Clinton's would-be opposition had been won over in the intervening years. Both Vitter and DeMint were sworn in as senators in 2005, and seemed to have little if no relationship with Hillary during their short overlapping times.

"This nation has come together in a way that it has not for some time," McCain said, praising the confirmation of Hillary.[1]

Until January 22, 2009, Hillary Clinton had managed only two things of any major significance: her universal health-care plan, during the early days of her husband's administration, and her 2008 presidential effort. Both, even her staunchest supporters would admit, were notorious disasters—practically from start to finish. So with her third time up to the plate, and with a chance to show her managerial bona fides, there was enormous pressure for her to succeed when she arrived for the first time at the State Department offices in Foggy Bottom to cheering employees.

While running the department once led by Thomas Jefferson and George Marshall provides great prestige, it also poses unique challenges to even the most experienced diplomat: It's a massive federal bureaucracy with a budget of over $45 billion per year, a staff of over fifty-eight thousand, and locations all over the world.

As secretary of state, Hillary Clinton was at first determined to do more than manage a large bureaucracy and improve her own image. For the top diplomat, the State Department is a great platform and Hillary Clinton was determined to make the most of it. According to sources, she made a genuine effort early on to push issues close to her heart, assert herself in meetings with other principals in the administration, and make her mark on the policies and priorities of Barack Obama's presidency.

Just as one would expect from a secretary of state, she immediately made plans to go abroad. But instead of a visit to Canada or Europe or to another traditional ally, Hillary decided to visit Asia—first Japan, then Indonesia and South Korea, before finishing in China. The entire trip was set up to show a "pivot" toward emerging allies in the East and to show that America under this new president would have different priorities.

She'd join the press on the back of her airplane for an off-the-record conversation, which a participant described as surprisingly frank. Most principals even in technically "off-the-record" sessions know better than to dish and to go off talking points. They assume that eventually the conversation will be leaked. In Hillary's case, she took some chances with the traveling State Department press corps. On her jaunt back across the Pacific, she was able to relax with a stiff alcoholic beverage. It was a good-will gesture—one that won over a few in the press who were skeptical of her intentions in joining the Obama administration. But there was still much work to be done.

Work that would focus on ending the wars in Iraq and Afghanistan, and then quickly pivoting to other areas of the world that the new administration wanted to focus on. "In the next 10 years, we need to be smart and systematic about where we invest time and energy, so that we put ourselves in the best position to sustain our leadership, secure our interests, and advance our values. One of the most important tasks of American statecraft over the next decade will therefore be to lock in a substantially increased investment—diplomatic, economic, strategic, and otherwise—in the Asia-Pacific region," she'd explain in an article in *Foreign Policy* a couple of years later. "The Asia-Pacific has become a key driver of global politics."

But in fact the reality was slightly different in that present moment: America was still heavily involved in two wars, and worse, the Middle East was once again about to go up in flames. A "pivot" would prove to be in name only.

No matter how much Hillary may have wanted to forge a new path, Team Obama had other ideas. The tone was set early on with cabinet meetings. As with other recent administrations, these were scripted affairs, opportunities for select cabinet officials to report on what their departments were doing, but not open for freewheeling discussions. "It wasn't a debating society, but more of a reporting session," one former cabinet secretary who served during Obama's first term tells me in an interview. Officials were informed who would be issuing reports and for how long. "It was a lot of window-dressing to show . . . the country and to show Washington that the president was consulting those cabinet officials," the former cabinet secretary says. The meetings usually ran about ninety minutes.

Instead of relying on his cabinet secretaries, Barack Obama relied on a small, insular team of White House insiders who have been calling the shots since the first day of his administration. People like Valerie Jarrett, Obama's loyal, longtime confidante; Tom Donilon, Obama's national security advisor; and a host of White House staffers who toil in anonymity but whose memos and talking points have the power to shape American foreign policy as much as, if not more than, any decree issued by the secretaries of state or defense.

If tensions between Obama and Clinton eased after the 2008 campaign, that never became true among staffers at the lower levels. This was due to "the campaign hangover," according to State Department employee Vali Nasr, who served as a special advisor to the president's special representative for Afghanistan and Pakistan. "Obama's inner circle, veterans of his election campaign, were suspicious of Clinton," he told me shortly after the publication of a memoir of his time in the Obama administration—one that wasn't received well inside 1600 Pennsylvania Avenue. "And even after Clinton proved she was a team player, they remained concerned with her popularity and approval ratings, and feared that she could overshadow the president."

Clinton and Obama's defense secretary Robert Gates, a Republican holdover from the Bush administration, shared a resentment of the maneuverings of a National Security Council (NSC) populated by people they found largely young, arrogant, and out of their depth. None of them had much of an affinity for Hillary Clinton. One of Obama's top campaign surrogates, Samantha Power, had called Hillary "a monster." She resigned from the campaign, but then subsequently was hired as a senior director on the NSC, undoubtedly making chilly some meetings in the Situation Room when both women were present. With the Power selection, Obama was also making another point—Hillary wasn't in control of national security policy. He was.

Obama had never run a government bureaucracy bigger than a Senate office (which generally has about thirty or forty staffers, a budget of around $2 million to $3 million, and a couple of state offices in addition to its main office on Capitol Hill). Still, his approach was to try to run the important things himself, such as foreign policy, where he had pledged to do things differently than his predecessor George W. Bush—and to restore the trust and confidence the world once had in America.

When Obama recruited Hillary for his cabinet, he told her that *his* top priority would be jobs and the economy. The economy had tanked. Big banks had collapsed and unemployment had surged to highs not seen in recent years. It was for this reason, among others, that he'd need her to take the reins on foreign policy. Whether he meant it or not—he probably didn't—the reins in fact never left Obama's hands.

"Part of the fighting was that—where does policy get initiated?" Vali Nasr recalls as I question him in his office at the Johns Hopkins School of Advanced International Studies, where he's now dean after leaving Hillary's State Department. "The national security apparatus is such that the agencies suggest policies, provide intelligence, provide information. The job of the National Security Council is to organize this for the president and set up a decision-making process for the president based on the input of these groups, so they're really giving the president policy options."

But it was different with Obama. "When I was there, that's not the way NSC worked," Nasr says. "They wanted to basically shape the policy there and then for these agencies to implement it. Basically, it became a singular policy-making apparatus, which then begs the question what is the quality of the decision making there, and what is the quality of the people making these policies there, and what is their objective? Is the objective to protect the president from foreign policy? Is the objective to manage his image? Or is the objective to further America's national interest?"

As Hillary, the pragmatist, had demanded before taking the job, she did have regular "one-on-ones" with the president. For Clinton this offered the visual, at least to the Washington press corps, that she was an integral player. To Obama it was a chance for respectful listening and making sure that Hillary personally felt looped-in to the happenings at the White House. But it never seemed to stop him from doing whatever he wanted to do once she left the room.

"As secretary of state I think that her relationship with the president was cordial, but never close," says Senator McCain, who served as the top Republican on the Senate Armed Services Committee and observed her up close. McCain's a foreign policy hawk—one more aligned with Hillary than Obama, so it is with a tinge of regret the former Republican presidential nominee makes this observation one morning in his Senate office. "I don't believe that when crucial decisions were made that she was necessarily in the room. . . . [W]hen it came to some crucial decisions I don't think that Mr. Donilon was swayed by her opinion. I'm not saying she wasn't consulted, but I think it's very well known she was not in the inner circle of decision makers on national security."

"I think she had very little interaction" with the president, says one veteran State Department employee. "A lot of this was, you know, she would go to meetings of the NSC when she was in town and called, but it was a very distant relationship."

The NSC sidelined Clinton at every turn—as it did other cabinet secretaries from Gates to his successors at the Pentagon, Leon Panetta and Chuck Hagel. "They would send [the defense secretary] to someplace like Botswana while they crafted North Korea policy at the White House," one former Defense Department official says.

"The structure of the White House was set up particularly by people who are not experienced in foreign policy, often came from a domestic policy background, and had their eyes on 2012 and the poll numbers," says State's former special advisor Nasr. "They were micromanaging. They were micromanaging the strategic review on Afghanistan. They were micromanaging the Pakistan policy. They were micromanaging Egypt. They were micromanaging all of these issues."

Contemplating how Bill Clinton would have adapted to the workings of the Obama cabinet, one person who served both Presidents Clinton and Obama laughs. "My prediction is that . . . he would have been a disaster," he says, "because he would have had a hard time keeping in his lane." Hillary didn't have that problem.

"Obama brought her into the administration, put her in a bubble, and ignored her," says a former high-ranking diplomat. "It turned out to be a brilliant political maneuver by Obama, making it impossible for her to challenge him, unless she left the administration, and not giving her an excuse that she could resign in protest. So she was stuck."

One early signal to Hillary about her real place in the administration involved formulation of policy toward Afghanistan, which came during the first year of Obama's presidency. The decision was whether to escalate the war or not. It would be Obama's first major foreign policy decision, centered on what he had called the "good war," a contradistinction to the bad war, which he considered Iraq. This one was Afghanistan, which the United States had invaded soon after the September 11, 2001, terror attacks—the largest and most devastating in America's history. He felt less good about the war upon coming into office.

Hillary, for her part, suggested President Obama listen to his commander on the ground—General Stanley McChrystal—who had requested a surge of forty thousand troops. Gates basically was in agreement, though he could have lived with a smaller commitment.

"I want an exit strategy," Obama reportedly told Gates and Clinton, according to Bob Woodward's account, in a private Situation Room war meeting.

But he ended up deciding that a surge of thirty thousand troops on a limited and preordained timeline was what would be appropriate. The deciding factor? Not so much Hillary, though it wouldn't have exactly been a position of strength to retreat from war without his cabinet behind him. It goes deeper. Obama's natural instinct was to retreat, to pull back from the world and let the Afghans deal with the problem of Afghanistan. He had made that promise in Iraq—it was a central campaign promise that set him apart from Hillary, who had voted along with most other Republicans and Democrats to support the war in Iraq. The problem was that full retreat was the least politically tenable option, and it would require his crossing the entire military establishment. Pulling back entirely would have resulted in charges of abandonment.

A first-term president already looked at with caution by the hawkish wings of the Democratic and Republican parties did not feel he had the strength to make such a decision.

Hillary had appointed Richard Holbrooke, a longtime Clinton aide, to be her point person on Afghanistan. This didn't sit well with the president and his loyalists.

From the start, Obama didn't trust him. And as a result he didn't listen to him. The president deferred instead to an insular circle of loyalists, many of whom had far less experience in foreign policy. That list included Tom Donilon, a political type with midlevel stints at the State Department who had been an executive at mortgage giant Fannie Mae; Denis McDonough, a longtime Senate aide with a low profile, who was personally close with Obama; UN ambassador Susan Rice; family friend and confidante Valerie Jarrett; and chief political advisor David Axelrod, who was on hand at the weekly "Terror Tuesday" meetings in the Situation Room, where President Obama developed his "kill list" of terrorist targets. These were the trusted advisors in the White House. Not Hillary—or her hand-selected staff.

The selection of Holbrooke, some think, was a classic Hillary mistake: Rely on a dear friend from over the years instead of someone who might be better suited to managing the war on which President Obama was most focused. Holbrooke was in some ways a brilliant foreign policy thinker, but he set out to align himself with the opponents of Afghan president Hamid Karzai in part because Karzai was considered George W. Bush's man in Kabul. When it came time to work with the complicated and imperfect Karzai, the relationship was sour almost from the start.

Hillary's loyalty to Holbrooke was unwavering. After he fell ill in 2010 and his condition deteriorated, Hillary visited him every day at George Washington University Hospital. "The night that he was dying or when they decided to pull the plug, she just, wherever she was, she just left and came straight there," Nasr remembers. When Holbrooke died, his whole crew—all his staff—was waiting downstairs in the hospital. Hillary hugged everybody.

"Let's go to the closest hotel," Hillary told the shocked and mournful staff. "Let's go there and have an Irish wake."

They left the hospital for the Ritz-Carlton, less than a half mile away, where Hillary stayed until about midnight. "She told stories. She listened to other people tell stories. She cried with everybody, and had tears in her eyes," Nasr recounts. "That's the side of her we saw."

Once she realized she would never really be a major player in Obamaland, Hillary Clinton did what she always did: adjusted her course. "She kept her head down on large issues," says a former Obama administration official. "She did a nice job of tamping down any tension between her and the White House." And she focused on her own future. With Clinton taking to the skies and traveling the world, her post at the State Department became a platform for the United States and Hillary Clinton. Except not in that order.

To handle mundane State Department activities, she set up a traditional State Department operation, filled with people comfortable with, and to, the foreign policy establishment.

Her first press secretary, P. J. Crowley, was typical. Crowley's professional history was steady, but far from sparkling: twenty-six years in the air force; an assistant to the president in the Clinton White House; a vice president for public affairs for the Insurance Information Institute; a senior fellow at the liberal Center for American Progress, the organization that had been designed to be a White House in waiting for Hillary while she was in the Senate.

As a spokesman for Hillary's State Department, Crowley was not nimble enough for the Foggy Bottom press corps. Clumsy at the podium, he would often create news at times when the State Department wanted to play down stories. By contrast, a good press secretary can conduct an hour-long, on-the-record briefing that makes no news. To be fair, the State Department podium is one of the most difficult to man—it requires knowing America's position toward every nation in the world. One slipup and an international crisis can be created.

Most infamously, Crowley broke with the U.S. government on the issue of Bradley Manning, the man who leaked secret U.S. documents to Julian Assange of WikiLeaks. "What is being done to Bradley Manning is ridiculous and counterproductive and stupid on the part of the Department of Defense," Crowley would tell a group at the Massachusetts Institute of Technology.[2] The break from the administration was so sharp President Obama had to address it later that week at a press conference. Crowley was soon out.

To replace him, Secretary Clinton turned to State Department veteran Victoria Nuland, an immensely talented and knowledgeable foreign policy hand. It was widely thought in Washington that Hillary picked her to preempt criticism from the right. She held previous appointments in the Bush administration, and her husband is Robert Kagan, a conservative foreign affairs columnist for the *Washington Post* and former foreign policy advisor on John McCain's 2008 presidential run. Nuland's appointment prevented many establishment Republicans from crossing the prominent Kagan by going after his wife in public.

Hillary even appointed Kagan to her Foreign Affairs Policy Board, which was headed by Strobe Talbott, who had long ago forgiven his former roommate, Bill Clinton, for once hitting on his girlfriend while they were in school. The board, like so many in Washington, was perfunctory—and indeed it's not apparent any substantive policy recommendations from the board were ever adopted by Hillary. That was hardly the point. Instead, the primary function was similar to the reason Nuland was appointed: If the Washington foreign policy establishment is working for you, and serving you in some way, it's much less likely that they'll publicly criticize your actions.

There was a second, almost entirely separate operation set up by Clinton, which might as well have been dubbed "2016."

In a sign of just how much Obama was determined to corral her into his cabinet, the president and his top aides had reluctantly agreed to let Hillary, unlike other cabinet officials, refrain from hiring the usual political appointees and campaign staffers and bundlers who had worked to help Obama get elected. Certainly, she wouldn't have to hire anyone who had worked in 2008 to defeat her. She and she alone would pick political appointees for her department. By contrast, Senator John Kerry, chairman of the Foreign Relations Committee, complained that he couldn't get any of his people through the White House personnel system. (Kerry had endorsed Obama in 2008.)

There were occasional limits to that power. Hillary proposed bringing aboard Sidney Blumenthal, for instance, a trusted Clinton advisor who had fired some of the heaviest artillery directly at Obama in the 2008 campaign. Rahm Emanuel, the brash former Clintonite brought on as Obama's chief of staff, was given the job of telling her no. It's long been suspected that it was Blumenthal who during the campaign sent around a photo of Obama dressed in African garb in what was seen as an attempt to make Obama, whose father was born in Kenya, look foreign. It helped feed into the baseless rumors that Obama himself had been born in Kenya—a trope that appears to have originated in Clintonland in a nasty and subversive attempt to dismiss the young senator during the outset of the campaign.

Otherwise, Mrs. Clinton was able to largely reassemble her political operation at State. This included her longtime speechwriter Lissa Muscatine, her press-hating press secretary Philippe Reines, and of course her devoted Huma Abedin, who traveled with her on almost every one of her trips to more than one hundred countries.

"Huma and Philippe were very close personal managers of her affairs," Nasr says.

Indeed, so close was Reines to Hillary that he was spared what otherwise might have been a firing offense. Because of his actions Hillary was humiliated in front of the Russians, when the cockiness of the press aide prevented him from using wise judgment.

In March 2009, less than two months into the Obama administration, Hillary was meeting her Russian counterpart on neutral ground in Geneva. She brought along a gift: "an emergency stop button that had been hastily pilfered from a swimming pool or Jacuzzi at the hotel," according to the book *HRC*, cowritten by a former staffer for Democratic National Committee chair Debbie Wasserman Schultz.[3] The red button, printed in Latin script and not Cyrillic, said *peregruzka*, meaning "overcharge." It was supposed to read "reset," a reference to a line Vice President Joe Biden had offered the previous month about offering a "reset" in U.S.-Russia relations following George W. Bush's rule, but Reines got the translation wrong.

"You got it wrong," Clinton's Russian counterpart, Foreign Minister Sergey Lavrov, said.

Hillary could only counter, "I got it wrong." She was humiliated.

Reines tried to blame someone close to Obama, Michael McFaul, who'd go on to serve as President Obama's ambassador to Russia. Fortunately for Hillary, the press went a little easy on her. "Lost in Translation: A U.S. Gift to Russia," the *New York Times* declared, playing down the embarrassing gaffe.[4]

But once again, it was a sign of Hillary's being ill-served by people who were too close to her to allow for accurate judgments of their work and character.

"Clinton put a team in place to make sure that her hair was in place, her lighting was good, and she was seen with major leaders," says a former ambassador.

For the first time in modern State Department history, reporters who covered Hillary recall, the secretary of state had her own spokesman on the government payroll for issues that *didn't* concern American foreign policy but only concerned the secretary herself. The crusty Reines would deal with all press questions that related to Hillary Clinton the public figure. Questions concerning politics and her personal life would go through him. He would answer to varying degrees, depending on whether he liked you (which was unlikely, considering his *hatred* of reporters) or thought you were useful.

The most essential person running Clinton's political operation was, of course, her choice of chief of staff. All powerful leaders need a loyal alter ego who sits at their right hand, offering sage advice, executing sensitive orders, and managing underlings whose loyalties may or may not lie with their leader. Don Corleone had Tom Hagen. Bill Gates had Steve Ballmer. For Hillary Clinton, the consigliere is Cheryl Mills.

In the battle to turn the tide against Barack Obama's primary victories, Mills was candidate Clinton's de facto campaign manager. At Foggy Bottom, she was Secretary Clinton's chief counsel and chief of staff. And if the Clintons make it back to the White House, Cheryl Mills will be the second most powerful woman in the world. She will be Hillary's Hagen.

The daughter of a lieutenant colonel, Mills grew up on army bases across Europe, in Belgium and West Germany, and like many in the military, her loyalties run more toward people than toward ideologies. Just two years out of Stanford Law, Mills left her high-paying job at one of Washington's most prestigious law firms, moved to Little Rock, and joined the transition team planning the opening phases of Bill Clinton's presidency. The campaign against George Bush and Ross Perot wasn't even finished, but Clinton led in the polls. Mills was willing to bet on the Clintons, and when victory came, the impressed Clintons were willing to bet on Mills.

The twenty-seven-year-old was appointed associate counsel to the president, and four years later, she became deputy White House counsel. Her most important job was handling the parade of scandals and investigations that culminated in impeachment. Mills's allies would say she had a talent for protecting the Clintons from out-of-control investigators with political agendas. Her enemies say she was simply good at covering up illegality.

Mills's approach was to play hardball with enemies, investigators, and inquiring journalists. If there was a way to avoid sharing requested documents, she found it, never backing down or giving up ground in what she treated as a prolonged trench war for the Clintons' legal and political survival. Everything from her screen saver ("It's the lioness that hunts . . .") to the slogan hanging above her desk ("Don't Go There") reflected the attitude she brought to her defense of Bill and Hillary Clinton.[5]

According to a congressional committee, when it began investigating allegations that the administration had used government workers on government time to create a government database of potential donors that was sent to the Democratic National Committee and the Clinton reelection campaign—a relatively minor scandal by Clinton standards—Mills withheld documents. Then, when testifying before the committee, her veracity was challenged.

According to the Congressional Record, this matter was referred to the Department of Justice for investigation of possible perjury and obstruction of the investigation. No charges were ever brought against Mills.

Similarly, after a technical glitch allegedly caused the White House to withhold more than 1.8 million emails from investigators, Congress, and outside groups, Mills was asked to look into the problem. She didn't. In a sharply worded judicial opinion, a federal judge said Mills's response to news that the White House was in possession of a huge amount of documents it was legally required to disclose was "totally inadequate," a "critical error," and "loathsome."[6] (The most notable exception to her instinct for withholding documents occurred when she recommended releasing government records and private communications by Kathleen Willey, in an attempt to discredit the woman who accused Bill Clinton of groping her in the White House.)

From her first day in the White House, Mills demonstrated the quality that had first impressed the Clintons in Little Rock: her loyalty to them. "She is incredibly loyal to the president," an anonymous White House aide told a reporter. "If something's on the other side of a brick wall and the Clintons need it, she'll find a way to get to it: over, around, or through." After the House of Representatives impeached Clinton, Mills had a public outlet for her loyalty to the president. On the second day of presentations by Clinton's lawyers, Mills spoke in Clinton's de-

fense. With her proud parents looking down from the Senate gallery—
the thirty-three-year-old was only the third or fourth African American
in history to speak from the Senate floor—Mills said she was "very proud
to have had the opportunity to serve our country and this president." In
response to accusations that Clinton lied to thwart Paula Jones's civil
rights case, Mills assured the Senate that Bill Clinton loved civil rights.
His "grandfather owned a store" that "catered primarily to African
Americans," and "the president has taken his grandfather's teachings
to heart." After all, he had hired Cheryl Mills: "I stand here before you
today because others before me decided to take a stand," and "I stand
here before you today because President Bill Clinton believed I could
stand here for him."

Her peroration capped a speech that North Dakota's Byron Dorgan
called "one of the most remarkable that I've heard in the Senate or in
my political career."[7] Summing up the case for Bill Clinton, she repeated
the phrase "I am not worried" four times—building to her punch line: "I
am not worried about civil rights because this president's record on civil
rights, on women's rights—on all of our rights—is unimpeachable." What
any of that had to do with lying under oath and obstructing justice was
irrelevant—Mills and the rest of the Clinton team had successfully helped
to "OJ" the Clinton impeachment trial. It was somehow about race. .

After her virtuoso performance—and Bill Clinton's acquittal—Mills
could have had almost any legal job in Washington. The president even
offered her the position of White House counsel. But Mills was burned
out. She moved to New York in 1999 to become a vice president at Oprah
Winfrey's Oxygen Media, and after two years, she took a job as general
counsel at New York University—leaving far behind her more than six
years of subpoenas, congressional investigations, independent counsels,
and investigative reporters. She may have been one of the few lawyers in
history who moved to Manhattan for a taste of tranquility.

Mills's quiet life away from politics lasted for eight years—until Hillary Clinton announced her campaign for the presidency. Mills came
on board as a counselor, and when Hillary fired her campaign manager

after a string of primary defeats, the trusted, combative, and indefatigable Mills took the reins de facto. "Sometimes on campaigns," said traveling press secretary Jay Carson to a reporter, "you can end up in a situation where there's not a clear single person, no clear leader, no clear power center. When Cheryl is in charge, that's never a problem."[8]

Others were not only impressed but also terrified of her. "I really like Cheryl," says an aide who worked with her on the 2008 campaign. "She'd kill me if she knew I were talking to you." The aide adds, "I never, ever saw the, like, the crazy Cheryl moments that I've heard about. But I've definitely heard about them. I know they exist."

After Hillary Clinton's defeat and move from the Senate to the State Department, Mills followed her to Foggy Bottom, where she was an efficient, devoted, and occasionally notorious guardian of all things Hillary Clinton. Clinton loyalists were quick to praise her. "Cheryl Mills ran that building extremely well," says Vali Nasr.

Among those in the building she ran so well were the two people in the positions Congress created in 2000 when it split in two the normally administrative job of deputy secretary of state, the number-two position at the department. Clinton filled one of those jobs with a typical Foreign Service type. The other position went to a seasoned political operative, Tom Nides, who protected Hillary's political future.

"Tom [Nides] was just a big protector of Secretary Clinton," says one former State Department official who also served in the Bush administration. With a wife working as a senior executive at ABC News (she'd later move to CNN), Nides also had excellent ties to the mainstream media.

Together Nides and Mills did the department's dirty work, while Clinton maintained a statesmanlike distance as she worked to enhance her image. (One insider predicted in fact that Nides would get the coveted White House chief of staff job if Hillary won in 2016—not Mills.)

"They would decide what would go in to Secretary Clinton and what they would secretly get her to sign off on, but not make any public announcements on, so that she was protected in the decision-making process," says one State Department employee. "She needed to be able to officially stay away from the issues, so that she could deny that she knew anything" if something went wrong.

"She was able to kind of stay above it," says an official, "and as the policy began to really fail, she stayed away from it."

Mrs. Clinton's celebrity was the one clear advantage she brought to the job and the Obama administration. She was far better known going into the office of secretary of state than any of her predecessors—from Henry Kissinger to Colin Powell to Condoleezza Rice. And this helped put a pleasing public face on the administration around the world.

It also helped her attract unlikely admirers, like Secretary of Defense Gates, who seemed to beam around Hillary whenever they were in the same room. One Gates aide described him as coming across like a groupie with a rock star. They allied together on many issues against the Obama NSC, even if they usually lost.

No doubt with an eye to avoiding a repeat of 2008, she placed a special focus on strengthening relations with members of Congress—the Democrats she'd need for endorsements and the Republicans who might run against her. One Republican senator who once had an acrimonious relationship with the Clintons remembers the secretary of state being extremely receptive to his ideas—and willing to listen whenever he had thoughts he wanted to share with her.

One of her potential challengers in 2016, Congressman Paul Ryan, also counts himself as a Hillary fan, having worked with her during her State Department tenure. "I think we both respect each other as, you know, talented—she's a talented leader in her party," he tells me in an interview. "And so she has my respect and I get the feeling that Hillary's mutual."

Keenly aware of the Senate's massive egos, Clinton had a reputation for returning calls quickly, following up on congressional requests, and giving the impression of personal attentiveness to even their most mundane, even kooky, ideas.

One senator called her up to share some ideas about the nature of Islam. Hillary returned his phone call almost instantly. "My suggestion was that we needed to look for forums by which we can gather Islamic leaders, and then we ask simple questions like, 'Well, do you believe a Christian should be given equal rights in Saudi Arabia?' And when these 'Islamic leaders' publicly admit not to believing in equal rights for Christians and Muslims and Jews, then we could have a public airing of these differences," he explains.

The senator compared his plan to the way he believed segregation was ended in America. "When CBS News put the microphone to the preacher's face and said, 'Can a black person come to your church?' It's all right not to have any and not to do it for a hundred years, but are you going to say on TV he can't come to my church because of the color of his skin? I'm thinking that these guys are getting away with saying all kinds of things in their mosque, and all this hateful stuff, and you get them in public and ask them some simple questions they're going to have a hard time."

After a rather lengthy conversation with the senator, Hillary told him, "Well, I'll think about it." The senator had voted to convict her husband on both articles of impeachment and had been a fierce opponent of her legislative initiatives. But he felt like he'd been listened to, which is all most members of Congress want anyway. By the time Hillary left Foggy Bottom, he felt affection and respect for her.

The issue her aides try to emphasize the most—suggesting what they might consider Hillary's most impressive accomplishment—is women's rights, which she brought up, famously, when in the Democratic Republic of the Congo toward the beginning of her tenure. She was asked (according to the translator on the scene at the time), "What does Mr. Clinton think, through the mouth of Mrs. Clinton?"

She ripped the translating device from her ear. "Wait, you want me to tell you what my husband thinks?" shouted an indignant Hillary, dressed in a purple pantsuit with a matching purple shirt. "My husband is not the secretary of state, I am. So, you ask my opinion, I will tell you my opinion. I'm not going to be channeling my husband."

The question was about Chinese contracts in the Congo, but it mattered little.

Back stateside, video of the event, which also featured former basketball star Dikembe Mutombo, went viral.[9] The tabloids mocked Hillary, however. "Hill: I Wear the Pants," read the *New York Post*. "Hey, I'm the Boss, Not Bill," is what the *New York Daily News* went with.

It was a theme Hillary tried to bring to the rest of the world—and usually with a bit more forethought and a bit more calm. "Women's equality is not just a moral issue, it's not just a humanitarian issue, it is not just a fairness issue," Hillary said at a conference. "It is a security issue, it is a prosperity issue, and it is a peace issue . . . it's in the vital interests of the United States of America." These were lines that were widely quoted—and ones, it's safe to assume, that she wants defining her tenure as America's top diplomat.

It would echo what she said in China in 1995. "It is time for us to say here in Beijing, and the world to hear, that it is no longer acceptable to discuss women's rights as separate from human rights," the then first lady said at a women's conference.[10] "It is a violation of human rights when women are doused with gasoline, set on fire, and burned to death because their marriage dowries are deemed too small . . . when thousands of women are raped in their own communities and when thousands of women are subjected to rape as a tactic or prize of war." Hillary's good friend Melanne Verveer would credit that speech for "help[ing] spark a movement around the world for women's progress."[11]

It was a powerful message in 1995—and when she returned as secretary of state, she claimed progress. "I think we have made an enormous amount of progress, and we have women able to chart their own lives much more than ever existed in human history. But there are external barriers and internal barriers. Externally, there are still many places where education is not available, health care is not available, jobs are not available, training, credit, you know, just the basics of being able to construct your own approach to your life," Hillary would say at a meeting with women leaders in Beijing in May 2010.[12]

"And then, internally, each woman has to make the right balance in her life, and we have to respect the decisions that women make, because we're all so different. But there are still some attitudes in the minds of men and women that keep it very hard for women to feel like they are achieving and being able to get supported in their choice."

She'd also make an effort to talk up gay rights. In a video released by the State Department, Hillary made a domestic plea: "Like millions of Americans, I was terribly saddened to learn of the recent suicides of several teenagers across our country after being bullied because they were gay or because people thought they were gay," Hillary said as she stared into the camera. "Just think of the progress made by women just during my lifetime, by women, or ethnic, racial and religious minorities over the course of our history—and by gays and lesbians, many of whom are now free to live their lives openly and proudly. Here at the State Department, I am grateful every day for the work of our LGBT employees who are serving the United States as foreign service officers and civil servants here and around the world. It wasn't long ago that these men and women would not have been able to serve openly, but today they can—because it has gotten better. And it will get better for you."[13]

It was odd only in that it was a rare entry into American domestic politics. Not something a secretary of state normally does, but it demonstrated how important Hillary finds the issue. She'd talk it up abroad, too, perhaps becoming the first secretary of state to embrace gay rights as such an important issue to American foreign policy.

These are all issues she'll tout as defining moments of her tenure. And although there aren't clear victories showing progress—it's hard to claim victory on women's rights or gay rights—it's helped build the foundations for a presidential run. She'll say that electing her will ensure that the fight for these issues continues.

Hillary also worked to cement her relationship with Obama, which, while never warm—the president was known to have warm relations with almost no one—was cordial, correct, and businesslike. Those were the qualities an aloof leader like Obama prized most highly.

Hillary's staff made it very apparent to the press where the two had disagreed. Clinton portrayed herself as more hawkish than her boss. First was in the summer of 2009 in Iran, where a presidential election was stolen by the hard-liner Mahmoud Ahmadinejad, an avowed hater of America and our allies. The people took to the streets there to rise up and express their displeasure. The unrest was widespread and sincere. It was a real moment, the first in more than three decades, where it looked like the repressive regime might be able to be challenged.

Hillary, her aides have maintained, wanted to get the United States involved in playing a role in shaping a post-Khomeini outcome. Even her aides, acting under the unsubstantiated belief that it was a social media revolution, driven by the collective power in social media platforms like Twitter, tried to harness that into something more substantive. It was in part a reaction to losing the election to Obama, who they believed had beaten them using the collective power of the Internet. But Obama viewed the Iranian uprising differently, as a purely internal matter. "It is up to Iranians to make decisions about who Iran's leaders will be," Obama said. So nothing substantive happened and eventually the protests subsided under withering attacks and arrests by pro-regime forces—and that moment to help the Iranian people perhaps topple their repressive regime was lost forever.

Similarly, in Syria, where an internal civil war turned into a regime crackdown on the uprising, Hillary wanted the United States to come to the aid of the Syrian rebels. She wanted America to do *something*. President Obama didn't. These are the sorts of distinctions that are in no way lost on some of Hillary's staunchest supporters. Likewise, the distinctions bred skepticism throughout the Obama years.

Obama seemed to give her a pass when she quietly let out word of such disagreements. He still needed her, especially as he approached his 2012 reelection campaign. And he especially needed her renegade husband. Bill would be happy to help out, if there was something in it for him.

With Obama's poll numbers sagging by the middle of 2012, and the president seemingly unable to articulate a coherent rationale for his reelection, it increasingly fell to Bill Clinton, of all people, to serve as Obama's champion. It was not a job the former president came to naturally, or easily.

"They had moments where it was really ugly," a senior Clinton and Obama aide says. "I was in the [2008] campaign and I think for whatever reason, the Obama people resented what he did more than what she did, because he said some things that really stick in their craw."

Obama looked at the former president with something just short of contempt. Both men found the other grossly overrated. But Obama, a political realist, also knew that Bill Clinton had his uses, which helps explain why top Obama officials, including Secretary of the Treasury Timothy Geithner, made sure to see that the former president's views were solicited during the 2009 financial crisis.

At one point, Geithner himself trudged up to Clinton's office in Harlem to hear the thoughts of the Democratic Party's political "genius." He was disappointed.

Throughout the conversation the notoriously unfocused Clinton placed a single-minded emphasis on one seemingly irrelevant idea: He urged Obama to create better financial incentives to commercial builders so they could make their buildings more energy efficient. It was a proposal he'd read about in a white paper published by a think tank. If banks could finance a thirty-year mortgage, Clinton argued at one point, why can't the government find a way to finance a five-year payback on energy efficiency retrofits?

"We kept wanting to talk about TARP, China, and the financial crisis," says someone who was in the meeting that day. "He kept coming back to retrofitting skyscrapers. . . . He was weirdly focused on it."

Before long, Geithner had had enough of Bill's "advice." He was baffled by the performance, as he indicated to aides on his return, but others wondered whether Clinton was being dumb like a fox. Obama had defeated Clinton's wife. His campaign had called the forty-second president a racist. Why should he give Obama any good ideas to get him out of a mess?

As late as 2011, Clinton was chastising his wife's boss. In a book about the economy called *Back to Work*, Clinton implicitly criticized Obama for class warfare rhetoric that drained support from voters in the top income bracket: "Many of them supported me when I raised their taxes in 1993, because I didn't attack them for their success." Clinton also blamed the dismal 2010 midterm elections on the failure of Obama and the Democrats to "counter the national Republican message with one of their own."

Then, by the middle of 2012, something clearly changed. Clinton began to campaign for Obama with such gusto and force that many believed his forceful and relentless advocacy helped propel the sitting president to victory. At the same time, Clinton made sure that *everyone* noticed that he was the popular one in the Democratic Party. He wanted to use the election to unite the party once again around him and his machine.

Clinton's golden opportunity to do just that was his 2012 speech at the Democratic National Convention—a tour de force that made Obama's case for reelection better than Obama ever could, reminded voters that Clinton was the most clever and charismatic leader of the Democratic Party, and brought down the house.

On the surface, the speech was just another long-winded tribute to Bill Clinton, written by Bill Clinton, and delivered as only Bill Clinton can. While mentioning Obama thirty-three times, Clinton said "I," "me," or "myself" more than one hundred times. He talked about (his) work-

ing across the aisle, with Ronald Reagan and both George Bushes—while
mocking Republicans for bothering to tell voters their candidates "love
their families and their children and were grateful they'd been born in
America and all that." He flaunted his mastery of data with more than
forty-five statistics, ratios, and numbers. He implored viewers on no fewer
than six occasions to listen closely to the vitally important points he was
making, with lines like "listen carefully to this; this is really important."

What his listeners heard was a romp through almost every issue
imaginable, from jobs to taxes, spending, the auto industry, gas standards, energy production, education, student loans, Obamacare, Medi-
care, Medicaid, welfare, the debt, national security, immigration, and
voting rights. By the end of the speech, the audience had cheered after
every applause line, laughed at every joke, and made clear that the bond
between Bill Clinton and the Democratic Party was the longest, most
loyal, and most intense of the Big Dog's many, many love affairs.

"The convention speech was enormously helpful in helping them solidify the economic narrative, something that Obama himself hadn't really
done effectively in four years," says a former Obama aide. "It used to drive
me crazy when I was in the administration because I felt like the economic
message was very incoherent. Clinton really did a pretty good job creating
the synthesis and the narrative around it that they had not done."

The former president framed the election as a choice between two
narratives, and he did it in a matter of seconds. As Clinton saw it, Republicans were saying, "We left [Obama] a total mess. He hasn't cleaned
it up fast enough. So fire him and put us back in." The case for Obama
was equally simple and "a lot better. Here it is: He inherited a deeply
damaged economy. He put a floor under the crash. He began the long,
hard road to recovery and laid the foundation for a modern, more well-
balanced economy that will produce millions of good new jobs, vibrant
new businesses, and lots of new wealth for innovators."

Clinton told the convention that "since 1961, for 52 years now, the
Republicans have held the White House 28 years, the Democrats, 24.
In those 52 years, our private economy has produced 66 million private

sector jobs. So what's the job score? Republicans, 24 million; Democrats, 42 [million]."

Clinton also told his audience why Democrats—including, most especially, Clinton himself—were better at creating jobs than Republicans. "It turns out that advancing equal opportunity and economic empowerment is both morally right and good economics. (Cheers, applause.) Why? Because poverty, discrimination and ignorance restrict growth. (Cheers, applause.) When you stifle human potential, when you don't invest in new ideas, it doesn't just cut off the people who are affected; it hurts us all. (Cheers, applause.) We know that investments in education and infrastructure and scientific and technological research increase growth. They increase good jobs, and they create new wealth for all the rest of us. (Cheers, applause.)"[14]

"Clinton got out there and created a new narrative on the economy, which took some of the needles out of Obama," says Republican strategist Mike Murphy. "It was the biggest single number-moving event in the entire campaign. It was devastatingly important to the Obama guys. And he put him back in business." (It also helped, Murphy adds, that "the Romney campaign was totally incompetent.")

In 2000, Clinton had famously faulted Al Gore for not letting Clinton rally the base in key swing states. It was not a mistake Barack Obama was going to repeat. In addition to his convention speech, Clinton stumped for Obama in swing states like Florida and Ohio. Unlike Gore and his campaign team, "the Obama people, despite whatever hard feelings they had, were pretty dispassionate and not afraid to let him come in and steal the show, if they thought it would be helpful," says a former Clinton official who worked in the Obama administration. Clinton even starred in a widely seen advertisement for Obama, declaring that "President Obama has a plan to rebuild America from the ground up, investing in innovation, education, and job training. It only works if there is a strong middle class. That's what happened when I was president."[15]

Clinton's efforts did not escape the notice of Mitt Romney, who understood how effective the former president could be. "Campaigns can be grueling, exhausting," Romney would joke at the lighthearted Al Smith Dinner in New York City, mere weeks before Election Day 2012. "President Obama and I are each very lucky to have one person who is always in our corner, someone who we can lean on, and someone who is a comforting presence. Without whom we wouldn't be able to go another day. I have my beautiful wife, Ann. He has Bill Clinton."[16]

The roomful of Catholics laughed uproariously. Everyone knew it was true. Even President Obama, who was seated just a couple of seats from the grinning Romney. It would no doubt make him hate Romney more for saying it out loud.

Many politicos and reporters watching the fast friendship between Bill and Barack found it curious. Most guessed that Clinton was just being the consummate Democrat, a team player who came onto the field when his party badly needed a home run hitter. That's how many top Republicans saw it.

"I see President Clinton as sort of the elder statesman of the Democratic Party," says Paul Ryan, Romney's 2012 running mate, in an interview with me. Clinton was, he says, "doing his duty."

"Clinton likes being on the stage," says Karl Rove. "He has suffered every moment since he left the White House by not being in the center of the drama."

Others who knew the Clintons better wondered if something else was afoot. Bill Clinton, after all, was never known to be a selfless team player. Never. In other words, what was in it for him? That question, and its answer, would lead to increasing speculation, especially when the Clintons came to Obama's defense during his biggest election-year crisis—the death of Americans by terrorists in Benghazi, Libya, less than two months before a close presidential vote.

President Obama's otherwise benign neglect of his secretary of state and her State Department operations left many problems to fester, until they became PR problems. Then under Mills, they were covered up. Indeed, the same kind of accusations that had swirled around Mills at the White House surfaced again during Clinton's tenure at State. An inspector general's memo outlined eight State Department cover-ups, including an ambassador's alleged solicitation of sex from prostitutes and minors. One of the eight cases involved the president's nominee to be ambassador to Iraq, and it reported that Mills may have "attempted to block an investigation" into allegations he had improperly leaked sensitive foreign affairs intelligence to his girlfriend at the *Wall Street Journal*. But nobody seemed to have too much interest in that. Especially not the press. That was until a crisis occurred in a place no one had ever heard of. It was called Benghazi.

Mills's name returned to the headlines when Benghazi whistle-blower Gregory Hicks testified before the House Oversight Committee. At the Benghazi, Libya, post, Hicks was second in command to the murdered ambassador, Chris Stevens, and in the wake of the terrorist bombing, he defied State Department attempts to silence him. After Hicks ignored orders not to be interviewed by an investigating congressman, Jason Chaffetz, he received an angry and intimidating call. Hicks could not have been surprised that the call came from someone extremely close to Hillary Clinton—the woman the *Washington Post* once dubbed her guardian angel: Cheryl Mills. "Mills called from the United States and pulled Greg Hicks out of my briefing," Chaffetz tells me. "[She] chewed him out for allowing this to happen without [a State Department minder] being there present. . . . She is the fixer."

The events of that day are by now familiar. On September 11, 2012, the American "consulate" in Benghazi was targeted by suspected al-Qaeda-linked terrorists who killed four Americans, including the ambassador to that country, Chris Stevens.

The Benghazi terror attack took place less than two months before Obama would face the voters in his reelection bid—a bid, it must be said, in which the Obama campaign ran on the notion that al-Qaeda had been decimated. "Al-Qaeda is on the run," Obama would say. The strongest point Obama would be able to rely on was that Navy SEALs had killed

Osama bin Laden, the longtime al-Qaeda leader, in Pakistan. And on his watch, under his direction. The weakest talking point—which might have made the American public question the official narrative being perpetuated by the campaign—was of course Benghazi. And so it was an inconvenient truth then to find out that al-Qaeda had been behind the terror attack. It was not spurred by some Internet video. It had been a well-planned, coordinated, powerful attack against Americans working in an official capacity abroad.

The administration's initial response to the attack was to connect the attack with a YouTube movie that mocked Muslims. According to the initial Obama administration version of the story, Muslims across the globe decided to riot against American embassies to protest the video. Muslims protested in Egypt, Yemen, and elsewhere. But in Benghazi, things got a little out of hand. What had been a protest became a mob. The mob got out of control and overwhelmed security at the little compound in Benghazi. The entire scenario was spontaneous—no intelligence service could have anticipated and prevented the attack. And, in the end, and though it was regrettable, four Americans ended up dead.

Hillary played along with this argument, at least at first. "This has been a difficult week for the State Department and for our country," she said in a nationally televised memorial service at Andrews Air Force Base three days after the attack. "We've seen the heavy assault on our post in Benghazi that took the lives of those brave men. *We've seen rage and violence directed at American embassies over an awful Internet video that we had nothing to do with.* It is hard for the American people to make sense of that because it is senseless and it is totally unacceptable."[17]

The coffins wrapped in American flags holding the remains of the four Americans were the backdrop to the speech in the air force hangar. The bodies were escorted by uniformed soldiers from a large cargo airplane in the background, and brought directly into plain view—for all to see around the world.

It had been the first time in two and a half decades that an ambassador had been murdered in the line of duty. The ambassador, Chris

Stevens, by all accounts was particularly special. He was patriotic. He knew the risks of his line of work, but cared so deeply for the future of America, and the future of America's future allies (such as Libya), that he happily accepted the post.

"People loved to work with Chris," Clinton said. "And as he rose through the ranks, they loved to work for Chris. He was known not only for his courage but for his smile—goofy but contagious—for his sense of fun and that California cool." Stevens was also gay, a rare distinguishing trait for an American ambassador abroad.

"When you do these jobs," Clinton said by way of explanation, "you have to understand at the very beginning that you can't control everything." *There was only so much she could have done.*

Clinton's allies and aides agreed. "I think the way she has dealt with this has been admirable," the reliably loyal Paul Begala later said. "And Republicans are treading awfully close to the tin foil hat." The State Department's undersecretary for management, Patrick Kennedy, blamed a lack of funding, claiming that "the best defense is the ability to construct new facilities." P. J. Crowley, a former assistant secretary of state for public affairs under Hillary Clinton, said, "You've gotta look at this in the full picture. It's a tragedy that happened on her watch, but I don't think it will diminish what is a very significant record." Clinton aide Philippe Reines was more concise, telling a reporter asking questions about Benghazi to "Fuck Off."

Sensing a rare opportunity to damage Clinton for 2016, Republicans pounced on her role in the attack. "There was a clear disconnect between what security officials on the ground felt they needed and what officials in Washington would approve," said California congressman Darrell Issa, chairman of the House Oversight Committee. He added, "Reports that senior State Department officials told security personnel in Libya to not even make certain security requests are especially troubling."[18] Later, former vice president Dick Cheney summed up what will likely be a common attack on Clinton in any run for the White House: "She clearly wasn't hands on . . . she's doing everything she can to avoid responsibility for what clearly fell into her bailiwick."

For a time, Clinton avoided many requests to testify on Benghazi, citing the mysterious collapse at home that left her incapacitated and out of the public eye for a month. It was the same attack that had led some observers to assume she had had some form of a stroke, or mini-stroke, that she was covering up from the public.

When she finally did appear for questioning, on January 23, 2013, Hillary Clinton looked her entire six and a half decades. It was a week before her final day as secretary of state, and her years at Foggy Bottom had not been easy on her. Clinton's face had wrinkled, and her skin sagged even lower than usual. But worse than health and her bodily appearances was the black mark on her record as secretary of state—the tragedy that left four Americans dead.

"For me, this is not just a matter of policy, it's personal," she read from her prepared remarks, choking back prepared tears. "I stood next to President Obama as the Marines carried those flag-draped caskets off the plane at Andrews. I put my arms around the mothers and fathers, the sisters and brothers, the sons and daughters."

During her questioning, Clinton repeatedly relied on the classified review of the State Department's procedures of the evening of September 11, 2012. When she was in a bind, or hit a tough question, she insisted that all the answers were in the classified report (but, since the report was classified, she would have to pass on answering their questions in public, or be at risk of breaking the law). It was a beautiful strategy, which she cunningly employed throughout the day, often making her interlocutors look like fools who hadn't done their homework.

In fact, members of Congress, as well as their aides with security clearances, say there's little in the classified report that is not in the public report. It does not explain the failures of the State Department and other intelligence officials to properly diagnose what had gone wrong in Benghazi. And it does not explain why the Obama administration, including Hillary Clinton, sought to cover up what had really happened that terrible night in Benghazi.

Not that any of that mattered to the Democrats on the House and

Senate committees. Nearly every Democrat to question the embattled secretary of state spent the first half of their allotted time lavishing her with praise and practically begging her to run for president. "I think I speak for all the freshmen," said Ami Bera of California, "that we're not gonna get much time to serve with you, but we hope in a few years we'll get that chance to serve again." Congressman Joseph Kennedy of Massachusetts called her career and dedication to public service "truly exemplary" and said he looked "forward to what the future holds for you as well." One congressman from New York even asked Clinton, a "fellow New Yorker," to show her around town.

The sycophants were so over-the-top that they prompted one Republican congressman to mock Clinton's suitors. "I bring greetings from many of our mutual friends in Arkansas," Congressman Tom Cotton said. "Some of our peers on the other side have expressed their ambitions for your future. I'd like to say that I just wish you'd won the Democratic primary in 2008."

Jokes aside, the Republicans who had been demanding for months that she appear before Congress to explain why four Americans had been murdered and why the U.S. response had been an utter failure came completely ill-prepared, and were soon overwhelmed by a battle-ready Clinton, who alternated between smiling, laughing, lashing out, and choking up—all with a timing so perfect she might have been mistaken for the most talented performer in her family.

At one point, in response to questioning about the administration's misleading statements that the attacks were a protest over a YouTube video, Clinton exploded with a seemingly well-prepared retort. "With all due respect, the fact is we had four dead Americans." She was shouting. "Was it because of a protest or was it because of guys out for a walk last night who decided to kill some Americans? *What difference, at this point, does it make?* It is our job to figure out what happened and do everything we can to prevent it from ever happening again, senator."[19]

The secretary of state then gave a warning, to the senator questioning her and to those who would follow: "Honestly, I will do my best to answer your questions about this, but the fact is people were trying their best in real time to get to the best information." In other words: Don't you dare try to blame these attacks on *me*.

As a point of fact, learned only after Clinton left office, she had been AWOL the night of the attack. Chairman of the Joint Chiefs of Staff General Martin Dempsey later testified under oath that the military "never received a request for support from the State Department, which would have allowed us to put forces" in motion. Secretary of Defense Leon Panetta was even more direct: "We did not have any conversations with Secretary Clinton" on the night of the attack, he testified, sitting next to Dempsey.

Nevertheless, at Hillary's hearing, her strategy worked. After her "what difference . . . does it make" outburst, she was hardly challenged the rest of the day, and she won widespread praise in the media for her forceful testimony. The *Washington Post* began an article on her testimony by reporting, "In what probably was her final major public appearance as secretary of state, Hillary Rodham Clinton spent Wednesday delivering a forceful defense of the Obama administration's response to the killings of four Americans in Libya last year and praising the commitment of the United States' diplomats."

MSNBC's Chris Matthews was far less reserved in his praise. In a "magnificent display of smarts" and "guts," Hillary "showed acuity, eloquence, humanity and charm," gushed the liberal talk-show host who once described "this thrill going up my leg" during an Obama speech and who was a frequent source of anti-Hillary invective during the 2008 primaries.[20] "To the reasonable question, she offered candor and humility. . . . In response to hostile questions, she came back with strength and a challenge of her own." Perhaps in an attempt to make up for his frequent attacks in earlier years, some of which media critics and Hillary staffers described as "misogynistic," he added, "Hillary, Hillary, Hillary—she never looked better. . . . She looked every bit like a person who could run for president, run well, win big and serve confidently."[21]

The "forceful defense" storyline was all many Americans heard about Benghazi in January 2013, but her performance was far weaker in substance than it was in style. Clinton's role in Benghazi was damning, as revealed both by her testimony and the testimony of other administration officials. Because Clinton did not speak with Secretary Panetta or General Dempsey, and because neither Obama nor the White House spoke with Panetta and Dempsey, Clinton left her men under attack to fend for themselves.

Under oath, Panetta and Dempsey revealed one other bombshell that would in retrospect make Clinton look like a fool: They knew immediately, the night of September 11, 2012, that the attack in Benghazi was a *terrorist* attack. It was not the outgrowth of a protest over a video; it was a planned terror attack carried out by enemies of America. That means either Clinton had not talked with Panetta and Dempsey about the attack for days after it, or she knew the deadly attack had nothing to do with the video and intentionally misled the American people.

As Jason Chaffetz, a sharp young representative from Utah, says, there are three main "buckets" regarding the attack—and about how Secretary of State Hillary Clinton handled it—worth considering.

"One is the lead-up to the actual attack itself. Why were these people in essentially a death trap?" Chaffetz tells me as we discuss the attack in his House office. There were multiple signs that al-Qaeda was active in Benghazi and that they had their eyes set on attacking U.S. forces. The consulate, as well as the CIA annex that came under attack the same night, would appear to have been the obvious targets of these attacks, and that would explain why Stevens, the murdered ambassador, had written a cable to Hillary Clinton back in Washington to request tighter security. Alas, the security was not sufficient—and steps were not taken by the State Department to ensure that diplomats abroad would be safe.

"Bucket two is the hours during the attack," Chaffetz says. "I think there are a lot of questions there." He points to what Hillary was doing— and, more important, what it appears she was not doing—while the attack was taking place. "It's Libya after a revolution on 9/11. Our facility had been bombed twice. The British ambassador had an assassination attempt. How does that not get to her desk?" Chaffetz asked. "I mean, she said she takes full responsibility. I can't imagine that of all the facilities in the world, there's none that I'm aware of that have been bombed before, let alone twice, let alone the ambassador, let alone the Red Cross, al-Qaeda flying flags over government buildings and she's unaware of anything? What does that say about her? I think it says a lot. If she wasn't paying attention, then what in the world was she doing other than logging a lot of frequent flyer miles. I don't know. I think it's a very legitimate question."

The third and last "bucket," according to Chaffetz, is the aftermath. The State Department knew immediately that al-Qaeda, the terror organization responsible for attacking America on September 11, 2001, was responsible. And yet there appears to be evidence of a suppression campaign in which administration officials did not tell the truth about what had happened in Benghazi.

John McCain, who himself knows a thing or two about running for president, says, "You know, I mean it just cries out for outrage because it was in a political campaign." He adds, "Hillary, I don't know how much she had to do with the decision making as to what the president of the United States should say, but I sure didn't hear her say, hey, wait a minute! It wasn't [a protest over a video]. In fact, she gave a speech saying it was a hateful video, as you might recall."

Former aides to Hillary Clinton worry about the impact of Benghazi on a 2016 presidential race. "If Benghazi hadn't happened, she would have had a cakewalk," one aide tells me inside a busy New York City eatery.

"What is their concern about Benghazi?" I ask.

"I just think it looks bad. Someone died on her watch. It just looks bad. But I mean, look: 9/11 happened on fucking George Bush's watch and he got reelected. It just looks bad, and politics is perception. People will try to use that against her. But people die all the time. Because she doesn't have the Susan Rice problem of having gone on TV and saying something that was a lie, she's kind of inoculated against it. No one has video of her lying," the aide replies, apparently unaware of the video evidence of Hillary blaming the attack on an Internet video.

In short, when the testimonies of Clinton, Panetta, and Dempsey are considered with Clinton's public statements in the days after the terrorist attack, it's easy to conclude that Clinton did not do all that was in her power to save her men in Benghazi. She did not even lift a finger to call the Defense Department to see if there was any military action that could possibly be taken to save an American ambassador's life. Ambassador Stevens and his men were not offered all the resources at America's disposal. And they were not saved. The only thing saved—so far—was the reputation of a secretary of state who did not make a single phone call, or even a plea, for help.

"She made, I believe, personal judgment calls that turned out to be the wrong call and it cost people their lives," says Congressman Chaffetz. "She's the one that was running ads [against Obama's lack of national security experience in 2008] about, 'Okay, the call comes at 3:00 in the morning . . .' Remember that ad? Her call came in the middle of the afternoon and she blew it and they know it."

The impression of Mrs. Clinton's being a successful secretary of state—only Benghazi really scarred her record, and most Democrats have given her a pass on it—is even more remarkable since her record of accomplishment at the State Department proved so lacking. It says something about her tenure that one of her main achievements was how many miles she traveled—956,733, to be exact. There was still no peace in the Middle East, and she had negotiated no grand treaties or landmark solutions to a single diplomatic crisis.

"There's no doubt in my mind that the world in the last five years has become a far, far more dangerous place than it was in 2009," says John McCain. "I mean, we are seeing an upheaval in the Middle East, worsening relations with Russia, emerging China, having Iran . . . I mean [on] any spectrum of national security policy the country is far worse off.

Now how much of that is her fault? Not much, but certainly it is a legacy that I think Obama will carry for a long time."

Somehow none of that record seemed to tarnish Hillary Clinton.

On February 1, 2013, Secretary of State Hillary Rodham Clinton left office the most popular actor on the American political stage. And with a new best friend.

8

THE DEAL

"I think there's probably more animosity there than people will care to report."

—a well-connected Clinton aide on the Obama-Clinton relationship

"This was the biggest political payoff in American history!"

—a former Biden advisor on an Obama-Clinton deal

Joe Biden was mad. Not just mad. *Pissed.*

Those who followed Biden closely, and worked with him, saw the fury firsthand. He had worked hard at the job of vice president. He had basically been successful—in his eyes at least, very successful. He was always, to use Washington parlance, "in the room," offering opinions, helping the president see his options, making a difference. His extensive foreign policy expertise and wealth of close relationships with world leaders—honed during his time as chairman of the Senate Foreign Relations Committee—had been indispensable to Obama. In his thinking, at least, he'd done more for the administration than its celebrity secretary of state ever did.

But Joe Biden wasn't being rewarded for being the *last man* in the room before President Obama made the most important decisions America faced. He wasn't being rewarded for giving it his all and doing everything he had been asked. Instead his boss was there, on his television screen, rewarding *Hillary Clinton*, a largely absent cabinet member, whose contributions, in Biden's mind, didn't come close to measuring up.

The event that really drew his ire—and renewed D.C. gossip about the Obama-Clinton relationship—was the president's joint appearance with Clinton on CBS's *60 Minutes* in January 2013, as she departed her position as secretary of state. In the Democrats' world, no media forum is more influential or important than the long-running, usually Democrat-friendly CBS News program. Obama had come to rely on the show a number of times to help define himself and certain issues he felt passionate about.

Perhaps more crucial, *60 Minutes* was an important fixture to the Clintons, who grew up in politics when network television mattered much more than it does today. It was how to reach an audience, the largest audience, of mindful Americans interested in politics. It's where President Clinton in 1992 "acknowledged wrongdoing" in his marriage (he was responding, if obliquely, to questions about his relationship with Gennifer Flowers). And, during his presidency, he sat for at least two interviews for the TV program. Indeed, so important was the TV show that Clinton himself briefly worked for the program in 2003, offering commentary in a short-lived "Clinton/Dole" series, where the pair who went head-to-head in the 1996 election would offer perspectives from the left and right, respectively. It didn't last long because it wasn't good TV—Clinton and Dole were too nice to each other, and the producers from *60 Minutes* didn't have the guts to do what they really wanted: to pit Clinton against Fox News host Bill O'Reilly.[1]

When the January 2013 Clinton-Obama interview aired and raised questions about Obama's 2016 loyalties, the White House's official explanation for offering Hillary the honor of a joint interview was deceptively simple. "I just wanted to have a chance to publicly say thank you, because I think Hillary will go down as one of the finest secretary of states we've had," the president said on *60 Minutes*, with an endearing glance over to Mrs. Clinton. "It has been a great collaboration over the last four years." The president even let it be known that the decision to depart was not his, but hers.[2]

In fact, the hyperconfident president, sitting with his right leg crossed over his left, wearing a finely tailored dark suit, a blue tie, a matching purple shirt, and an American flag pin, seemed unusually deferential. He leaned back as Mrs. Clinton spoke, at times stared down at the ground between him and interviewer Steve Kroft, and at other times interrupted to offer uncharacteristically gracious compliments. But for the most part, he let Clinton carry the interview while he positioned himself as a cheerleader, or even understudy. He sat by her side, offering fulsome praise and reassuring looks throughout the entire thirty-minute interview.

Kroft, the longtime, slightly shlubby CBS correspondent, sat across from the two. Despite the program's reputation for fearless reporting and nonpartisanship, he was solicitous and supportive, careful not to offend his hosts at the White House. "I spent time with both of you in the 2008 campaign. That was a very tough, bitter race," Kroft recalled, as the camera focused on a wide shot of Clinton, who vigorously nodded her head, and Obama, who stoically stared him down. "And I'm going to spare you reading some of the things that you said about each other during that campaign."

"Please do," Clinton pretended to implore, letting out a laugh. It wasn't necessary; Kroft was going soft. "But how long did it take you to get over that? And when did it happen?" he asked.

Obama took this one. "You know, the—it didn't take as long as I think people would perceive it. As I said, once the primary was over, Hillary worked very hard for me. Bill worked very hard for me. So we were interacting on a fairly regular basis. I think it was harder for the staffs, which is understandable," said the president in an unusually soft tone.

But the really interesting question was the simple one asked of Hillary earlier. "What did he promise you? And has he kept the promises?" It was a question many had asked. And the two seemed to have trouble answering it, stumbling in the interview.

"It was going to be hard. But, you know—" Clinton started, before being gently cut off by the man by her side. "And I kept that promise," Obama said.

"Welcome to hard times," Clinton continued, leaning her right elbow on the arm of her wooden chair. "I mean, because the one thing he did mention was he basically said, 'You know, we've got this major economic crisis that may push us into a depression. I'm not going to be able to do a lot to satisfy the built-up expectations for our role around the world. So you're going to have to get out there and, you know, really represent us while I deal with, you know, the economic catastrophe I inherited.' But, you know, we're both gluttons for punishment. And, you know, my assessment was, 'Look, we are in a terrible fix.' And, you know, I felt like this president was going to get us out of it, but it wasn't going to be easy. And it was going to need everybody, you know, pulling together."

By sidling up to Hillary, Obama had dissed his own man, his own choice as running mate, on national television. "The president and his outgoing secretary of state were so laudatory of each other on the CBS news program that they were practically cuddling," the *Daily Beast* would observe.[3] And for all the world to see. A *Gawker* headline screamed, "BFFs Barack Obama and Hillary Clinton Say Giddy Goodbye on *60 Minutes*."[4]

Whether intended or not, and it's hard to believe the overly cautious Obama did many things without careful consideration, various media outlets thought the president was sending a fairly obvious signal. "Obama and Clinton chuckled as they described their partnership and stoked speculation that Obama may prefer Clinton to succeed him in the White House after the 2016 election," noted the Associated Press, which also noted that the appearance "teetered on an endorsement of a 2016 presidential bid."[5] "Hillary Clinton 2016: Obama Basically Endorses Clinton for President on '60 Minutes'" was the headline on one blog.[6] "Obama Delivered a Not Too Subtle Hillary 2016 Endorsement in *60 Minutes* Interview," wrote another.[7] Few seemed to think much of what this meant for Joe Biden, though *Politico* was one exception. "Jiltin' Joe?" it asked in a headline, noting that "it is also the first sit-down television interview that Obama has given with anyone other than first lady Michelle Obama."[8] As *Gawker* reported, "Clinton refused to speculate on a possible 2016 run—'You guys in the press are incorrigible,' Obama said when Kroft asked—but it was hard not to look at the appearance as a kind of pre-pre-pre-endorsement." The *Examiner* website also chimed in: "After Obama made a statement of support for Hillary Clinton in her job as Secretary of State, the interview invited speculation that Obama might be favoring Hillary for President in 2016."[9]

In other words, media outlets across the political spectrum were in effect asking variations of the same question: Considering their once-notorious rivalry, what gives?

In the more than two dozen years since Bill and Hillary Clinton came onto the national scene, conspiracy hung on their every action. As Mrs. Clinton left office, a new conspiracy made the list: that Barack and Hillary had made a secret deal—the Clintons' support for his presidency in return for his support for theirs. Like so many activities surrounding the former first lady, it can be difficult to support the speculation from facts, myth from reality. What is clear is that President Obama, contrary to his public and occasionally private assertions, has clearly expressed a preference for Hillary Clinton as the next president of the United States.

As for the conspiracies, some are more persuasive than others. Perhaps the least persuasive of the arguments is that a deal was struck in the aftermath of the 2008 campaign—that Hillary would support Obama if Obama would support her eight years down the road. For one thing, Obama was in a powerful position—at the height of his power, beloved by his base. He didn't need to make such an overt arrangement—one that would be radioactive if the news ever leaked—with a family he did not trust.

Still, some observers wonder what motivated her to have a change of heart in 2009, when she already had drafted a press release dropping out of consideration for the position of secretary of state. "I spoke this morning with President-Elect Obama to convey my deepest appreciation for having been considered for a post in his administration," the draft stated. "[I]n the end, this was a decision for me about where I can best serve President-Elect Obama, my constituents, and our country, and as I told President-Elect Obama, my place is in the Senate, which is where I believe I can make the biggest difference right now as we confront so many unprecedented challenges at home and around the world."[10] According to this version of events, in a midnight phone call, President-elect Obama had said something to change Mrs. Clinton's mind. What else, one wonders, would explain Mrs. Clinton's sudden, eleventh-hour reversal of her decision to serve? Obama had wooed his former rival for weeks, even flying her to Chicago for a full-court press. Nothing seemed to work. Did Obama offer to clear the field for her in 2016 if she decided to join the team?

"I've never heard, never seen anything in print that suggested there was any pledge of support if she were to run for president," Larry Sabato, the University of Virginia professor who has been a well-connected observer of presidential politics for thirty years, says in an interview. Then he adds, "I've always wondered. It would be the only thing that you would think of politically that would matter to her. The arguments to me were always stronger for her to stay in the Senate. She had her own independent base from a major state right in the heart of media-dom. She could have run a parallel administration, and gotten in a position to run either in 2012 or, if she'd prefer, 2016 on her own terms. And instead, she basically gave up her independence and signed on to his record, whatever it might turn out to be. And she had said, I think she believed it, in 2008 in the primary campaign, that [Obama] would not be a successful president for the reasons she outlined."

In fact, there were many reasons for Senator Clinton to take the State Department job, without an explicit "deal" with Barack Obama. By many accounts, Hillary was done with the U.S. Senate by 2008. She sure as hell didn't want to go back to a Democratic caucus that embarrassed and betrayed her, to be one of the crowd rubber-stamping Obama initiatives lest she look like a bad sport.

The State Department job offered Hillary credentials she lacked for another presidential run—foreign policy gravitas, the chance to be photographed with important foreign leaders, an opportunity to look above partisan politics. The job also offered Hillary the possibility of being a constant thorn in Obama's side.

For a moment, she dwelled on the chance of primary-ing Obama in 2012. Even to Bill Clinton, that notion seemed insane. "Bill's the one that told her you got to be crazy, you're not going to run against him," an observer says. He urged her to take the job as the best possible option. "Everyone's going to look to [Obama]," he said. "You'll be nothing."

"Look, serving as secretary of state is a much more important job than simply being one of a hundred in the Senate," Karl Rove said in an interview for this book. "And look, it's hard to go back to the Senate after you've run for president, I mean if you've, you know, it's hard for anybody to go back to doing what they were doing before when they thought they had a chance at moving up in the scheme of things."

"She enhanced her political position significantly," John McCain tells me. "I think it catapulted her from probably the favorite for 2016 to an overwhelming favorite for 2016."

Of additional note, the negotiations that led to Clinton's acceptance of the job were, according to sources, "adversarial" rather than cordial. They were negotiated on the Obama side by John Podesta, the former Clinton aide. The Obama team demanded what one participant described as "chickenshit small-ball" concessions, such as releasing the list of donors to the Clinton Foundation. Team Obama's demands were all but laughable to the far more calculating Clintons. In exchange, Mrs. Clinton got exactly what she wanted.

Through an agreement with President Obama himself, Hillary secured weekly meetings with the big man, giving her direct access to the most powerful person in the world. She also, importantly, had the newly elected president agree to allow her to pick her own staff, a truly unprecedented distinction that Hillary and her staff would insist on in those formative first months. The deal would take the form of a "Memorandum of Understanding," dated December 12, 2008, signed December 16, and released to the public two days later. The agreement, signed by Bruce Lindsey, representing the Clinton Foundation, and Valerie Jarrett, for Team Obama, committed to "ensur[ing] that the Foundation may continue its important philanthropic activities around the world" but sought "to ensure that the activities of the Foundation, however beneficial, do not create conflicts or the appearance of conflicts for Senator Clinton as Secretary of State." Hence "a set of protocols"—"mutually agreeable protocols related to the activities of the Foundation during the period in which Senator Hillary Clinton serves in the Obama Administration"—were adopted by all parties. Team Clinton agreed to "publish its contributors," to ensure that "President Clinton personally will not solicit funds" or seek contributions.[11] It was all meant to keep Clinton, Inc. at bay while Hillary served President Obama. In other words, the Clinton enterprise would not trump the Obama administration, as long as Clinton was confirmed by the Senate and served as secretary of state. Those were terms that both ClintonWorld and Team Obama were happy to accept.

The notion of a 2008 Obama-Clinton deal is further undercut by the fact that Bill Clinton kept attacking Obama, in the press and in private, all the way up to his 2012 reelection. After all, as late as 2011, for example, Bill Clinton was reportedly telling friends, "Obama doesn't know how to be president. He doesn't know how the world works."[12] In the middle of 2012, Clinton further raised eyebrows by praising Mitt Romney. "I think he had a good business career," Clinton said on Piers Morgan's

CNN program, when the Obama campaign was ratcheting up attacks on Romney's work at Bain Capital. "There's no question that in terms of getting up and going to the office and basically performing the essential functions of the office, a man who has been governor and had a sterling business career crosses the qualification threshold."[13]

A far more popular, and persuasive, version of a potential Clinton-Obama "deal" centers on 2012—when Obama, struggling in the polls against Romney, really needed the Clintons' help.

Author Ed Klein cites a meeting in 2012 in Chappaqua, where he quotes Bill Clinton as saying, "I've heard more from Bush, asking for my advice, than I've heard from Obama," Klein's sources quoted Clinton as saying. "I have no relationship with the president—none whatsoever. Obama doesn't know how to be president. He doesn't know how the world works. He's incompetent. He's an amateur!" Recognizing they have a problem with a furious Bill Clinton, Klein contends that "chief political strategist David Axelrod convinced the president that he needed Bill Clinton's mojo. A deal was struck: Clinton would give the key nominating speech at the convention, and a full-throated endorsement of Obama. In exchange, Obama would endorse Hillary Clinton as his successor."

Over breakfast at a hotel outside Washington, D.C., one former aide to Joe Biden insists to me, "Bill brokered that deal that led to the *60 Minutes* interview." According to this Democratic strategist, Obama needed to make a deal to cover for his dereliction of duty on the night of 9/11/12, when four Americans were murdered by terrorists in Benghazi. Bill is always looking to make a deal to further the couple's interests, and to help keep things in order for the 2016 campaign. So the deal was struck: Bill would campaign for Obama, and Obama would help the Clintons out sometime later.

"It was the biggest payoff in political history at the presidential level," the advisor says. "It was run nakedly in front of the entire country." Turkey bacon in hand, the former aide adds, "And now the person with the Machiavellian influence in the White House is Bill Clinton."

Bolstering the case was the unusual, even bizarre turn taken by Clinton's husband, who all but single-handedly dragged reluctant Democrats and independents back on the Obama bandwagon in 2012.

"'As you can see, I have given my voice in the service of my president,' Mr. Clinton said, wheezing while introducing President Obama at a late-night set at a Bristow, Virginia, amphitheater on Saturday. He kept coughing, patting his chest and mouthing words that carried only muffled strains in chilly air. Black tea with honey and a steady diet of cough drops between events helped little," the *New York Times* would report days before the election.[14]

"They and Michelle had dinner and his numbers were tumbling. Bill Clinton saved his ass," the Democratic strategist declares.

At the time, many Republicans too seemed to think something sinister was afoot. "I am told that there are some that think this may have a lot to do with 2016 and the president's wife, Secretary of State Hillary Clinton," McCain said about Bill Clinton's sudden change of heart.[15] "I suspect that Bill Clinton is collecting IOUs in case Hillary Clinton wants to run in 2016," said Newt Gingrich.[16]

A former Clinton associate who knows the former president well but did not work for him in 2012 can envision such a scenario involving his former boss. "If there was a deal cut, it wouldn't surprise me," the source tells me, "but Obama himself doesn't do that."

Obama is not a wheeler-dealer like many of his predecessors, the source said, and certainly not like Bill Clinton. At events at the Clinton White House, the president so much enjoyed socializing, kibitzing, and plotting that he had to be dragged upstairs so that his guests could go home. Obama, by contrast, is known to spend as little time as possible until he can head upstairs to the residence. "He indulges people," says one Democrat, "whereas Clinton likes that kind of stuff." More likely, he suggests, is that a deal of sorts was brokered on his behalf, probably by a man close to both teams.

In some ways, the actual circumstances of the Obama-Hillary arrangement are incidental. What cannot be disputed is that an alliance of some sort is clearly in place, one that began in 2012 and has been augmented with each passing year. There is no other explanation for the litany of senior Obama aides who have signed on, implicitly or explicitly, with Hillary 2016. In the cultlike atmosphere of Obamaland, none of this would happen over the opposition of the boss.

Hillary Clinton likely knew that he would come to see her as the most logical, if improbable, choice. After all, she spent four years in his administration dutifully working him. She didn't come on too strong. When she was sidelined, she didn't fight back; she kept her head down. Did her job. Took every chance to chat him up. Was nice to Michelle and the kids. And finally managed to get Bill in line. She lobbied Obama by not lobbying him. And it paid off.

Traditionally, Joe Biden's position as vice president might pose problems for Hillary. After all, vice presidents, even lackluster ones, tend to win the nominations of their parties—notably Richard Nixon, who served Eisenhower in 1960; LBJ's vice president, Hubert Humphrey, in 1968; George H. W. Bush in 1988; Al Gore in 2000. With Biden, however, there is a problem. Contrary to the conventional wisdom, Obama increasingly has come to dislike him. (Perhaps the better word for someone like Obama is that he "disdains" him.)

Though many press accounts describe a warm relationship between Obama and his vice president, the truth is that the two men have extremely different personalities. Biden is publicly at least a backslapping, engaging, blue-collar guy with decades of government experience. Obama, by contrast, is not a creature of Washington. Nor is he anyone's idea of the old-time pol.

Their relationship always has been a little rocky. Biden had always been respectful of Obama in public. Always. Except for that time Biden was caught trying a little too hard. "I mean, you got the first mainstream African American who is articulate and bright and clean and a nice-looking guy," Biden told the *New York Observer* at the outset of the 2008 campaign, when he too was running for the top spot. "I mean, that's a storybook, man."[17] When Biden called former black presidential candidate Al Sharpton to apologize, Sharpton told him, "I take a bath every day."[18]

Smelling blood in the water, Obama released a statement critical of Biden, saying, "I didn't take Sen. Biden's comments personally, but obviously they were historically inaccurate. African American presidential candidates like Jesse Jackson, Shirley Chisholm, Carol Moseley Braun and Al Sharpton gave a voice to many important issues through their campaigns, and no one would call them inarticulate."[19]

Biden made up for that verbal gaffe—an exercise he had lots of experience with over the years—the next day in a conference call by heaping mountains of praise upon the then–junior senator from Illinois, while leaving out any more inelegant exultations about Obama's cleanliness. "Barack Obama is probably the most exciting candidate that the Democratic or Republican Party has produced at least since I've been around," Biden clumsily told reporters on a conference call. "And he's fresh. He's new. He's smart. He's insightful. And I really regret that some have taken totally out of context my use of the world 'clean.'"[20]

Though relations warmed enough that Obama selected Biden as his running mate in 2008, the discomfort between the two has remained a constant. "In private, Biden mocks the president's people skills and chilliness, and even his ability to curse properly," *Time* magazine noted. "And he still sees himself as the Washington wise man showing his young ingenue how politics works. When they served together in the Senate, Obama saw Biden as a gasbag, a classic example of the dangers of Senatoritis. During the 2008 campaign, he was infuriated by Biden's lack of discipline, a mortal sin in Obamaworld. And he's still a bit bewildered by Biden's goofy side; like everyone else in Washington, he sometimes rolls his eyes at Joe-being-Joe stories."[21]

The *New York Times*, in a story on Biden in 2012, similarly made note of "a sometimes uneasy term, one marked by triumphs and occasional tensions with a boss markedly different in style and temperament."[22]

According to sources who have watched the interaction between the president and his vice president and who spoke to me for this book, there's little indication the president relies on his vice president for much of anything—except for doing tasks that Obama sees as beneath him. Contrary to Biden's own spin, the vice president has become in effect a "nonperson" within the administration, sources say. Those in close proximity to the vice president see what Biden is oblivious to, by nature or by choice. That Obama, perhaps unfairly, thinks he's a fool and a blunderer. Someone who can't be trusted not to fuck something up. Biden in fact has spent an increasing amount of time in Delaware, where a source claims he once had hoped to establish his official vice presidential residence—an early request to the Obama people that fixed in them a perception that he was an oddball.

In particular, there was the time Biden embarrassed Obama by coming out for gay marriage before him—winning accolades from the base of the Democratic Party while making the president look, like, well, Joe Biden—flat-footed and behind the times. It wasn't that Obama, who was for gay marriage before being against it, didn't truly believe in gay marriage. He had long wanted to publicly reverse his position on it again—but he was worried about the politics—and wanted to set it up so that he would be greeted as making a clear step toward civil rights.

"I am absolutely comfortable with the fact that men marrying men, women marrying women, and heterosexual men and women marrying another are entitled to the same exact rights, all the civil rights, all the civil liberties," Biden said on NBC's *Meet the Press*.[23]

The White House summoned ABC reporter Robin Roberts to the White House. (That Obama knew that Roberts is a lesbian is likely. She would later come out of the closet in 2013.) ABC executives couldn't immediately find her, because at the very moment the White House was beckoning her to interview the president for his "I-have-evolved" interview, she was being diagnosed with breast cancer.

But being the professional that she is, Roberts made it down to Washington the next morning to talk to the president about how his views on gay marriage had shifted. "I've been going through an evolution on this issue," Obama said in the interview, only days after Biden got out ahead of him. "I've just concluded that—for me personally, it is important for me to go ahead and affirm that—I think same-sex couples should be able to get married."[24]

But he also had to use that interview to apologize for Joe Biden. "I had already made a decision that we were going to probably take this position before the election and before the convention," Obama insisted. The vice president, he said, "probably got out a little bit over his skis, but out of generosity of spirit."[25]

It was a stinging rebuke, a coldhearted comment to make on national TV. Especially considering it was a boss mocking his subordinate.

Even if he liked Biden, Obama would still be a realist. It is hard to imagine how the vice president, who has already suffered from two brain aneurysms that required brain surgery, can be elected to the presidency at the age of seventy-three. And he definitely seems to be trying hard to make it clear to Biden that he should not pursue the option. If he did, he'd only muck things up for Obama's all-but-obvious candidate of choice.

What's in it for Obama? Like all second-term presidents, Obama looks to his legacy. With over two years to go in his presidency, he quietly has assigned key staff members to figure out what he should do with his presidential library—where it should go, and how it should be run. This is a man who intends to take his postpresidency seriously.

Obama has no more elections in which he will run. No more opportunities to see his name on the ballot, make his case to voters, and push his favored views and positions. All that is left are the remaining years he has in office and the ability to help choose a successor best able to carry forward his vision. Electing a Republican in 2016 would repudiate his vision, perhaps dismantle it. That wouldn't do. For Obama not to think about who could replace him as Democratic Party leader would be political malpractice.

Obama's was hardly a unique circumstance. In 2000, Bill Clinton cast aside his own misgivings about the maladroit and wonky Gore to champion his cause. To this day, he is baffled why Gore refused to run as if he were seeking a third Clinton term. And why he refused to allow Clinton to campaign for him—even in states like Arkansas, where he might have been able to make a difference—perhaps the *decisive* difference.

The 2004 move by Kerry to rebuff Clinton's suggestion that he pick his wife is still a source of tension between Kerry and Clinton—and perhaps the main reason the current secretary of state, Hillary's successor, is still scared of Bill Clinton, according to a former diplomat who knows Kerry well.

In 2008, George W. Bush swallowed his concerns about his onetime enemy, John McCain, gauging him the best possible choice to win that year's election. He knew McCain would cement in place his Afghanistan and Iraq policies and in effect demonstrate that the voters didn't dislike Bush as much as the polls seemed to indicate. But just as Bill Clinton was kept away from the Gore campaign in 2000, Bush was considered too toxic to be seen too often on the campaign trail in 2008. The most help he could provide, the McCain people determined, was to be close but not too close.

In 2016, Obama faces the same decision—a search for someone who will keep his pet projects in place, whose election would serve as a vindication of sorts of his record. If a Republican succeeds him as president, that person will almost certainly work to enact his party's number-one political priority—the repeal or neutralization of Obama's signature health-care plan. A Republican victory would look like the voters had turned against the increasingly unpopular Obama, that Obama might even have fatally damaged the Democratic brand. Barack Obama, a proud, even vain man, does not want that as his political epitaph. He needs someone who can solidify his legacy. And so he needs someone who will not treat him like he is a scandal-ridden Bill Clinton or a trigger-happy George W. Bush. Someone who can win.

Of course, Obama would not want people to see it this way. He probably does not want to see himself that way. Petty politics—well, he might think that is beneath him. Successors, party unity, legacies—those were the sorts of things that *a Washington insider* worries about. Not him. His aides were equally emphatic, assuring reporters and biographers how little he cared about party succession. He was neutral in the potential rivalry between Hillary and Biden, or whatever other Democrat might want to run. It didn't matter to him. That he would involve himself in the contest in any way would be "inconceivable."[26] This is the line being fed to political reporters to this day. It is of course demonstrably untrue.

In a clear affront to the sitting vice president—again something Obama could easily have stopped—Mrs. Clinton has been *publicly* blessed by those closest to the president.

One of the most notable signals came from an unlikely source, the usually discreet David Plouffe, who is often considered "[t]he architect of Obama's successful 2008 presidential campaign," as the *Washington Post* put it, with "one of the best political minds in the Democratic Party." Obama himself praised to the sky his political handler by calling him, after he secured election in 2008, "the unsung hero of this campaign, who built the best—the best political campaign, I think, in the history of the United States of America."

So it was altogether startling that Plouffe would say such nice things not about Obama's running mate Joe Biden but of his rival—Hillary Clinton.

"I think all of us who went through that primary just have the highest degree of admiration for her. She obviously would be an enormously strong candidate if she decided to run; we've got others obviously who will look at it certainly if she doesn't. But it's too soon to know," said Plouffe at a public event.[27]

"She is in both parties right now by far I think the most interesting candidate, probably the strongest candidate. But she has right now the opportunity to take some well deserved and rare time for her with her family and figure things out."

Calling her the "strongest" candidate was an enormous vote of confidence—and one that made the sitting vice president, Joe Biden, look particularly weak, since Plouffe ostensibly worked for Biden, too, when he was at the White House.

Plouffe made the comments toward the beginning of 2013 at a public event in New York City at the 92nd Street Y. And while he said that he wouldn't work for her campaign, that's not to be taken as a slight—those who've engineered winning presidential campaigns (from James Carville's 1992 win with Bill Clinton to Karl Rove's 2000 and 2004 wins with George W. Bush), it's basically unprecedented for winners to come back for a second time with a completely new candidate to achieve something they've already achieved.

But that doesn't mean top political advisors don't have a keen insight into politics—and doesn't mean they can't and won't help from the sidelines. So that means that when David Axelrod, the strategist who helped bring the young state senator from Illinois to the White House and helped to shape the president into the man he is now, says something, Democrats will listen. "[S]he is an indefatigable candidate and very, very powerful, and she's only stronger now for having four years of I think splendid leadership," Axelrod recently said. "I think she'd be in a very, very strong position."[28]

Even President Obama's first chief of staff, Rahm Emanuel, has been publicly touting Hillary. "I'm behind Hillary if she runs. And I think she will, but that's up to her. If she runs, I'm in," Emanuel said. That by itself might not be considered too surprising: Emanuel served in President Clinton's White House and has always remained close to Hillary Clinton, as well as to key Clinton insiders like James Carville and Paul Begala.

Except Rahm, who has been referred to as "The Godfather" by websites like the *Drudge Report*, now has a political machine of his own: It came with his election to mayor of Chicago, which position he secured shortly after leaving the Obama White House. And some close to him think he might be gearing up himself for a run. "I don't know, because you can't tell what Hillary does and how she's viewed. She gets her first right of refusal. That's not to say other people will look at it, but it's clear, she gets first right of refusal. People like Rahm. I think they'll look at it depending on what she does," says a former cabinet member who served in the Obama administration with both Hillary Clinton and Emanuel.

But this friend of Rahm's pulls back a little when I push him on whether the Chicago mayor would really run. "Rahm and I talk on a very regular basis. We still talk about once a week and he and I are just very good friends. He is still focused on trying to . . . he's got fiscal problems in the city and he's really focused on being mayor and he'll run for re-election and that's really what he's focused on. I mean, if you were asking my opinion, I've never had an in-depth . . . the things that Rahm and I talk about are what's going on in the city."

"Absolutely not," Rahm told CNN when asked whether he was interested in pursuing a bid for the White House. "I have no interest."[29]

Regardless, plenty of other Obama minions are going all in behind Hillary. Obama field director Jeremy Bird has signed up with the Ready for Hillary super PAC. And the lanky campaign manager for President Obama's reelection campaign, Jim Messina, has already joined Priorities USA, the leading super PAC behind President Obama in 2012, which is now positioning itself for a possible Clinton White House bid in 2016.

That super PAC was run last election cycle by Paul Begala, a key Clinton aide since the very beginning of President Clinton's rise to national prominence. Begala would be expected to remain involved in the super PAC as it positions to get behind Hillary. Some say that the Clintons, fearing a more amateurish super PAC, specifically implored Begala to get more involved with Priorities USA. "The PAC would act as the centralized pro-Clinton advertising wing," news outlets reported.[30]

Stephanie Cutter, another top Obama advisor, who is now a public relations specialist, trading on her close ties to Obamaland, and a cohost of CNN *Crossfire*, told reporters, "If Secretary Clinton runs, she'll be the nominee—the first female nominee of either party."[31]

The media has taken notice. "Three of the president's former political hands have all but declared publicly Clinton the Democratic nominee if she runs," reported *Politico*'s Maggie Haberman. "It at times has been a cringe-inducing—even if unintended—diss to the man who was on the Democratic ticket with Obama less than a year ago, Joe Biden."

Then of course there are the moves that are being made by Obama himself. First was the *60 Minutes* segment. But even after Hillary left office, Obama has gone out of his way to keep Hillary and her husband, Bill, close.

There was the summer lunch at the White House in 2013, carefully choreographed for the press. At President Obama's invitation, Hillary and Obama dined on grilled chicken and pasta jambalaya, along with a salad. They sat outside at a table set for two. A photo of the lunch was released by the White House—something the White House wouldn't have done if it hadn't wanted to be asked about it.

"As you know, over the course of the last four years, and as much as has been written about over the last four years how Secretary Clinton and the president have developed not just a strong working relationship but also a genuine friendship," said a White House spokesman. "And so it's largely friendship that's on the agenda for the lunch today. So it's not a working lunch as much as it is an opportunity for the two who saw each other on a pretty frequent basis over the course of the last four years to get a chance to catch up." When asked whether they'd be talking about work, the spokesman replied, "The purpose of the lunch was chiefly social, but given that the president and Secretary Clinton worked on [Middle East peace] pretty closely together over the course of the last four years, I'd be surprised if it didn't come up."[32]

"I bet Joe Biden loves this," one former White House speechwriter joked in an email to me at the time. Indeed, if Obama wanted to dispel the idea that he was showing preference to Hillary, he could have invited Biden along. Or closed the lunch to the press.

Hillary tried to ease the tension by having breakfast with Biden the next morning—but that sort of missed the point: that Obama was going out of his way to publicize a meeting with Hillary, not that she had accepted the president's request for a lunch date.

On November 20, Obama offered Bill Clinton the nation's highest honor—the Presidential Medal of Freedom—and again, it was something he did not have to do. In the East Room of the White House, the same place Clinton's official portrait had been unveiled a decade earlier by George W. Bush, Obama awarded the highest civilian honor to the president who had been impeached for not telling the truth to sexual harassment investigators.

"We honor a leader who we still remember with such extraordinary fondness," Obama said in his public remarks. He painted the portrait of Bill Clinton that the former president loves best—the devoted mama's boy who cares about nothing more than helping the poor and downtrodden. As Obama put it, "[Bill] still remembers as a child waving goodbye to his mom—tears in her eyes—as she went off to nursing school so she could provide for her family. And I think lifting up families like his own became the story of Bill Clinton's life. He remembered what his mom had to do on behalf of him and he wanted to make sure that he made life better and easier for so many people all across the country that were struggling in those same ways and had those same hopes and dreams. So as a governor, he transformed education so more kids could pursue those dreams. As president, he proved that with the right choices you could grow the economy, lift people out of poverty, shrink our deficits, and still invest in families, health, our schools, science, technology. In other words, we can go farther when we look out for each other."[33] Bill Clinton appeared deeply affected.

"This year it's just a little more special because this marks the 50th anniversary of President Kennedy establishing this award," Obama said. As a youngster, Clinton came to Washington to meet his hero, John F. Kennedy. The photo of a dashing young Clinton shaking the hand of the liberal hero would often be exploited during Clinton's own ascendancy to the White House—with the photo linking Clinton to

Kennedy and implying that Clinton was destined to be president of the United States.

That day, November 20, would be an entire day with the Clintons by Obama's side. After the ceremony, the Clintons and the Obamas, the president joined by his wife, Michelle, took the short trip in the official motorcade across the Potomac River to Arlington National Cemetery. There the foursome laid a large wreath at the grave of John F. Kennedy, America's thirty-fifth president, who had been assassinated five decades earlier in Dallas, almost to the day.

It was a chilly November day. Dressed in long overcoats, the four would place their hands over their hearts as a military bugler played taps. The White House pool reporter would note that taps was played "to the accompaniment of clicking cameras," a sound the Clintons must have been pleased to hear.

"This afternoon, Michelle and I were joined by President Clinton and Secretary Clinton to pay tribute to that proud legacy. We had a chance to lay a wreath at the gravesite at Arlington, where President Kennedy is surrounded by his wife and younger brothers, and where he will rest in peace for all time, remembered not just for his victories in battle or in politics, but for the words he uttered all those years ago: 'We . . . will be remembered . . . for our contribution to the human spirit,'" Obama would say that evening at a dinner at the National Museum of American History in Washington, D.C., to honor recipients of the award, the third public appearance he would make with the Clintons in less than twelve hours.[34]

That night, they'd be serenaded at the Smithsonian by Arturo Sandoval. Bill Clinton would sit next to baseball great Ernie Banks, but would break to partake in his favorite pastime: schmoozing the press. "They told me I had to wear it," he told the press about the heavy ornate medal he had hanging around his neck, which Obama himself had draped over him. Hillary, accompanied by Huma Abedin, would give a warm hug to Jesse Jackson Sr.[35]

Through all this, Joe Biden was hardly a thought. Which was kind of the point—and must have been what upset him. The vice president, along with his wife, Jill Biden, would be introduced at the first event of the day, the medal ceremony. But their very presence was perfunctory at best.

Two weeks later, it would happen again. This occasion would be the death of Nelson Mandela.

After news broke of Mandela's death, President Obama, who had visited the South African nation the summer before, took to the airwaves to express his heartfelt sympathy. And the next week, he'd travel to the memorial service to pay his respects. He had invited Bill and Hillary Clinton to ride with him aboard Air Force One, as well as President George W. Bush and his wife, Laura. Bill was in Rio de Janeiro, Brazil, convening the Clinton Global Initiative Latin America. But Hillary was stateside and had the honor of riding aboard the presidential aircraft.[36]

In the Air Force One conference room, Dubya would pull out his iPad to show Hillary and Barack, and Eric Holder, Susan Rice, Valerie Jarrett, and Michelle Obama, the paintings he had created in his post-presidential life.

The White House would do them all the favor of releasing a couple of photos of the activities on board. It would, most important for them, be beneficial to the White House, too. Obama's a man who does not play well with others. Especially those who are his equals, or, worse, those around whom he feels self-conscious. By releasing photos of the Obamas ably hanging out with Hillary Clinton and George W. and Laura Bush, the White House was taking a page out of the Clinton playbook: rehabilitating the president's image by showing him spending time with past rivals.

The events all made one thing very clear—for whatever reason, the Clintons have Obama in their corner.

One longtime Clinton aide expressed amazement at the maneuverings to me, given his knowledge of recent history. "I think there's probably more animosity there than people will care to report," he says of

Obama and Hillary Clinton. However, their alliance is clearly not one of warmth, but rather of necessity. Which is why Chelsea Clinton, who according to sources actively detested Obama all throughout the 2008 campaign, offered fulsome praise for him in 2014.

In ClintonWorld these days, nothing counts more than the opinion of the former first daughter.

9

DADDY'S LITTLE GIRL

*"The whole way she's approached her emergence
has been very self-laudatory and kind of selfish."*

—a Clinton aide on Chelsea

Sitting onstage in June 2013, Bill Clinton looked downward, studiously avoiding the stunning former Miss America contestant in her tight pinkish orange dress and her dangling crossed legs. His hands were clenched together and resting between his legs.

She tried to get his attention. "President Clinton, before I let you go," the woman, TV personality Trish Regan, said as Clinton's gaze remained transfixed on a random piece of the stage floor. A mischievous grin crept across her face. "Any chance we might see another Clinton in the White House in 2016?"[1]

As she asked the question that everyone wanted answered, she turned to the audience as its members collectively let out a spirited chuckle.

"Last question, I promise," Regan said, as her interlocutor considered how to respond.

Bill Clinton's hair was completely white and his skin, too, showed signs of age, at sixty-six. He looked skinnier than in his presidential days, and while he was far from frail, his body looked a little droopy, as if it were failing its fight with gravity and a life lived hard.

He and Regan were seated before a filled hotel ballroom in Chicago, packed with thousands of guests of one of his pet projects, the do-gooder-sounding Clinton Global Initiative. This was why he was working so hard to be on his best behavior, working so hard to avoid gaping at the buxom woman before him. He wanted to show potential donors—to the foundation and of course to Hillary—that he was a reformed man.

So the former president smirked, nodded, and turned his head even farther away from Regan's as he delivered a well-practiced line. "Chelsea's still too young." He smiled as he quickly moistened his lower lip before lightly biting it.[2] (In fact, Clinton was wrong—Chelsea will be thirty-six in 2016.)

Finally he released his hands, letting them fall to the side of his chair, where they quickly grabbed the sides and were used to move his body around for a second as if he were struggling to break free from some invisible restraint.

The very mention of Chelsea as a politician might have come as a surprise for some who hadn't been following the Clintons' repositioning over the last years. Yes, it was a clever way to deflect the real question, which of course centered on Hillary. And yes, he said, she's too young to be president. But the thought *had* crossed his mind. And there's at least one person who was surely not surprised at all at the mention of Chelsea as a future politician: Chelsea herself, who had long been repositioning herself in her family's power structure to be something of a coequal with her parents.

The Chicago event was in its way a coming-out party for Chelsea. Her name, too, after all, was being added to the Clinton Foundation— her new place, directly alongside her parents, finally secured. That was her idea, to add her name alongside her parents', finally getting into the family business.

Bill Clinton has always been a believer in the Third Way. In politics, the term refers to the effort to reconcile left-wing social positions with right-wing economic policies. Indeed, Clinton prided himself as president as governing as something of a moderate or centrist Democrat friendly to business interests whose record won praise even from senior economists under Ronald Reagan.[3]

In a larger sense, Clinton is constantly seeking a third way, another alternative, a third possibility. In the Clintons' family dynamic, that third way is Chelsea Clinton. For most of her life, the Clintons' only child has been the bridge holding them together. She's also the former president's backup plan, groomed to be a political force in her own right if Hillary blows it again.

Considering that she's been in the public eye most of her life, it is surprising how few people really know anything about Chelsea Clinton. This is true even of those who know Bill and Hillary Clinton very well. To their credit, the senior Clintons have done an excellent job sheltering their daughter from examination or discussion in the popular press— just as they vowed to do since entering the White House in 1993. So in the absence of information about the past (and future?) first daughter, most people revert to their default memory: of that seemingly sweet, awkward, and shy girl with raspberry blond curls and braces whom they first encountered when she was twelve years old.

But that is not the Chelsea Clinton of today, at least as described by those who've worked closely with her. Bill, who by all accounts is devoted to his daughter, has trained her well. In fact, Chelsea seems to have quietly emerged as a political power player with many of her parents' best and worst qualities. She is also perhaps the biggest victim of the decades-long turbulence and scandal that often have marked the Bill and Hillary partnership.

When Bill Clinton decided to run for reelection as governor of Arkansas in 1986, he and Hillary sat with their daughter at the dinner table to prepare her for what was to come.

"We explained that in election campaigns, people might even tell lies about her father in order to win, and we wanted her to be ready for that," Hillary recalled in her book *It Takes a Village*. "Like most parents, we had taught her it was wrong to lie, and she struggled with the idea."

Then Bill rose from his chair and pretended to be one of his election opponents. "Bill said terrible things about himself," Hillary wrote. "Like how he was really mean to people and didn't try to help them."

Chelsea started to cry. According to Hillary, Chelsea's parents acted out the mock attacks on her father over and over again, until Chelsea could listen to them without sobbing. She was six years old.[4]

It is hard not to feel sorry for Chelsea Clinton. She has had one of the oddest lives in the history of American politics. Not only as the daughter of a president, but the child of a father accused of philandering, sexual assault—and, among the more inflammatory (and unproven) charges flung by opponents, even rape. And a mother routinely called a liar, a cheat, and a crook. She had to endure Gennifer Flowers telling the world that Chelsea was the reason her parents didn't divorce. Without Chelsea, said Flowers improbably, she, Flowers, and Bill would be together today. Such a strange, invaded life would take a toll on even the strongest of personalities, and almost certainly changed the trajectory of the shy and awkward thirteen-year-old with the curly strawberry blond hair and braces who grew up in the controversy-filled Clinton White House.

For eight entire years, her voice was rarely heard, her face rarely seen. In the White House there was a long-standing and strictly enforced rule: Leave Chelsea Clinton alone. "It was pretty much an ironclad rule, even when Chelsea was having semi-public moments like her high school graduation, or when she went on trips with her mom, it was kind of understood that she was off-limits," former White House press secretary Mike McCurry once told *New York* magazine.[5]

It didn't mean folks like radio host Rush Limbaugh didn't criticize her—because he did. And it didn't mean that shock jock radio DJs didn't call up the White House to offer Chelsea a car when she turned sixteen—because that happened, too. What it meant was, Chelsea might appear with her parents in public, but she was not to be written about and not to be questioned.

"I've always been in the public eye," Chelsea told a reporter in an interview.[6] "My father was governor of Arkansas when I was born. I was on the front page of the newspapers the next day. I don't remember that. I do remember—I guess a better way to say it is, I don't remember a time in my life where people haven't recognized me or come over and talked to me about something they've loved that my parents have done or something that they've hated that my parents have done."[7]

To be sure, her lot in life came with some benefits. Few young women get to dance with a Beatle (Paul McCartney) or have been sung to by a pop star (Barbra Streisand) or have received a personal escort to the restroom by a sitting vice president and future president (George H. W. Bush). As Bill Clinton has told the latter story, "My daughter was 3 years old, and I introduced her to George Bush. I said, 'Chelsea, this is Vice President Bush, and this is his wonderful home.' She looked at him and she said, 'I have to go to the bathroom.' He took her by the hand and took her to the bathroom."[8]

But with Chelsea Victoria Clinton's good fortune came this hard truth: All her life she'd been used. By her parents when they wanted to dismiss rumors of womanizing or an open marriage or a sham family structure. And especially by her father after the Lewinsky scandal, when she was trotted out as the person, literally, holding her parents together.

A very public nonperson, Chelsea has had a difficult time forming an identity of her own. The general refrain from people who've met her is a simple one. "She's weird," says a Washington journalist who, like all of them, knows well the lesson of David Shuster and will never discuss her on the record.

Chelsea's experiences, quite understandably, must have caused her to have a deep mistrust of reporters and the larger group of the public known as outsiders. Not many young women in junior high school would reach an understanding, such as Chelsea did, "that it was important to understand a given media report's intent, message, and interests, whether political, profit, or something else altogether." She said, "Sometimes my parents would start the conversations; sometimes I would, prompted by something I had read in the morning paper or something someone had said to me at school. What was true in a given story? What wasn't true? Why did the truth sometimes not seem to matter? Those conversations helped me develop a broad and healthy skepticism about the media, as well as a respect for its ability—in a news story, song, computer game, or movie—to empower or disempower people."[9]

The off-limits rule followed her from the hoity Sidwell Friends School, a top private school in the nation's capital, to Stanford University, also a top private school—but on the other side of the nation, in Palo Alto, California. Only when she was graduating, in June 2001, when Bill Clinton was no longer president but Hillary Clinton was a senator from New York, did the *New York Times* recognize that despite her familiarity, America knew hardly a thing about her. She had grown up, the newspaper put it, "in wordless pantomime."[10]

"She may be the ultimate anomaly of the multimedia age, a household face whose voice has so seldom been heard that she could be a silent movie star," the *Times* wrote. "She was not yet 13 when she first slipped onto the national stage in her parents' shadow, and at 21, having traveled the world at her parents' side, she is barely better known."[11]

How could Chelsea Clinton be anything but "weird" when her father is the president of the United States and is forced to tell her, to her face, that he had oral sex—in the Oval Office—with a woman not much older than she was? (Chelsea would later cause her father to break into tears by reading the Starr Report online.) Acting out of hurt and shortsightedness, one of Hillary's punishments for Bill after he confessed his role in the Monica Lewinsky scandal was to have him confess his sins directly to the daughter who idolized him and had defended him. Chelsea was then at Stanford.[12]

Clinton felt worse for Chelsea than for anyone else caught up in the scandal, he told associates. The president has prided himself on the attention he paid his daughter. Fiercely protective, open with his affection, and generous with his time, Clinton once cited his daughter's midterm exams as a reason for refusing his vice president's plea that Bill and Hillary travel quickly to Japan to make amends for an unintentional snub of the Japanese. "Al," he said, "I am not going to Japan and leave Chelsea by herself to take these exams."[13] After the scandal, as Clinton confided to biographer Taylor Branch, "[Chelsea] had to endure the searing exposure of her father's sex life at an age when peers meant the whole world. His presence at Stanford has been unbearable for her."[14]

Days after Clinton told Chelsea about the Lewinsky affair, she received a call from the only adult outside her family who had her cell phone number.[15] He said he knew she was going through a terrible time and wanted her to be sure to remember that both her parents loved her, that it was important to stay loyal to your family, and that if she ever wanted to vent or ask for advice or pray with someone, she should call him—the Reverend Jesse Jackson.[16] Bill Clinton and Jackson long had had a "checkered" past, as Bill once described it, but he never forgot that outreach to his beloved daughter when his own relationship with Chelsea was all but shattered.[17]

The Lewinsky scandal, by the accounts of close associates of Bill and Chelsea, reshaped the father-daughter relationship just as profoundly as it did for Bill and his wife. A source very close to the Clinton family put it to me this way when discussing "what people are missing" about the Clintons: "When you screw a young White House staffer, or whatever they did, you're paying the price for the rest of your life. When your daughter wants to buy a ten-million-dollar apartment, the question isn't 'Are you crazy?' It's 'Where do I wire the money?'" The guilt over Chelsea, according to the source, is not confined to her father. Hillary similarly feels tremendous responsibility toward Chelsea for "being gone all those years." Chelsea's evolution into adulthood also calls into question what long had been a point of pride for the Clintons—their parenting skills.

Since those days, Chelsea has seemed largely adrift, trying one thing and then another in a quest to form an identity. With a history degree in hand from Stanford, she set off in her father's footsteps, going to Oxford to pursue a master's, and then to Columbia, where she studied public health.

"She enrolled in NYU and then she didn't like that," says a person who knows Chelsea well. "And then she enrolled in Columbia, and didn't like that. And then she went back to NYU. She couldn't figure out what to do with her life."

In describing her personality, a source uses the same words often attributed to her father—*exhausting.* She's ambitious, working hard to get whatever it is that she wants, letting nothing stand in her way.

Eventually Chelsea settled for a life in New York City, where her famous name must have helped her jumpstart a career in the business world. She'd begin at the premier consulting company McKinsey & Company, where she made an estimated $120,000 a year as a starting salary.[18] Clinton was the youngest recruit to her McKinsey class and was hired at the same level as consultants with MBA degrees.[19] By 2006, she'd leave that job and head to Wall Street to work for the hedge fund Avenue Capital.[20] Her boss there was Clinton donor Marc Lasry, who's estimated to be worth $1.7 billion.[21]

For many years Chelsea eschewed involvement in her parents' endeavors. One source tells me of the time her father was having heart surgery. Asked to pitch in at the Clinton Foundation, Chelsea refused. "She wanted nothing to do with it," the source says. "She made that pretty clear to everybody for many, many years."

Then, suddenly, she did.

Chelsea made her first foray into public life during her mother's run for president in 2008. Initially her involvement came during her vacation time, but then her role became enhanced. Hillary enjoyed having Chelsea with her on the campaign trail and Chelsea proved an effective and fiercely protective advisor.

Borrowing the trademark spin of her mother, always publicly reluctant to enter the political fray, Chelsea told *Time* magazine that campaigning for her mother was "not something I'd ever expected to do." In the same interview, Chelsea demonstrated a knack for seamless grand-standing. "Then I literally found myself in New Hampshire after she won the primary, and I just thought, 'I can't go back to work. I need to go tell whomever will listen why I so strongly believe in her, as a daughter, as a young woman, as an American, as a self-identified progressive.'"[22]

She quit her job at the investment firm and went on the trail full-time, still surrounded by a cocoon of Clinton aides shielding her from the press. (Sometimes, as in the case with David Shuster, she'd have to shield herself from the press's advances.)

It was there, in front of crowds large and small, that she began to find her public voice—at least in part. She made the case to Americans that her mom would be a great next president. "I went out on the campaign and I answered questions about my mom and why I so fundamentally believed in her. And sometimes it would be two people and sometimes it'd be 20,000 people. I did more than 400 events in 40 states in about 5 months. And through that process, I really understood why politics was so important and why . . . everyone needed to participate and have their voices heard at the ballot box. And so at this point in my life, what that deep belief has translated into is talking about why I think it's so critical that people register to vote, and then vote," she'd explain years later. [23]

But to onlookers trying to figure out who she was, the voice did not appear to be authentically hers—since she was acting as a surrogate for her mother. They still had no clear idea who she was and what she be-lieved in, other than her mom's political fortunes. Her own outlook on the world went unrevealed—and though she was a strong, passionate, and forceful advocate for her mother, she was only that. They believed they had no sense of her inner core.

Not that most outsiders seem to care. Chelsea is a beloved celebrity, though not everyone is sure why.

"The most ridiculous thing I ever saw was after Hillary's campaign was over—*HuffPo* wanted to have 'who is the most likely first woman president?'" says a longtime Clinton associate, who was shocked to see the name Chelsea Clinton on the list. "She's just right out of college.

Why?!? Just because she's got their name? She's suddenly someone you should mention in the first-female-president conversation because she's their daughter? She's not accomplished anything."

Chelsea still wears the scars of growing up in the White House, and displays them whenever it suits her purposes. In the runup to the presidential reelection of Barack Obama, a calm Chelsea in an animal print dress, with the length of her arms showing and straight hair flipped out, charmed a New York City crowd.

"She and I actually have something in common," Chelsea told the crowd, referring to Sandra Fluke, the former Georgetown law student who was criticized after testifying on Capitol Hill about the need for healthcare coverage for contraception. "We both have been attacked by Rush Limbaugh." The crowd laughed, and participants on the stage—all women—joined in and began to clap.

"Thank you, thank you," Chelsea said, reveling. "Yes. I do also believe if you have the right type of enemies you're doing something correct." More light laughter.

"She was thirty, I was thirteen." The crowd groaned. "It's true, actually. In 1993, he said, and I'm grateful I don't remember the exact phrasing, but something like, You may know that the Clintons have a cat 'Sox' in the White House, they also have a dog. And then he put a picture of me on the screen."

Chelsea began to nod. "And yet thankfully I had grown up in public life. And knew that having thick skin was a survival skill," she said, then turned, visibly saddened, toward Sandra Fluke.

"But, Sandra, you have reacted with such nobility to everything that has happened and clearly have chosen to empower yourself over what has happened and not become disempowered by it."[24]

The truth about the once shy and awkward Chelsea Clinton is that as close as she is to Hillary, Chelsea is tip-to-tail her daddy's little girl. She's politically attuned and immensely influential in her parents' decision making—more so, these days, than any other aide around the former president and secretary of state. Indeed, it's quite possible that there is no one more integral to Hillary Clinton's decision of whether to run for president than Chelsea herself. That is a scary thought for longtime Clinton supporters. A friend of Paul Begala says the Clinton loyalist has previously expressed his dislike for Chelsea and thinks she is not the sweet girl image she projects.

A former associate who left ClintonWorld amicably calls Chelsea tremendously coddled and entitled. "It bothers the shit out of me that everyone thinks she's the greatest thing since sliced bread."

This perception, which revised the earlier view of Chelsea as an innocent naïf, was shared by other observers.

A journalist accompanying Chelsea and Hillary to Italy in July 1994 recalls that the visitors' section of Pompeii was completely shut down so Chelsea and her mother could have a private visit. That's the kind of world (in some ways, through no fault of her own) the young woman has grown accustomed to.

"Nothing seems very authentic," a close observer says. That may be because her image is managed by a slick, high-powered PR firm in New York, Rubenstein Public Relations, and because Chelsea surrounds herself with a tight circle of loyalists, one more impenetrable than either of her parents'. Like her mother, she can't seem to let people go. To add to the boundary-less weirdness that is the hallmark of her family, Chelsea's married ex-boyfriend hangs around as part of her entourage, sometimes attending family functions with her.

That would be Jeremy Kane, a former White House intern, who dated Chelsea for about a year and a half in college. The fact that she'd date a White House intern has led some to say, "Like father, like daughter," a clear dig at her father also being engaged romantically with another intern.[25] She'd also be linked to Rhodes scholar Ian Klaus, an author of a book on Kurdistan, and even, somewhat outlandishly, to Hollywood actor Ben Affleck. "Chelsea came very close to exiting the White House without a Hollywood controversy on her hands, but when she and her father were mere weeks from leaving office—and the U.S. was captivated by the undecided presidential election—tabloids began circulating rumors that Ms. Clinton had ignited an affair with Hollywood heartthrob Ben Affleck, who had recently ended his relationship with Gwyneth Paltrow," reported the *Daily Beast*.[26]

It's perhaps not surprising that Chelsea Clinton has had a series of well-paying jobs, and that doors have opened for her due to her famous name. A sore spot with many observers is her lucrative gig with NBC, which hired her in 2011 for a reported large sum to profile people who are "Making a Difference" through volunteerism in their communities. This didn't sit well with everybody. A former Clinton staffer says, "Think about all the real journalists out there who are struggling, who have been working for ages to do this."

Clinton's biggest feature was an embarrassing interview she conducted with the insurance company GEICO's mascot—an animated gecko. It resulted in mockery across the Internet, as bloggers derided Chelsea digging up the GEICO gecko's supposed yearbook photo. The bit was hardly worthy of a journalist, let alone a high-profile correspondent like Chelsea.

"TV critics have not been impressed with Chelsea Clinton's reporting skills at NBC. This certainly won't change after Friday's *Rock Center*, wherein the former presidential daughter actually interviewed—wait for it!—the GEICO gecko," wrote one conservative media critic.[27]

"For some background—in case you're actually interested!—the segment was about various commercial personalities such as the Old Spice guy, the ATT guy, and, of course, the GEICO gecko. Great get, huh?" asked the critic, who called Chelsea's interview style "amateurish" and credited her famous parents and "friends in high places" with getting her "such a plum position."

It's not just Chelsea's conservative critics—liberals haven't been too kind either. "[R]ight now, we're stuck in another awkward Chelsea Clinton phase, a kind of perpetual sheltered adolescence, still getting to know you after all these years. And who wants to watch that?" a *BuzzFeed* reporter dared, reporting that she's not well liked or highly regarded in the NBC family.

"The days of Chelsea having it both ways are over. It's one thing to want your total privacy, and stay totally private; it's another thing to want your total privacy while reaping all the rewards and privileges that contemporary celebrity has to offer," the *BuzzFeed* reporter announced.[28]

Following her parents' lead, Chelsea chose a partner around whom rumors and conspiracies seem to endlessly circle. In the summer of 2010, at the age of thirty, she married Marc Mezvinsky. The two were friends at Stanford, and they don't appear to have started dating until many years later. It's likely their somewhat similar family lives played a role in bringing them together.

Like Chelsea, Marc—whom the *New York Post* called "youthfully dashing," with "wavy hair" and a "lanky frame"—is the child of Democratic politicians.[29] His mother is Marjorie Margolies (formerly Marjorie Margolies-Mezvinsky), a one-term Democratic congresswoman from Pennsylvania, who, it's often said, lost her reelection campaign because she was a bigger fan of President Clinton than the rest of her district. (She voted for Clinton's tax increases, against the wishes of her constituents.) Marc's father is Edward M. Mezvinsky, a two-term Democratic congressman from Iowa who pleaded guilty to stealing $10 million from investors and tried to use his son's relationship with Chelsea Clinton to ease prosecutors away from pursuing his case. It didn't work, and the elder Mezvinsky spent five years in prison.[30]

Marc Mezvinsky is an investment banker himself, and started his own fund in April 2012 with the help of Clinton benefactors. "He is using [his father-in-law] to go to conferences or dinners or lunches with potential investors" and "hitting them up to invest in [Marc's] funds." If Doug Band could be marginalized, there would be a potential vacancy for a new surrogate son: Chelsea's husband, Marc.

In the fall of 2011, Bill, Hillary, Chelsea, and Marc met in Little Rock to dedicate the Bill Clinton Presidential Park Bridge. Completed with an infusion of $10 million from the Clinton Foundation, the bridge was an obvious play on one of the former president's best-known lines during his 1996 reelection campaign: "I want to build a bridge to the 21st century."

As the quartet was about to make their way before the cameras at the dedication ceremony, Chelsea stopped and turned to her husband, with whom she'd celebrated her first anniversary the previous June.

"Stay here," she told him, urging him out of the camera shot. "You're not a Clinton."

Chelsea is said to be an adherent to the view espoused by many other senior Democrats—and advanced by Bill and his aides—that he is a changed man now. In his midsixties and hoping to be a grandpa, the lecherous Bill of the 1990s is a thing of old. A former aide tells me Chelsea is oblivious to the truth that her father "is still fucking around."

Veteran Democratic strategist Bob Shrum once recalled a moment in the 1990s when Clinton brought a woman to the home of prominent D.C. socialite Pamela Harriman and spent the night with her. "Pamela was hardly a prude," Shrum noted, "but she was angry with Clinton; it was reckless."[31]

By 2013, Shrum was a believer in the Bill the Redeemed storyline. "I think the recklessness is the past," he says to me. "I don't think that's true anymore."

Throughout Barack Obama's first term, as Hillary Clinton maintained her statesmanlike persona and subsisted on a government salary—as secretary of state, she earned $186,600 per year—Bill's money-raising efforts continued. His speeches were well received and well compensated. (He even brought George W. Bush in on the act, who throughout his own presidency had fretted about not having enough money.) His foundation was flourishing. And now he and his right-hand man Doug Band had a new moneymaking scheme—a company called Teneo. It caught Chelsea Clinton's attention.

Sometime before the 2012 presidential election, Band approached

Clinton with the idea of a multifaceted and comprehensive consulting business that could well make him, and by extension his patron Clinton, a ton of money. Along with Band was the man who would be Teneo's chairman and CEO, Declan Kelly.

Kelly previously had served as the U.S. economic envoy to Northern Ireland, appointed to that position by Hillary Clinton in 2009. He was born in Tipperary, Ireland, and his brother Alan served in the European Parliament representing his home country. (Alan is now minister of state at the Department of Transport, Tourism and Sport in Ireland, where he's a member of the Labour party.) A good-looking, dark-haired Irishman, Declan favored pinstriped suits, accented with a white-collared and -cuffed dress shirt.

A former colleague, who compared him to a snake oil salesman, says, "He was amazing to watch. Declan was the best salesperson I ever saw in my life."

The idea for Teneo was to have Fortune 400 companies pay large monthly stipends in exchange for access to Band, Clinton, and their massive international network. The group would "consult" with the companies, offer strategic advice, and help them overcome issues in various countries across the globe. That was how it was billed.

I asked a former Teneo employee what these companies actually received. "Nothing," says the employee. "There was this sort of implicit promise of access to Clinton or Clinton knowledge or people who are close to him or whatever. And that they did sell. But there was something really seedy about it." (Defenders of Teneo would say that the president was already for sale—available to come to events or speak at conferences for the right price—and that the consulting company wasn't necessary for the former president's own multimillion-dollar business of selling himself.)

Nonetheless, the Clinton allies used their connections with senior executives at companies like Coca-Cola and Dow Chemical to bring in millions. And there were other companies, too—Bank of America, Harrah's, Hess, UBS Wealth Management.

Clinton was of course the key to Teneo's success. "The two needed the president," a source says. "It was he who they were selling to their corporate clients. Or, more precisely, it was their proximity to power—President Clinton, and his wife, who was then secretary of state—and their own Rolodexes, which were a natural extension of the work they had done over the years for the Clintons."

Because of his wife's position, Bill wasn't going to receive an actual piece of the company. That raised too many perception questions even for him. Instead he had a contract.

The contract was worth $3.5 million, a handsome fee even for the ex-president. "Everything the president did for Teneo he got paid for," says a former Teneo employee. He would attend events where there were a hundred CEOs or a hundred big investors coming together. And with his speaking fee, Clinton would make hundreds of thousands of dollars just for an hour or two schmoozing with his corporate friends.

"I bet Dow was paying close to a million a month," says a source, a former Clinton staffer. "And Coke probably, too, because Coke, when they [signed on] they got rid of all their other consultants." They had contracts with at least four consultant companies and pushed all that business to Teneo.

The Manhattan-based Teneo built an impressive board of advisors, including former chairman of the Securities and Exchange Commission Harvey Pitt, former Reagan campaign manager Ed Rollins, a collection of loaded investment managers like Karim Shariff, and prestigious academics like Georgetown professor Victor Cha.[32]

There was only one problem that might stop the money from rolling in. At their preliminary meeting with Clinton to get his go-ahead on Teneo, the group was joined by two other guests who had until then stayed largely out of the family business: Chelsea Clinton and her husband, Marc Mezvinsky. They saw the promise of Teneo. They wanted in.

Chelsea, with Marc and her dad by her side, asked Band and Kelly for an equity stake in the company.

Band and Kelly demurred. As much as they might personally like

Chelsea, they thought it would be a bad idea. Teneo was going to have offices around the world, in São Paulo, Melbourne, Hong Kong, Beijing, Dubai, Moscow, Brussels, London, and Dublin. It would raise too many questions to give a piece of the company to someone who was actually the daughter of the current secretary of state.

"They weren't happy about that," a source close to the situation says, referring to Chelsea and Marc.

Doug Band was clearly on his way out of Clinton Inc., but he already wanted to transition to a different kind of relationship with the former president. The business was an easy out—a way to maintain a relationship with the Clintons and maximize the network he had developed, but without having to travel around with the former president and be his direct aide.

And Chelsea wanted in. Going from not caring about the foundation and refusing to take part in foundation-related events before the 2008 presidential campaign, Chelsea had come around to seeing how useful it might be to her. And that no matter how much she might have wanted her own path in life, she'd always and forever be the daughter of Bill and Hillary Clinton.

By 2012, the combination of Band's business dealings and brash self-promotion was causing trouble for the one man he couldn't afford to alienate—the former president on whom everything built by the former bagman depended. There were reports that the Obama campaign—from whom the Clintons were looking for an alliance—hated him, that Hillary was worried about perceived conflicts between clients of Band's consulting company and the State Department, and that Chelsea had concerns about conflicts of interest between Band's business interests and her father's foundation. As a friend of Bill Clinton told the *New Republic*, "the last thing anyone wants is noise."

Indeed, over time, Band began to take some liberties with Clinton's name. Band controlled Clinton's most valuable commodity—his schedule—and a former White House colleague called Band "a gatekeeper who charged tolls."[33] With or without Clinton's knowledge, the price Band charged for access to Clinton was enough to buy himself a $2.1 million condo in 2003, move to a $7.1 million condo in 2008, and add a $1.7 million expansion in 2009.[34]

Occasionally, Band's dealings raised eyebrows. When the U.S. Postal Service exercised a purchase option of a Sarasota, Florida, post office building owned in part by Band's father, Doug Band jacked up the price with an appeal to a Clinton ally on the Postal Service Board of Governors, who later resigned after an inspector general's report said he failed to uphold his fiduciary duty to the service. Similarly unsubtle was the sales pitch Band arranged in 2012 at a small private gathering of wealthy VIPs in a Manhattan ballroom to hear Clinton, George W. Bush, and Tony Blair discuss terrorism and globalization. The sales pitch was for the corporate consulting company Band founded in 2009 (while also working for Clinton), and according to one guest at the gathering, the pitch was long-winded, "flagrant," and "inappropriate."[35]

The problem was less about what Band was charging as Clinton's gatekeeper and more about who he was letting in the door. Victor Dahdaleh got in; he was later arrested in Britain and charged with bribing a Bahraini company with $9.5 million. Frank Giustra got in; he received a uranium-mining contract in Kazakhstan after Clinton traveled to the country and praised Kazakhstan's corrupt and repressive dictator. Most notably, Raffaello Follieri got in; the con man (and then-boyfriend of actress Anne Hathaway) later pleaded guilty to fraud, conspiracy, and money laundering, forfeited $2.44 million, and served four years in federal prison.[38]

The *New Republic* accused Band of profiting off his relationship with the Clintons and said it concerned Chelsea. But, of course, none of this profiteering had been a problem for Chelsea when it involved other aides. Why didn't it bother her that Huma Abedin would profit off her many associations in ClintonWorld? Why didn't it bother Chelsea when her former minder Philippe Reines went on "contract," which would allow him not to be full-time and to take on private and corporate clients through the consulting firm he founded, Beacon Global Strategies, whose mission and pitch sounds an awful lot like Teneo's? At least Reines had waited to leave the State Department. Abedin hadn't.

Beacon now boasts a roster of top executives with ties to the Clintons—as well as ties to the investigators into Benghazi and those who were supposed to have been on watch. There's Andrew J. Shapiro, who served as a senior advisor to Hillary and later as an undersecretary in her State Department; there's Jeremy Bash, Leon Panetta's former chief of staff; Michael Allen, former staff director to the House Permanent Select Committee on Intelligence, one of the House committees investigating the Benghazi terror attack; and Michael Morell, who was number two at the CIA during the attack. "Business records reviewed by Fox News show that in April 2013, Beacon Global Strategies registered as an LLC," Fox News's Catherine Herridge reported.[39] In other words: just in the middle of an ongoing investigation into Benghazi, principal actors were colluding to start a firm together—to take on high-paying clients and to turn a nice profit.

Throughout all of these mini-controversies, Bill Clinton stuck with Band, his traveling partner and all-around accomplice. They traveled around the world many times, visited celebrities and billionaires, hobnobbed with Nicolas Sarkozy in France, and even met with the late Kim Jong Il in North Korea.

Doug Band was the son Bill always wanted, according to numerous accounts. He was the closest thing Bill ever seemed to have to a friend. He knew too much about the president and his scandalous personal life to just kick him to the curb. And he was indispensable until he wasn't.

And although he had been off the foundation payroll since 2010, a series of articles began to appear in the *New York Times* and elsewhere about financial improprieties at Clinton's various foundations. All of them were in one way or another overseen by Doug Band. He was mentioned more than thirty times in *Vanity Fair*'s "The Follieri Charade,"[40] and the *New Republic*'s Alec MacGillis wrote a hard-hitting and well-reported exposé in September 2013 called "Scandal at Clinton Inc.: How Doug Band Drove a Wedge Through a Political Dynasty."[41]

At least one of the most damning articles on Band was written by the *New York Times*' Amy Chozick, who at the time was one of the only reporters awarded an extensive interview with Chelsea.

Meanwhile, there was renewed focus on the financial questions surrounding Bill Clinton's various enterprises, particularly how little money the Little Rock–based Clinton Foundation, designed as a charitable nonprofit, actually devoted to charitable causes. In 2011, for example, the William J. Clinton Foundation was listed among the 591 top U.S. foundations in terms of assets ($197,890,114). Its income that year alone was $62,769,161. In terms of grants given out, however, the Clinton Foundation was ranked a paltry 1,673, having given out only $4,728,000 in 2011, or less than 10 percent of the money it had taken in.[42]

Over its lifetime the foundation has supported some good causes. In 2011, for example, a $2,374,669 grant went to the Alliance for a Healthier Generation to combat childhood obesity; in 2009, $2,223,000 went to the American Heart Association.

Larger sums were sent to organizations and entities that seemed to help the Clintons themselves. A whopping $43,200,000 was given from the foundation to the National Archives and Records Administration to support an"[e]ndowment and partial transfer of building." NARA, as it's known, administers the Clinton Presidential Library. Almost $3 million went to the city of Little Rock, Arkansas, to support the Clinton Presidential Center Park there. The Clinton Foundation gave $1,981,227 in 2004 to another Clinton organ, the Clinton Foundation AIDS Initiative. Five grants, given each year from 2004 to 2008, went to the Miller Center in Charlottesville, Virginia, housed at the University of Virginia, with one to support an "[o]ral history project of Clinton presidency."[43] The total amount granted to that organization by the Clinton Foundation was $851,250.[44]

Executive compensation for the foundation during this time period, given to people like Bruce R. Lindsey, a longtime close friend of President Clinton, amounted to more than $5,393,900, according to tax records. And the salaries and benefits of all staff at the foundation are an eye-popping $220,218,840—well above the total grants for the lifetime of the foundation. Travel expenses paid by the Clinton Foundation far exceed the total of grants outside the top three, and for the years 2003–2011 totaled $55,628,306. Accounting alone has cost the foundation more than $1.5 million. Advertising and promotion are slated at $3.5 million. Even information technology has cost it more than $3 million. Occupancy is $22 million. And fundraising for the foundation has cost more than $25 million.[45]

Suddenly many of these embarrassments were noted in the press, and usually linked to criticisms of Doug Band's mismanagement. It wasn't long before President Clinton decided Band was a liability. Pretty soon Bill was living without the man he said he "wouldn't be able to get through the day without." The two men, inseparable for more than a decade, now speak only a handful of times a year, and their conversations are reportedly awkward at best. "It's like when your wife cheats on you," said a witness to the relationship, "and after the divorce, you have to see them at the friend's wedding or at the supermarket. There's a strangeness to it."[46] (Others have hinted that the two sneak private conversations a little more frequently.)

After twenty years of service to Clinton, Doug Band was unceremoniously dumped from the payroll of the William J. Clinton Foundation, his reputation taking one hit after another. In the spring of 2013, the organization was renamed the Bill, Hillary and Chelsea Clinton Foundation. And it was clear to all who was now firmly in charge.

In the press and within the foundation, Chelsea is portrayed as a white knight bringing some order to the mess her father and Band made. One can wonder whether a young person of such limited experience was really capable of running such an enterprise.

"She is going to be the new face of the Clinton Foundation from this point forward," says a former Clinton aide who worked with her. "She is running the foundation. She is the head of the foundation. I think that she's sort of thinking that she's going to pick up the mantle and run with it." Which is much easier now that Doug Band is no longer working at the foundation.

According to new reports, tensions simmered between the former first daughter and Doug Band. "Chelsea's handlers are likely auditioning for White House gigs, should Hillary become president, and they bring to their current jobs all the paranoia that may serve them well in Washington. One . . . sits in on her interviews holding an iPhone like a stopwatch ('you have two minutes'), whisks her away when she's in the middle of answering one final question, and scolds this journalist for even mentioning Doug Band's name in Chelsea's presence. It's all an odd, occasionally funny blend of control and confusion," read a recent *Fast Times* profile of Chelsea.

One of Chelsea's handlers is chief of staff Bari Lurie, who's in her early to midthirties and (like Doug Band) was a former Clinton White House intern and an alumna (just like Huma Abedin) of George Washington University, and who has worked for the former first daughter since 2011. (Even the idea of a former first child having a chief of staff strikes many Chelsea watchers as ridiculous.) Indeed, it's at the White House, where she was working in the East Wing for the First Lady, where she first met Chelsea Clinton. She's a committed loyalist, and her relationship in that role spans over a decade. "Bari Lurie joined the Clinton Foundation in August 2011 as chief of staff to Chelsea Clinton. In this capacity she helps shape and implement the strategic direction of the office, including Chelsea's engagement across the Foundation," reads her official bio on the website that says she works in the Office of Chelsea Clinton. "Before moving to New York, Bari worked on Secretary Hillary Rodham Clinton's presidential campaign as well as her 2006 Senate race and for her political action committee, HILLPAC."

The whole fight seems a bit amateurish, since Band is not an enemy that the Clinton family would want. He more than any other outsider (with the possible exception of Huma Abedin) knows the family's secrets. The Band situation is so delicate that as I was working on this book I received a call from the office of one of Clinton's tireless defenders, James Carville. His assistant, Kees Nordin, asked one question: Would this book focus at all on Band? I sidestepped the question.

However, James Carville's wife, the Republican strategist Mary Matalin, would answer a couple of questions for me via email. I asked, What's a good story that might illustrate how the Clintons work that you've heard or personally observed?

"Once, in Buenos Aires, we got into a conversation waiting for an elevator about Zoroastrianism, which lasted for almost an hour, as many elevators came and went. Another time, we went to an antique store and he found the perfect bracelets for my daughters. He is a great shopper."

And they've never held the fact she worked for a GOP president, George H. W. Bush, against her. "We have had many occasions to talk issues, family, music, religion, antiques, books, etc.; I greatly enjoy the breadth of his knowledge and curiosity on so many topics; also appreciate his cheerfulness and energy. He is a fun person to engage with and very open and honest. Never thought about the GOP thing; we appreciate each other's fidelity to our principles and loyalty to our brethren. I appreciate the Clinton's [sic] kindnesses to my girls and husband and the Bush family," she would write to me.

After Doug Band was rolled by the Clintons, simultaneously embarrassed by the national press and distanced from the former president and his family, I was talking to an aide about what happened and why Band, who had so many times been on the giving end, was now on the receiving end.

"People warned [Doug] that this was going to happen and he didn't listen," says a friend. "Doug's a little naive when it comes to loyalty, which is funny because he works for the ultimate people who claim to care about it, but also don't give a shit about it."

How does Clinton loyalty work? I ask the friend, as we sit in a crowded New York lunch spot.

"I think it's a fallacy."

In their lives, the Clintons have been loyal to only one person. Their one true thing. And that is their daughter, whose worst traits, according to a number of Clintonites who've worked with her, are the residue of a weird, distorted life. A life largely lived in the shadows of her famous mom and dad.

"That's probably their only real line in the sand—or true thing: their relationship with Chelsea," says a longtime aide. "Everything else is transactional . . . everything. It's a hard way to live." It certainly has been for Chelsea. And it may well prove to be the undoing of the Clinton comeback, a bigger Achilles' heel for Hillary than even her reckless husband.

Chelsea might not know everything that goes on around her. Nevertheless, "She's really inserted herself," says a source, building a reputation as something of a ruthless operator prone to self-pity and entitlement. Just like dear old dad, who is now actively encouraging her entry into another aspect of the family business. Some sympathetic to Band quietly wonder whether Chelsea will be able to manage the sprawling network given her young age and limited experience. As for her mother's 2016 hopes, Chelsea's emergence poses similar problems, ones which her rivals hope to take advantage of.

10

CHASING HILLARY

"I'm hearing it could be death by a thousand cuts."

—a Clinton aide on Hillary's 2016 chances

Among Democrats who hope Hillary Clinton doesn't run—and their number is larger than one might think—the complaints are familiar. Age and stamina are the obvious considerations. "Look at Obama's hair color, just like George Bush's," says a prominent Washington insider. "Somebody who's seventy shouldn't be president. And I think that's going to be an interesting issue against her, but who in the Democratic Party is going to have the guts to take on that machine?" A former Clinton campaign advisor is equally blunt. "This is gonna sound superficial"—which is an understatement—"but men do age better than women," he says. "At seventy she's not gonna be—it's not gonna be great."

Democrats fear she is too radioactive. One of many prominent D.C. Democrats who will only comment on background out of fear of inciting Clintonian wrath complains that "she will lose the general because her negatives are so high." Then there is the not-so-secret fact that she is not a very good candidate. Hillary is often compared to the kind of politician always better in concept than as an actual flesh-and-blood candidate. Many compare her unfavorably to Al Gore or John Kerry or even Mitt Romney, stiff policy wonks with difficulty making personal connections.

Some will chalk this up to sexism—or at least the difference between men and women politicians. It is not that Hillary is not a good politician, they will say, but that American politics is not used to female candidates. "We are only now growing used to the style of women in politics. You know, they're not backslappers, even if they are natural politicians," says political advisor Bob Shrum, who helped lead Al Gore's and John Kerry's presidential campaigns. Hillary, he insists, has grown into a natural politician.

But the real question being asked in Washington is not whether Hillary can be beaten as such, as it is whether any prominent Democrat has the guts to try to stop her.

The most obvious primary challenger, of course, is the one most often discounted. Vice President Joe Biden will turn seventy-four in late 2016. Gaffe-prone and perennially underestimated, Biden is expected to quietly step aside for the Clintons, with whom he's had a long and friendly relationship. Unless, of course, you ask Joe Biden.

Maybe Obama had forgotten all the trash talk Hillary leveled against Obama back then—but Biden hadn't. "You decide which makes more sense—entrust our country to someone who is ready on Day One . . . or to put America in the hands of someone with little national or international experience, who started running for president the day he arrived in the United States Senate," Hillary Clinton told a reporter in 2007. "He was a part-time state senator for a few years, and then he came to the Senate and immediately started running for president," she said in early 2007.[1] And that was just the stuff she said on the record.

After Hillary left the secretary of state's office, the world went on, and so did the administration. If anything, it was hard to notice she was gone. Except for personnel: Obama was free to shift over his traveling campaign press secretary, Jen Psaki, the dashing redhead who had been so harsh to Hillary on the campaign trail in 2008 that she was not allowed near the State Department until Hillary was out of Foggy Bottom. And most of the Clinton loyalists who had come to the State Department four years earlier left to cool their heels in various positions out of government while Hillary cooled hers.

On policy, John Kerry, some thought, did more for the administration in his first year than she did in her four years. He was able to carry out a key goal of President Obama's, by beginning to work out the structure of what could be a landmark deal with Iran. And with respect to Syria, Kerry gained plaudits from pundits—and the dovish Obama—for his ability to wage hard-nosed diplomacy by publicly signaling that a deal brokered with the Russians could avert an American strike in the Middle East country. Hillary didn't accomplish *any of that*. Instead, she claimed credit for the miles she flew, as if that mattered.

A former high-ranking official in the Clinton administration recently spoke to his friend Biden about Hillary's 2016 maneuvering.

"You going to step aside for her?" he asked.

"No," the vice president replied confidently. "Fuck no."

Traditionally Biden's stance might pose problems for Hillary. After all, vice presidents tend to win the nominations of their parties. But Biden has a major drawback. He lacks the support, even the quiet support, of the president he serves.

None of this has stopped the vice president from making plans, however. Biden has run for president twice before—in 1988, when he was forced to drop out over plagiarism charges, and again in 2008, when he was barely an asterisk against Obama and Clinton. And he still has the bug, fiercely jealous of the tendency in the press to write him off in favor of endless stories about Hillary's maneuverings.

"And let me not forget Joe Biden, because he will call me this afternoon and remind me," Democrat Donna Brazile once half joked during a Sunday talk show appearance where she discussed the Clinton campaign in waiting.[2]

She isn't the only one. The vice president or his senior aides at his behest will call reporters, pundits, anyone he feels is not giving his candidacy the credibility it deserves. He wants respect.

Though stranger things have happened in politics—like a one-term senator defeating the Clintons in 2008—few give Biden much chance of a surprise victory. One former Senate colleague says Biden could never be president. "He makes people like him, but lack of discipline is his weakness," the senator says. "She's far more disciplined and calculating."

"If you take a look at every important thing that's come out of the White House, Biden's had his finger on it," says a Clinton aide. "So, people underestimate Biden, and part of being a VP is being derided to a certain extent." Still, he adds, "He can't beat Hillary in '16 because she starts with eighteen million votes. Everyone that voted for her in '08 wants her to run again."

Shrum agrees. "I think [Biden] will recognize that reality," he says.

Allies of the vice president of course disagree with this assessment. Biden also knows there is a chance that the Clintons are bluffing. Signaling that she's running for president to get attention, speaking fees, book deals, but not really ready to hop in. Biden, too, is gambling on her health.

So are some Republicans. "I must admit I'm completely befuddled," admits Bush strategist Karl Rove. "My brain says yes, she's the frontrunner. My gut tells me we don't know everything about the health issue."

But if Hillary is bluffing, she's doing an excellent job. Leaving nothing to chance, the undeclared candidate has gone out of her way to take swipes at Biden—something she wouldn't likely do if her 2016 effort is just a feint. At a private event in Georgia in 2013, for example, she was asked a question about the bin Laden raid. "She took 25 minutes to answer," a Republican state legislator present at the gathering told the Atlanta newspaper. "Time and time again . . . Clinton mentioned the vice president's opposition to the raid, while characterizing herself and Leon Panetta, then director of the Central Intelligence Agency, as the action's most fierce advocates," the paper reported.[3]

Dr. Jill Biden, the vice president's wife, is said to be actively "counting down the days" until she can return to "normal" life. Some close to the Bidens speculate that she would "kill him if he decided to run for president." Especially a race she doesn't think he can win. That appears to be the only thing holding back a potential Biden 2016 run.

Among those not so secretly preparing the ground in case of a Hillary demurral: Senator Amy Klobuchar of Minnesota; Chicago mayor Rahm Emanuel; and New York governor Andrew Cuomo. But they seem to believe, as one Democratic strategist put it, that "Hillary gets the first right of refusal."

Observers believe the more potent threat is the little-known but aggressive governor of Maryland, Martin O'Malley. O'Malley would be fifty-four years old on Inauguration Day 2017—fifteen years younger than Hillary Clinton. He is a handsome man with impeccable liberal credentials, and "a fucking political animal," according to Maryland politicos who know him.

Two prominent political consultants in Maryland—both Republicans—said that O'Malley is someone who could do serious damage to Hillary Clinton in the primary. One of them listed his assets in a race against the front-runner: "He is mean. He has long a history of negative campaigning. He's a good fund-raiser." In other words, he's a younger Bill Clinton.

"He's very Bill Clinton-esque," the other consultant says. "He's very good shaking hands and politicking." He's even rumored to have women issues like the former president though none have ever been proven.

Former Vermont governor Howard Dean, who might have been expected to support O'Malley in a primary challenge, especially considering his implicit criticisms of the Clintons when Dean ran for president himself in 2004, has fallen under the Clinton sway. The once-maverick liberal firebrand has become increasingly establishment—in fact, he chaired the Democratic National Committee during the Obama-Hillary race. "I will support her against any other foreseeable Democratic candidate," Dean told me. But he held open at least a little wiggle room. "I like Martin O'Malley a lot."

Disclosing that he had a recent conversation with O'Malley—"I'm not going to tell you what the conversation was," he snapped—he adds, "I think O'Malley is very serious" about running for president in 2016.

By setting himself up as Obama's true heir, O'Malley is poised to run to Hillary's left. He's been an enthusiastic backer of Obamacare and vowed to lead the nation in sign-ups for the controversial program. Major Democrats know that he's going to be a problem for her. So they're trying to find a way to give him something to do. He's tested the New Hampshire waters, according to CNN, where he played a video summary of his career starting as mayor of Baltimore, which said, "Martin O'Malley formulated an assault on hopelessness." And it claimed that he transformed Baltimore while curbing crime and took his good governance to the Maryland State House in Annapolis. It was a three-and-a-half-minute-long campaign "video befitting a national political convention-style rollout," said CNN. And of course it was released in New Hampshire, traditionally the first state in the nation to hold a primary. As a Maryland Republican says, "He's running, unless they buy him off."

The most obvious payoff, of course, would be the vice presidency. A former Clinton aide envisions a scenario in which Hillary offers him the job to keep him out of the race, or to have him run as a "puppet" opposition candidate. "He's good looking, Irish Catholic, and young," the aide reasons. "She's gonna need some youth, so Martin is the logical pick."

Brian Schweitzer, a former Democratic governor of Montana, is another wild card. He's positioning himself as an anticorporatist, gun-toting populist who's not shy about bringing up Hillary's support for both the war in Iraq and the war in Afghanistan. He's already done that in Iowa, the state to hold the first caucus in the nation—and one where Hillary got tripped up in 2008 when she lost the contest there to Obama.

Antiwar rhetoric is a political weapon that's previously proven to be lethal on the political left—after all, it's not at all dissimilar from the public positions that Barack Obama was able to use to undercut the candidacy of Hillary Clinton in the 2008 Democratic primary.

Schweitzer might not be known yet, but that doesn't mean he can't level the primary field just by appearing in many debates (and performing well) before a national broadcast audience.

The same is true for Senator Elizabeth Warren of Massachusetts. Her very candidacy would undercut Hillary's bid to be the first female president and her liberal credentials are superb. Before being a U.S. senator she was the brains in the Obama administration behind the establishment of the Consumer Financial Protection Bureau. She is no pragmatist. She is purely an ideologue—which can be very helpful for riling up the base in a party primary.

Then of course there is the possibility of California governor Jerry Brown, who ran a stronger than expected primary campaign against Bill Clinton in 1992. Brown, a popular and well-known figure on the political left, has refused to rule out a run.[4] But at seventy-six, and with a personal life that long has been the subject of a whispering campaign, Brown is an unlikely threat. He most likely seems to be basking in the attention that comes from having his name mentioned.

As for the Republicans, an opposition campaign in waiting already is well under way. Republican National Committee chairman Reince Priebus has said that his party's major focus for 2016 is the Hillary Clinton record. Republicans hope to replicate the successful Democratic effort against Mitt Romney, who was painted in the press as a real-life Thurston Howell III before he even won his party's nomination.

"We have to be very aggressive on what she's done or hasn't done," Priebus said. "And the things that she is famous for, like a botched health care rollout in the '90s, and Benghazi, and the things that she is involved with that are or went obviously pretty badly, we need to focus in on."[5]

It reflects a tactic tried previously by the Republican National Committee. Beginning in 2005, right after Bush's Second Inaugural, a small group began to meet at the RNC's Capitol Hill headquarters. The mis-

camp. Why, I asked, did the Clintons care so much about these documentaries? I received a one-word reply.

"Monica."

The NBC miniseries was to begin with First Lady Hillary Clinton's discovery of her husband's affair with a twenty-two-year-old intern in the Oval Office. The stain of the Monica Lewinsky scandal—literal as well as figurative—has not dissolved. At least not in the minds of Bill and Hillary Clinton. It was a moment when the Clintons truly hit rock bottom and all was, for a brief moment, nearly lost. For Republicans, and many Democrats, that scandal is where the story of the 2016 campaign really begins. It is also a reminder of how impressive their comeback has actually been, as well as its potential fragility.

A likely GOP contender, Kentucky senator Rand Paul, already has made clear that the Lewinsky scandal and Bill's impeachment are fair game in any race that might involve Bill Clinton. Speaking on C-SPAN on a show that aired on February 9, 2014, Paul called the former president a "sexual predator" and argued that candidates should not accept money associated with him.

"They can't have it both ways," said Paul of Democrats accepting Clinton money.[8] "And so I really think that anybody who wants to take money from Bill Clinton or have a fund-raiser has a lot of explaining to do. In fact, I think they should give the money back. If they want to take a position on women's rights, by all means do. But you can't do it and take it from a guy who was using his position of authority to take advantage of young women in the workplace."

Many members of the GOP establishment blanch at such talk, remembering their experience last time with Bill Clinton's misbehavior.

The public and media seem to disagree. In early 2014, for example, the conservative media outlet *Washington Free Beacon* reported on the personal papers of Hillary Clinton's deceased best friend, Diane Blair.[9] The Blair files, decades old, led to a firestorm of publicity, particularly in relation to the Lewinsky affair and Hillary's contemporaneous reaction. The files were amplified by the popular website the

Drudge Report and discussed across the media spectrum for days if not weeks.

The reaction has opened the door for all sorts of trolling into the Clintons' personal lives and the scandals of the 1990s. A longtime intimate of the Clinton family tells me about being besieged by various reporters seeking to write about Bill's extramarital activities or reopen the Monica Lewinsky scandal with new allegations and information. "It could be death by a thousand cuts over the next year," a source well connected to the Clintons tells me. "I mean, just from what I'm hearing."

Associates of Lewinsky's have what might be called "The Monica Files"—obtained exclusively for this book—hundreds of pages of allegations about the former president of the United States, his former girlfriend Monica, and his wife. These include things as innocuous, if mildly humorous, as the umpteen media requests Lewinsky received from personalities such as Barbara Walters and Larry King to a long list of allegations against the former first couple of seemingly variable validity. All of these are likely to get into the eager hands of reporters and Republican operatives—as part of what might be dubbed the "thousand cuts" operation.

But there were also a number of more detailed allegations compiled by investigators, attorneys, and other Lewinsky advisors in the event that she might be involved in legal action against the president. Most supported claims of a pattern of sexual misconduct or adventurism by the president.

One of the more promising and detailed nuggets Lewinsky and her associates kept from Starr was the story of a woman who claimed to have met Bill Clinton decades earlier when she was a student at a California university. The year was unclear, but it was after Clinton returned from his studies as a Rhodes scholar in 1970. After a first date, Clinton arranged to meet with the woman again. Lewinsky's team were told they went to Golden Gate Park in San Francisco, where in a wooded area Clinton knocked her to the ground and attempted to have sex with her. Described by a friend as a "big girl" at about five feet eleven, she "scratched and kicked" Clinton until she was able to run away from him. No charges were ever filed. And the two did not meet again.

As the story went, the woman heard from a Clinton staffer decades later, when he was governor of Arkansas. The staffer had located her number in California and called to tell her he was running for president and asked if she would "support" him in the race. She was shocked by the call, but told the staffer yes. (She was a hard-core Democrat.) Though she was angry about the assault, she probably voted for him anyway, the friend guessed.[10]

And then there was another potential bombshell, never before reported, that Monica shared with representatives on her legal and public relations team and only vaguely with the independent prosecutor investigating the Clintons. According to Republicans, it demonstrated the distraction that Bill Clinton's behavior could have had on America's national security.

On March 29, 1997, Clinton called Monica to the Oval Office because he had something "important" to tell her. This also ended up as their last sexual encounter. The president was on crutches after a fall in Florida under dubious circumstances. The president had been walking down dark steps outside the home of Australian golfer Greg Norman at about 1:20 in the morning. The White House physician denied that Clinton had been drinking. Reporters were not immediately notified.[11]

"This was one of those occasions when I was babbling on about something," Lewinsky told prosecutors, "and he just kissed me, kind of to shut me up, I think." After another sexual encounter, involving oral sex in the study just outside the Oval Office, the president gave Monica important news: "We may have been overheard."

"I don't know what you're talking about," she replied, with concern. "How would they ever hear us? Who would do that?"

"Well, I don't know," Clinton said. He appeared cryptic. "If anybody ever says anything about the calls I've made to you, tell them we were just joking." At the time, Lewinsky told prosecutors that Clinton suggested that "they knew their calls were being monitored all along, and the phone sex was just a put-on." That is all the Starr Report offers on this encounter. But Monica and her team knew more.

They found evidence that the British, Russians, and Israelis all had scooped up the microwaves off the top of the White House. Offering some additional support, Boris Yeltsin, the former Russian president, wrote in his memoir that Russian intelligence had picked up on Clinton's "predilection for beautiful young women."

Foreign spies weren't the only ones who knew about the couple's phone sex. Monica's friends heard plenty of juicy details directly from Monica. "Let me ask you this," she once said to a friend. "If a man calls a woman for phone sex, don't they usually ask what the woman's wearing?" Referring to Clinton, she replied, "Well, he would say what he was wearing."

As Monica told it, the president of the United States would describe his clothing, over the telephone, while pleasuring himself. That uniform would usually consist of a gray University of Arkansas sweatshirt and what he called his "blue tighties."

He made similar calls like this to women while on presidential trips, such as one visit to the Seychelles. This was yet another of Clinton's reckless moves when it came to womanizing, since the British government ran eavesdropping operations on the island and Clinton's indiscretions might easily have been overheard.

In October 1998, Clinton met with Israeli prime minister Benjamin Netanyahu and Palestinian leader Yasser Arafat in a high-profile effort to move the Middle East peace process forward. The series of meetings, held at the Wye Plantation near Wye River, Maryland, also led to another negotiation, sources say. A negotiation kept well away from the headlines.

At one point, Netanyahu reportedly pulled Clinton aside to press for a pet cause for the Israelis—the release of Jonathan Pollard, an American spy for Israel who was sitting in prison. Netanyahu pressed Clinton to release Pollard, which in itself was not an unusual request. But the Israelis present at Wye River had a new tactic for their negotiations—

they'd overheard Clinton and Monica and had it on tape. Not wanting to directly threaten the powerful American president, a crucial Israeli ally, Clinton was told that the Israeli government had thrown the tapes away. But the very mention of them was enough to constitute a form of blackmail. And, according to information provided by a CIA source, a stricken Clinton appeared to buckle.

Intelligence officials in the United States or Israel will of course not confirm on the record the extent or substance of Israeli eavesdropping. Such a matter is of the highest sensitivity, since Israel is a close ally of America's and heavily reliant on American aid. In 2000 the conservative magazine *Insight*, after a one-year investigation by a team of reporters, claimed that the Israeli government had "penetrated four White House telephone lines and was able to relay real-time conversations on those lines from a remote site outside the White House directly to Israel for listening and recording."[12] At the time, an Israeli spokesman responded to the Associated Press, which confirmed that an FBI investigation was under way, that the claim was "outrageous." "Israel does not spy on the United States."[13] Of course one need only consider the long history of allies spying on one another—including the Americans on the Germans and Brazilians in 2013—to find such allegations plausible.

In any event there is ample evidence to support the Lewinsky story about an Israeli-U.S. confrontation. On November 11, 1998, for example, the *New York Times* reported that Netanyahu and Clinton had indeed discussed Pollard's release at Wye. And that the Israelis had told the president something that opened up the possibility of Pollard's release, something Clinton had explicitly ruled out during the first six years of his presidency. A White House spokesman told a reporter for the *Times* simply that Clinton was newly "impressed by the force of Mr. Netanyahu's arguments."[14]

So impressed was Clinton that he brought the notion to the attention of CIA director George Tenet. Tenet, according to a number of news reports, vowed to resign on the spot if the administration acceded to the request.[15] Faced with widespread outrage from his national security team, Clinton dropped the idea. He did, however, reconsider it one more time before leaving office.

That's not all the Monica files include. In postpresidential life, aides and White House servants to the Clintons talk about the former president's use of the White House theater, only steps away from the first lady's traditional offices in the East Wing, and which was said to double as a forum for presidential dalliances with various women. As long as their identities could be concealed, these aides were willing to be open about what transpired and how they were open secrets in the boys' club that was the Clinton West Wing. There were any number of young staffers who caught the president's eye, or hand, or "inadvertent" touch. An advisor to Monica Lewinsky was told a secondhand story, which he related to me, of a young woman along the campaign trail whom Clinton invited to "work out" with him at the Little Rock YMCA, and another to whom he slipped a private White House phone number. At Richard Nixon's funeral, Clinton was said to have made a pass at the wife of one of the former president's pallbearers.

A number of sources mentioned to me the former flight attendant whom, in true Kennedy style, Clinton had brought onto the White House staff, where she worked alongside another of his purported mistresses, this one a woman named Marsha. "She's a great character," one of her friends tells me at a lunch where she insists on anonymity.

During his first term in office, around 1994, Clinton is said to have called up his close confidant David Pryor of Arkansas to brag. They had known each other well since Clinton's days in Arkansas, and Pryor, who was then a U.S. senator representing Arkansas, had helped Clinton with his political rise in more ways than one.

The story goes that Clinton looked up to the politician and called to tell Pryor about a major accomplishment. He had been with a pop icon. Pryor, a reserved and conservative gentleman, was shocked. It was not just that Clinton would do something like that while president of the United States; it was that Clinton would go around and brag about it.

sion was simple: Defeat Hillary Clinton and destroy her 2008 presidential run.

"If you looked up *inevitable* in the dictionary, you'd find a picture of Hillary Clinton," said one of the members of the team back then. Hillary was going to be the next Democratic nominee, even if the Republican nominee was a long, long way from being picked. In a way the RNC effort was misplaced: Its singular focus on Hillary in 2008 belied the fact that she was vulnerable and a weak candidate. A barely scathed Barack Obama was able to slide past the Republican nominee John McCain and take the presidency. Running the risk that they might face the same eventuality, the RNC has doubled down on its opposition campaign against the once and future "inevitable" Clinton nomination.

In this current effort the RNC chairman has made reference to one of the major super PACs forming against the Clintons, America Rising. The group, run by former RNC opposition research director Matt Rhoades, who also ran the 2012 Mitt Romney campaign, plans a multimillion-dollar effort to research Clinton's record and redefine her to voters before she does. He's joined by Joe Pounder, who was research director for the RNC in 2012, and Tim Miller, who was a spokesman for the Republican Party that year, too. They're a shadow organization. And already they are off to a good start. There may not have been a "vast right-wing conspiracy" against the Clintons when Hillary coined the phrase in 1998, but in 2014, there certainly is something resembling one.

Their grand strategy includes early filing of multiple Freedom of Information Act requests for documents from Hillary's time at the State Department, as well as having a legal strategy to prepare for the inevitable stonewalling they're expecting from her successor at the department, John Kerry. Staffers have been assigned to Arkansas to interview former associates and reexamine past scandals. They've been combing the archives.

A comprehensive Republican-aligned polling unit of sorts is in place, one that already has picked up an interesting conundrum. Pollsters have found that voters have a reservoir of sympathy for Clinton, one that traces back to the final years of her husband's administration and his many womanizing scandals. Their impression of Mrs. Clinton improves each time she is seen as a victim of attacks, by Republicans, Democrats, or the media. It'll shape how Hillary's attacked.

"Clinton gains popularity as a 'victim,'" one Republican-aligned research firm discovered in an analysis of Clinton's poll numbers prepared in preparation for the 2016 presidential election—and never before revealed. "Clinton's personal popularity appears to rise when she is cast in a sympathetic light due to the perception that she is the victim of unfair attacks or being treated unfairly," the memo notes. "As a result of these attacks, Clinton's image is softened. Clinton's handling of the Monica Lewinsky scandal won her high praise from the public. Multiple pollsters noted that voters tended to sympathize, leading to her ratings rise."

Instead of a targeted assault on Mrs. Clinton's personal life or ethics directly, Republican strategists hope to revive in the minds of the voters the many financial scandals and improprieties of the first Clinton administration, to reawaken old scandals with new information, in the hope that Democrats and Republicans will remember why they'd tired of the Clinton circus in the first place. There is hope that more might even be mined from the biggest and most visible scandal magnet of them all— William Jefferson Clinton. This is also a chief concern of Team Clinton, who are hypersensitive about anything involving Bill's presidency or its accompanying scandals.

On July 29, 2013, CNN announced a planned documentary on the life of Hillary Clinton. Charles Ferguson, the Academy Award–winning director, was going to direct the piece. Ferguson was a left-wing filmmaker likely to be sympathetic to the former First Family. Almost simultaneously, NBC announced a four-hour miniseries called *Hillary* with Diane Lane in the title role.

Both efforts led to a furious reaction from the Clinton camp. Some might say overreaction. (Ironically, Republicans also threw a fit, assuming that any portrayal of Mrs. Clinton in the "lamestream media" would be biased in her favor.)

Nick Merrill, a close aide of Hillary Clinton's, became involved in what the *New York Times* labeled a "confrontational" meeting with the director, who had requested access and interviews for the piece. Ferguson reported that he was "interrogated" by Merrill. During a "three-month tug of war," the director claimed that "Clinton aides had told potential sources not to cooperate with his documentary."[6]

Getting attacked from all sides, on the last day of September 2013, CNN announced its decision to cancel the documentary. NBC, facing similar vitriol over its decision to air a Hillary-themed miniseries, followed suit.

In a column for the *Huffington Post*, a baffled and infuriated Ferguson explained in detail the hostile treatment he'd received from Team Clinton:

> The day after the contract was signed, I received a message from Nick Merrill, Hillary Clinton's press secretary. He already knew about the film, and clearly had a source within CNN. He interrogated me; at first I answered, but eventually I stopped. When I requested an off-the-record, private conversation with Mrs. Clinton, Merrill replied that she was busy writing her book, and not speaking to the media.
>
> Next came Phillipe [*sic*] Reines, Hillary Clinton's media fixer, who contacted various people at CNN, interrogated them, and expressed concern about alleged conflicts of interest generated because my film was a for-profit endeavor (as nearly all documentaries and news organizations are). When I contacted him, he declined to speak with me. He then repeated his allegations to Politico, which published them. . . .
>
> CNN and I decided to publicly confirm the film project to clear the air. Immediately afterwards, the chairman of the Republican National Committee announced that the Republicans would boycott CNN with regard to the

Republican presidential primary debates in 2016. Shortly afterwards, the entire RNC voted to endorse this position. This did not surprise me. What did surprise me was that, quietly and privately, prominent Democrats made it known both to CNN and to me that they weren't delighted with the film, either.

Next came David Brock, who published an open letter on his highly partisan Democratic website Media Matters, in which he endorsed the Republican National Committee's position, repeating Reines' conflict of interest allegations and suggesting that my documentary would revive old, discredited Clinton scandal stories. Coming from Mr. Brock, this was rather amusing. David Brock began life as an ultraconservative "investigative journalist," quotation marks very much intended, spreading scandal with little regard for truth. He first attracted attention with *The Real Anita Hill*, his nasty (and factually wrong) hatchet job on the woman who, during Clarence Thomas' confirmation hearings, said that Thomas had sexually harassed her. Years later, he apologized and switched to the Democrats.

When Brock published his letter about my film, I got in touch with several prominent Democrats who knew Hillary Clinton. I told them that this campaign against the film and against CNN was counterproductive. They conveyed this message to Mrs. Clinton personally, along with my request to speak with her. The answer that came back was, basically, over my dead body.[7]

Asked for a comment on the developments, Merrill emailed a statement to reporters: "Lights, camera, no reaction." This was a typical response for the Clinton media operation—flippant, seemingly disinterested in the entire issue, and thus highly misleading.

It was easy to understand why the Republicans were making a fuss about the programs. Bashing the liberal media and the Clintons is a sure bet for conservative fund-raising. More confusing was the Clintons' outsized reaction to a documentary and particularly an NBC miniseries that by almost all accounts seemed relatively innocuous, if not advantageous to them.

Out of curiosity, I emailed a person well connected to the Clinton

To former Clintonites, the explanation for the man's death was far simpler. He was a sad and troubled human being whose inner motivations and thoughts would always be a mystery. Simple too was the explanation for why White House aides were scurrying through his files—to see if he'd left behind any evidence about his affair with Hillary Clinton.

The relationship between Vince Foster and Hillary Clinton has long been an open secret among mainstream Washington reporters, but somehow hardly ever found its way into their reporting. It is beyond dispute that the married Foster and the married Clinton were extremely close (outside of her family members, no person is mentioned more often in Hillary's memoirs than Foster). As law partners in Arkansas in the 1970s and 1980s, the duo frequently lunched together, along with another lawyer, Webster Hubbell, at an Italian restaurant called the Villa. Her closeness with Foster "raised some eyebrows," Hillary once acknowledged. "In Little Rock at that time, women did not usually have meals with men who were not their husbands."[18]

That the married Foster and the married Clinton were involved romantically was an open secret in Little Rock, according to journalists who were there at the time. It was well known that they were "boyfriend-girlfriend," a former Clinton official says. "He really was infatuated with her."

A former reporter from the *Arkansas Democrat-Gazette* says that nearly everyone in the newsroom was aware of the relationship. One editor even claimed to have seen the two kissing. "A lot of people there knew [Foster] well, of course," he says, "and to a person they said he was having an affair with Hillary Clinton."

In the 1970s, when Mrs. Clinton was appointed to the Legal Services Board by President Carter and had to travel frequently to Washington, she is said to have shared a suite with Vincent Foster at the Hay-Adams Hotel in Washington that was paid for by the National Steel and Shipbuilding Corporation.

According to those I spoke to, certain investigative reporters were examining the relationship in the days before his suicide.

Regardless of the validity of the allegations, the Foster affair—if rekindled—would raise more uncomfortable questions about the Clintons' marital relationship. It's another indicator that even if her nomination is "inevitable," Hillary is in for a bumpy ride.

11

THE ROAD TO CORONATION

*"[Y]ou can't fire your daughter.
I mean, this is unexplored territory here because all of a sudden,
the person running the ship . . . you can't get rid of her."*

—a longtime Clinton family associate

Chuck Schumer came to Iowa prepared to make news. That was not at all that unusual for the flamboyant senior senator from New York. The media-loving politician is known to have press releases at the ready on almost any issue discussed on that morning's news shows, and long has been known to introduce legislation to fit any conceivable headline— waging "war" on a potentially hazardous caffeine-laced malt liquor drink, Four Loko, that suddenly became trendy; getting federal subsidies for Greek yogurt when the snack became popular; and seeking a ban on certain bath salts when they were the subject of an alleged act of cannibalism in Florida. Schumer even boasted of inventing a media-friendly family in his head—the Baileys—who advise him on the day-to-day struggles of the working class. "Though they are imaginary, I frequently talk to them," he once said. The aggressive senator is the perennial punch line for that favorite D.C. joke: What's the most dangerous place in Washington? Between Chuck Schumer and a TV camera.

Schumer's Iowa appearance, on November 2, 2013, was timed almost three years to the date before the 2016 presidential election. He was speaking before the ever-important Democrats in the state who will trudge through snow and ice to vote in the nation's first presidential caucuses, which will help set the course of the next election, and which mortally wounded Hillary Clinton's 2008 campaign when she lost Iowa to a hardly known man who'd been in the U.S. Senate for what seemed about fifteen minutes. The victory didn't seal Obama's bid for the Democratic nomination, but it sure made his candidacy, and the threat he posed to the front-running and so-called inevitable Clinton, suddenly seem more plausible.

Schumer, whose hair recedes to almost the middle of his head, took the stage wearing a dark suit and a light blue tie. His thick-rimmed glasses rested securely at the end of his nose. His left hand rested on his prepared remarks to help him keep his place as his eyes darted toward the 750-person crowd—and the cameras.

"I am urging Hillary Clinton to run for president," Schumer said in his nasal New York accent, as he pumped his right hand into the chilled air. TV cameras swept the applauding crowd, who by and large remained seated. "2016 is Hillary's time!" he announced.

He shuffled his upper body back and forth to try to get momentum or perhaps to feign excitement. "Run, Hillary!" Schumer punched the air again with his right hand. "Run! If you run, you'll win! And we'll all win!"

The unexpected announcement, odd for a number of reasons but perhaps mostly because it came so many years before the actual race, received the hoped-for response. "Schumer Endorses Clinton for President in Iowa Speech," read a headline in the *New York Times*. *Politico*, the influential Virginia-based trade publication, highlighted the New York senator's remarks with the following headline: "Chuck Schumer in Iowa: 'Run, Hillary, Run.'"

In addition to satisfying his attention fix for the day, Schumer made the announcement for larger strategic reasons. To show the Clinton team that he was their guy. A man who could make things happen for them. A man whom future president Hillary Clinton ought to support for the Senate majority leader's post, which just might be opening up, conveniently enough, in 2016, when Harry Reid is expected to retire.

The announcement also came with a complex backdrop, since the Clintons knew what tabloids such as the *New York Post* had speculated for years: Chuck Schumer hated Hilary Clinton and had worked against her from the outset of her time in elected office. So did most of the Democrats who worked with her in the Senate and went out of their way to humiliate her by endorsing Barack Obama in 2008. But that, as they say, was then.

The emerging story of the 2016 campaign is the careful, quiet, behind-the-scenes coronation that the Clintons are arranging for themselves. It's a feat reminiscent of what advisors did for Texas governor George W. Bush in the years preceding the 2000 election, when scores of Republican big thinkers and politicians began coalescing around a seemingly reluctant, torn candidate who hadn't even declared for the White House. As with Bush, the approach is working. Careful efforts are made to avoid the mistakes of 2008, when Hillary put herself forward too soon, failed to raise enough money, and underestimated her potential rivals.

"Hillary Clinton met with a handful of aides for a detailed presentation on preparing for a 2016 presidential campaign." That was in the summer of 2013, a good year before any campaign would really begin, and nearly three and a half years before Election Day 2016. "Three officials from the Democratic consulting firm Dewey Square Group—veteran field organizer Michael Whouley, firm founder Charlie Baker and strategist Jill Alper, whose expertise includes voter attitudes toward women candidates—delivered a dispassionate, numbers-driven assessment. They broke down filing deadlines in certain states, projected how much money Clinton would need to raise and described how field operations have become more sophisticated in the era of Barack Obama," reported Maggie Haberman of *Politico*.[1]

Key to their restoration are the pledges of fealty from people like Chuck Schumer, among the many prominent Democrats working to absolve themselves of their Great Sin—supporting, directly or otherwise, the man who stole Hillary's presidency away from her. Any number of those who cast their lot with Obama gambled that the 2008 defeat would rid them of the Clintons forever as a national political force—a wager they obviously lost.

"I endorsed Obama for two reasons," says one nationally known Democrat in an interview with me, echoing many others. "I thought he was something special and then the second reason was I was concerned that if Hillary was elected all the old Clinton people would come back. And to make a long story short, Obama brought all the old Clinton people back anyway."

The Democrats overestimated Obama, and they underestimated his most famous "frenemies," the Clintons. So now it is time for errant Washington, D.C., Democrats to make their amends. In addition to the shameless, and seemingly pointless, Schumer shout-out, all sixteen of his female Democratic colleagues in the Senate have circulated a letter endorsing Hillary for president.[2] The list includes a woman often mentioned as posing a possible primary challenge from the left—newly elected Massachusetts senator Elizabeth Warren. The early and enthusiastic embrace contrasts notably with 2008, when Hillary's Senate Sisters were largely silent or quietly rooting for Obama. The most notorious rebuff came from Missouri's Claire McCaskill, whom Hillary had lobbied furiously. Endorsing Obama, McCaskill poured salt into the wound by saying she had chosen Obama because he, not Hillary, had inspired her daughter. (Her daughter, McCaskill famously said, would not be allowed to go near Bill Clinton.)

To further demonstrate their fealty, many former foes like McCaskill have glommed on to any vehicle available. For the moment, that vehicle is a once-obscure super PAC called "Ready for Hillary," founded by a professor whose acquaintance with Hillary appears rather tenuous.

"Although I just met Hillary—we can't remember if it was '90 or '91, but it was before the campaign—I have known about her since '76 and '77," founder Allida Black says. "Do I trust her the same way I trust a close friend? Yes. Can I laugh with her? Yes. Do I want to bother her, the way I bother a close friend?" She laughs. "No."

Black is not anyone's idea of the polished political operative. She explains her tardiness for an interview by stating that her dog had thrown up that morning. Her voice is a bit gruff, her hair short and a little uneven, and she's dressed like a liberal academic, in a Native-American-style, zigzagged, loose-fitting shirt. A scholar of Eleanor Roosevelt and editor of books such as *Modern American Queer History*, she's quick to point out that she's "not some gazillion-dollar donor."

"I mean, look at me," she says, proudly holding out each of her fingers. "I don't have an eighteen-thousand-dollar ring."

The group's mission has been endorsed by such notables as Donna Brazile, Al Gore's former campaign manager; perennial Clinton cheerleader and TV pundit Paul Begala; California lieutenant governor Gavin Newsom; and Minnesota governor Mark Dayton. Even billionaire George Soros, a major funder of liberal causes (and a ringleader of the donor class), has pledged $25,000 to the group—the maximum the group is accepting right now. "It's just beyond our wildest expectations," Black says. "The enthusiasm, the response we've gotten, our Facebook and Twitter accounts, and Instagrams, have just exploded."

Others have gotten into the act to a notable, if not embarrassing, degree. ABC News labeled 2013 "The Year Everyone Gave Hillary Clinton an Award"—from the Pentagon to the Elton John Foundation's Founder's Award to something called the Michael Kors Award for Outstanding Community Service. The city of Little Rock opened up the Hillary Rodham Clinton Children's Library and Learning Center. In 2012, the Little Rock airport's name was changed to Bill and Hillary Clinton National Airport.

Yet all of this activity pales against the actual Hillary Clinton presidential campaign—behind the scenes, mostly below the radar, and now decades old.

"They've kept their network very much alive that they cultivated when he was running for president the first time, even before he was running for president," says one of Clinton's former press secretaries. "Look at some of the fund-raising he's done for state and local candidates and even getting involved in races from time to time, that you wouldn't necessarily think he'd get involved in. It's pretty extraordinary."

Their permanent campaign "has been never ending, never stopping, always on the ballot, always pushing, always driving forward," says another former Clinton aide. "Which is pretty insane." It's a candid reflection that they've been going in national politics for the last thirty years, an unheard-of commitment at such a frenetic pace.

Yet another offers his former employers praise that in retrospect sounds rather sad. "Look at the fucking hits that they've taken. Anybody else would've just fractured and gone away. Right? But they don't," he says. "Working and campaigning is all they know. That is their life."

The Clintons already have blunted one of the most formidable potential challengers, New York governor Andrew Cuomo, smart and telegenic, with access to New York money. As a former Clinton cabinet secretary, his ties to both Bill and Hillary are long-standing. His office in Albany, for example, is decorated with Clinton memorabilia.[3] Two decades ago, as both Bill Clinton and then-governor Mario Cuomo, Andrew's father, considered seeking the 1992 Democratic nomination, the families famously feuded. But if any bad blood still exists, it's not visible.

A few months after Hillary Clinton stepped down as secretary of state, a Cuomo administration insider, described as having "direct knowledge of the situation," informed the *New York Post* that the governor "has quietly told associates that he is resigned to the fact that he can't run for president in 2016 if Hillary Rodham Clinton enters the race, as is widely expected."[4]

Generally speaking, potential presidential candidates do not like to offer such unequivocal statements, especially three years before the next presidential election. Why Andrew Cuomo would go out of his way to make such a statement—and so early—says more about the fears he has about the Clintons than any they have about him.

A Clinton advisor offers one benign explanation. "Andrew won't run because he already ran against [African American Carl] McCall [for governor] and he pissed off the entire black community," he says. "So he's not gonna go piss off every woman for the rest of their lives" by challenging Hillary.

There was, however, a more urgent explanation for Cuomo's unusual move. Since her days as New York's junior U.S. senator, both Clintons have worked to build a financial juggernaut in the Empire State.

Cuomo went further to assure his loyalty. Not long after the *Post* article appeared, he and Hillary marched together in a Memorial Day parade in Westchester County, where the governor took every opportunity to kiss her ring. "It was a pleasure to be with Hillary Clinton today," he said. "I served eight years in the Clinton administration, so it was a pleasure to be with her and reminisce." Onlookers viewed the scene as confirmation of the *New York Post* story: He was going to stand down in 2016 to Hillary—in return, he received their warm embrace for governor.

If they weren't both running from the same state, they almost looked like ideal running mates. But Mark Warner might have something to say about that. The fifty-nine-year-old Virginia senator's vice presidential aspirations are an open secret in Washington. The action-oriented Warner, a former governor and business executive up for reelection in 2014, had actually considered retiring from the gridlock-laden Senate but changed his mind in part to remain a plausible Clinton running mate. On paper he is ideal—youngish, attractive, and ambitious with business savvy.

And hailing from Virginia, he may help hold a swing state that would be crucial to the Clintons' electoral math.

Bill Clinton already has given considerable thought to the vice presidential selection, which is crucial considering Hillary's age. (She would be sixty-nine years old on Inauguration Day in 2017, the second-oldest president in history—just a little younger than Ronald Reagan was when he became president in 1981.) He is known to favor the unorthodox approach. For his own running mate, he shied away from traditional consideration of age, experience, and regional balance in favor of someone who looked—on paper at least—just like him. Al Gore was another young, good-looking southerner who fancied himself as a moderate. Campaigning together with their wives and children, the duo conveyed a perfect image—of young, dynamic, reform-minded leaders. Similarly, in 2000, Clinton urged Gore to make an equally unorthodox choice—Maryland senator Barbara Mikulski, a four-foot-eleven-inch, unmarried liberal dynamo. It was a choice so seemingly unpolitical that it might have made the plodding, overly cautious Gore look something close to bold. Clinton's influence might have persuaded Gore to make his ultimate decision, which was another "outside the box" choice—Senator Joseph Lieberman, an Orthodox Jew and critic of Clintonian ethics. At the time Clinton called the Lieberman selection "brilliant."

Thus for his wife, Clinton would likely counsel someone equally unexpected or bold. Someone who might underscore Hillary's strengths while addressing questions about her age and health. Perhaps another woman. There are no shortage of Democratic females quietly auditioning, if not for VP then as a Hillary stand-in—McCaskill, Amy Klobuchar of Minnesota, Kirsten Gillibrand of New York, who succeeded Hillary as U.S. senator after Clinton became secretary of state.

With the prospect of the Clintons returning to the White House, it's only reasonable for Americans to ask: Under what capacity would they serve? Would they even be together? Would 2017 offer a return of marital infidelity, embarrassing scenes in the Oval Office, and a whole new round of investigations, allegations, and simple tawdriness? And besides, who's to say that Bill Clinton wants to return to the White House and be put under the same scrutiny he came to despise toward the end of his own presidency?

No one really knows the answer. Not even them. For the first time in basically thirty-five years, neither Clinton holds public office. They are richer, more powerful, and more popular than they have ever been. They are happy wanderers, both free to do whatever they want, whenever they want. To whomever they want. And they are doing it largely together, at least for now.

On June 13, 2013, in Chicago, Bill welcomed a glowing Hillary Clinton to her first job in the private sector in recent memory. The Clinton Foundation and the Clinton Global Initiative, where Hillary had formally come on board, had just been renamed to include the entire immediate family: the Bill, Hillary, and Chelsea Clinton Foundation. Three for the price of one.

"This last six months for our foundation has been a very interesting time," President Clinton said, a typical understatement considering the series of news articles and financial mismanagement scandals that were about to circle around Clinton and his consigliere, Doug Band.

He praised his new partner and, some would say, accomplice. "For the last couple of years, Chelsea's been spending about half her time on the foundation work," he noted. "She just got back from Asia, visiting our projects in Malaysia and Cambodia, and visiting the efforts of our CGI partner, Procter and Gamble, in Myanmar, Burma, where we, our foundation, is also slated to do a lot of work. And I'm very grateful to her for helping us to spearhead a reorganization to try to put all of our forces into one place."

Chelsea stood onstage smiling. Her cold dispatch of her rival for her father's affections was already in her rearview mirror.

"And I was thrilled when the third member of our tiny family, Hillary, said that she wanted to come into the foundation and resume her work," Bill gushed. With his tangents and awkward sentence structure, it was clear that he was once again winging his remarks. "I would depart from our normal rule that nobody gets to give a speech and let her give a fairly brief outline to you about what she will be doing in the Clinton Foundation, which has been renamed with Hillary and Chelsea as part of it. I can see this coming now, as I move into my dotage: My job will be to fund people who really know what they're doing." The audience offered a light chuckle. "Which I am very happy to do. So I'd ask you to join me in welcoming at her first—she's been at many CGI meetings in the past—but never as a principal in the Clinton Foundation: former senator and secretary of state Hillary Rodham Clinton."

The gathered attendees applauded, and a few added a smattering of whoops and hollers. Clinton embraced his wife, who was sporting a new hairdo and a teal oversize pantsuit. They kissed on the lips.

A wide smile came across her face as she looked out at the audience. "Good morning! Thank you!" The applause continued. "It is such a pleasure to be here in Chicago, participating as a *private* citizen."

This was her coming out at the foundation—and to the world—as philanthropic Hillary, the woman who cares about the Third World. Her brand-new official bio, which popped up on the foundation's website that day, indicated her latest rebranding, which would come as a surprise to many of her former colleagues at the State Department:

Hillary Rodham Clinton served as the 67th U.S. secretary of state from 2009 until 2013, after nearly four decades in public service. Her "smart power" approach to foreign policy repositioned American diplomacy and development for the 21st century. Clinton played a central role in restoring America's standing in the world, reasserting the United States as a Pacific power, imposing crippling sanctions on Iran and North Korea, responding to the Arab Awakening, and negotiating a ceasefire in the Middle East. Earlier, as first lady and senator from New York, she traveled to more than 80 countries as a champion of human rights, democracy, and opportunities for women and girls. Clinton also worked to provide health care to millions of children, create jobs and opportunity, and support first responders who risked their lives at Ground Zero. In her historic campaign for president, Clinton won 18 million votes.[5]

As she spoke, she appeared well rested and, as usual, meticulously well prepared. "I am thrilled to fully join this remarkable organization that Bill started a dozen years ago, and to call it my home for the work I will be doing, some of which I will outline today." And after a couple of acknowledgments to her hometown crowd—she had grown up in the Chicago suburbs six decades before—Hillary rained a series of trendy but meaningless buzzwords on her husband, thanking him for "giving philanthropy and problem-solving a new paradigm, and we've seen already this morning . . . what that means. To really look at solving problems through partnership and collaboration. And really I am very proud of what he has accomplished."

Hillary made it clear that she too was on board with the effort to brand Chelsea as the seasoned and competent NGO manager. "I am also a very proud mother," Hillary said, "because Chelsea's role is expanding and this is truly a labor of love for our entire family. In just a few short years, she has helped the foundation widen our reach to a whole new generation of young people through CGI U—CGI University. . . . Chelsea's really been our leader there."

As the crowd applauded, Hillary beamed at her daughter. "We are so excited and thrilled to have this be a full partnership among the three of us." It wouldn't be the last one for the trio, who stood onstage clearly as a unit. As solid a team as they had ever been. And just as much a mystery to everyone else.

"I don't understand the Clintons, either," says a former press secretary. "They're like any old married couple. When they're together, they get along just fine. They have their own very different styles. She's way more neat and organized and much more of a planner than he is."

For Newt Gingrich and others who have observed the Clintons for years, their latest evolution fits a familiar pattern. "These are very smart, very powerful people who are very, very intelligent, and who are very driven," says the former speaker. "She married him because he was going to be somebody. And he married her because she's going to help him be somebody. And they decided to be somebody together. . . . He has empowered her, while she has tolerated him. And it's been a mutually beneficial relationship."

Currently married to his third wife, Gingrich was animated talking about the Clintons' marriage. "They must have at some point had a very tough period of talking through—what the ground rules are, and how they relate to each other," he says. "I think they had a very clear discussion, whether it was the Lewinsky period or whether it happened five or ten times over their relationship, I don't know. But clearly they reached a very clear agreement on how they would operate and what they would do."

For the last decade, they have largely lived separate lives. Back in 2006, the *New York Times* found that the two spent only 51 of 73 weekends together. Their time together likely grew even rarer after she became America's most-traveled secretary of state, eager to board a plane across the globe because, frankly, she had nowhere else to go at home. With what spare time she had, she was usually at her house near Georgetown, where Bill rarely visited. There she would garden or redecorate. "They redo their house like every other week," says a former aide, somewhat facetiously. "And re-cover furniture. I think she does a lot of that."

That has changed, at least for the moment, now that both of them are out of public office. Hillary and Chelsea are around all the time, which does not entirely thrill the former president. "Why do you think he wants her to run for president?" a former aide asks half jokingly. "He just wants to have this lifestyle that he's grown accustomed to without them around, and now they are around all the time."

Hillary and her husband also look to buy more homes. They've been spotted in New York State, near the Connecticut border, looking at a $10 million home. It is a white colonial in South Salem and is described as having a "pool, lighted tennis court, studio, stable, indoor and outdoor ring and a 3-car garage." Bill Clinton wanted to turn the horse-riding ring into a conference center of sorts, which could be used by the Clinton

Global Initiative, according to someone familiar with their visit to the property. That would allow at least some of the property to be written off as business expenses.

The Clintons' concern was that the home should be close to the airport, which is a bit of a problem with the South Salem address since the closest airport is Danbury Municipal Airport, a twenty-five-minute drive away in Connecticut. That airport's runway is too short for the kinds of planes the Clintons would need to be able to use—which would make White Plains, New York, the next-closest airport and the one they would have to rely on. It's at least a thirty-minute journey to get to it.

The Clintons were even overheard talking about whether the home could, at some point, handle a helicopter pad—or at least some sort of helicopter landing space. Ultimately, they decided not to buy the home, showing a little indecisiveness.

In fact, property hunting is now a favorite Clinton pastime. "They always are looking," says someone familiar with their activities.

The key consideration, of course, was politics: How would it look if Hillary were to run again? They are concerned that it might not look too good to be buying a $10 million home before a presidential run. They are aware of the ridicule Mitt Romney endured in the 2012 election for his many homes, and for even putting a car elevator in one high-priced property. John McCain in 2008 and John Kerry in 2004 were likewise criticized for having too many houses. (Interestingly, the candidate in the last three presidential campaigns with the most number of homes would wind up being the loser—John Kerry in 2004, McCain in 2008, and Mitt Romney in 2012.)

And it might look especially bad to be buying a vacation home, though that too hasn't stopped the Clintons from looking into the possibilities.

"They were looking at property in the Hamptons for a while, but I think that they decided that, if she runs, that seems too tony or too exclusive. Which it is," says a Clinton insider. The Clintons love the Hamptons. While Bill Clinton was president, there were often reports that the

First Family had poll-tested places to vacation. They'd avoid the ritzier locales for something more "authentic" and down home. But out of office, they tend to enjoy a bit more flexibility on the vacation front.

"Bill and Hillary Rodham Clinton are renting a virtual Shangri-La in this lush, beachside paradise in the Hamptons. The $11 million mansion sprawls over 3.5 acres of prime real estate, with four fireplaces, six bedrooms, a heated pool and private path to the beach," the *New York Times* reported in the summer of 2013.[6]

There they hobnobbed with celebrities, held fund-raisers for their foundation, and gathered together with family.

In his self-pitying moments, the kind close acquaintances know well, the former president will tell people he only has five years to live. He has gone through heart surgeries, lost significant weight on a largely vegan diet, and worked hard to control his voracious appetite. For food anyway. Yet he hears the ticking of the clock. Hillary's election, he says, especially to donors, might be the last thing he ever does. The most important thing he could possibly do, with whatever time the good Lord has left for him.

The subtext, of course, is that this is not the Bill Clinton of old—the destructive narcissist who plunged his presidency through seemingly endless scandals. A kinder, gentler Bill Clinton, approaching seventy, is more discreet, more disciplined. He wants to be a grandpa, he tells acquaintances (unlike Hillary, he doesn't have many true friends). And he is the picture of the loyal, dutiful husband, one whose wife gamely jokes with Barbara Walters that if she were elected president, he'd want to be named "First Mate."

Her nonprofit rebrand aside, Hillary has joined Bill in the Clintons' real business—making money. She received a reported $14 million for her (second) memoir. She gives speeches around the country and around the world, often taking lessons from her husband, who by now has the routine down to a science. He shows up at a random place in the middle of nowhere, he makes a splash, steals the show, and, while he's still hot, he gets out of town. All the while, he makes as little news as possible—while still satisfying and flattering his high-paying hosts.

Wherever the Clintons are, they are plotting, constantly recalibrating their positions to stave off likely opposition to her candidacy on the Democratic left. In the span of Clinton's four years as secretary of state, the Democratic Party had essentially shifted underneath her feet. The consensus position among Democrats went from defining a marriage as between a man and a woman to the belief that gay marriage—marriage between a man and a man, or a woman and a woman—should be legalized.

Hillary obliged. "LGBT Americans are our colleagues, our teachers, our soldiers, our friends, our loved ones—and they are full and equal citizens, and deserve the rights of citizenship. That includes marriage," she said in a face-to-camera announcement posted online: "That's why I support marriage for lesbian and gay couples. I support it personally and as a matter of policy and law, embedded in a broader effort to advance equality and opportunity for LGBT Americans and all Americans. Like so many others, my views have been shaped over time by people I have known and loved, by my experience representing our nation on the world stage, my devotion to law and human rights, and the guiding principles of my faith." The video was published by the Human Rights Campaign, the biggest and most powerful gay lobbying organization.

The entire social issue shift Hillary engineered would also suggest another connection she was anxious to develop: one with younger voters, who were more socially liberal than their parents, and who used social media to follow politics. Hillary would try to tap into this at first by posting her video announcing her support for gay marriage on YouTube. She'd develop this outreach further by connecting to Twitter a couple of months later, in June. "Wife, mom, lawyer, women & kids advocate, FLOAR, FLOTUS, US Senator, SecState, author, dog owner, hair icon, pantsuit aficionado, glass ceiling cracker, TBD . . . ," her snappy and impressive Twitter bio would read. It would remind young Americans who might not be as familiar with all her official posts of her credentials. It would also intentionally leave an air of mystery surrounding her with the three-letter acronym *TBD*. Her future, she wanted everyone to know, was To Be Determined.

Over the course of the next year, she'd pose for selfies with her daughter, Chelsea, share pictures of her travels, and tweet at celebrities. You know, she'd use social media . . . just as the kids do these days. It wasn't any different from other politicians' mimicking social media practices—but it was a new experience for Hillary, who had fallen behind while at the State Department. Soon she'd have more than a million Twitter followers.

She'd also use the medium to push out statements on various policy issues that arose. After a Supreme Court decision on the Voting Rights Act, she tweeted, "I am disappointed in today's decision striking at the heart of the Voting Rights Act," with a link to a longer statement from her and her husband on the Supreme Court's decision.

That particular statement was part of something greater: a direct appeal to the black community. It's a core constituency of the Democratic Party and one that broke for Barack Obama, the first black president, in the 2008 primary election. Ironically, it was Bill Clinton, long before most Americans even believed a black president would be elected in their lifetime, who was famously called "the first black president," by author Toni Morrison. But signaling the shift away from the Clintons, she too would endorse Obama over Hillary and later explain, "I thought about voting for Hillary at the beginning. I don't care that she is a woman. I need more than that. Neither his race, his gender, her race or her gender was enough. I needed something else, and the something else was his wisdom."

Something like 90 percent of black voters support the Democratic nominee in normal presidential contests. These numbers went up to about 95 percent for Obama. In other words, looking at building support there made a whole lot of sense. Bill Clinton would personally go to great lengths to reingratiate himself with this constituency—one that had turned on him so sharply after he accused the Obama campaign of being a "fairy tale" and after he'd likened Obama's presidential prospects to those of a black man who had run unsuccessfully for president before him—Jesse Jackson. The former president would pick up the phone to call members of the Congressional Black Caucus, like Maryland Democrat Elijah E. Cummings to see how his mother, whose name Clinton (of course) remembered, was feeling. "He has made an effort to reach out over and over again through the years," the congressman told the *New York Times*, a sort of liberal bible.[7] The newspaper reported that Hillary would make an "appearance before the sisters of Delta Sigma Theta in July, which she opened by offering condolences to the family of Trayvon Martin, the 17-year-old who was killed in Florida last year, and her voting rights address to the American Bar Association in August drew significant attention among black leaders." Delta Sigma Theta, founded at Howard University, is an historic African American sorority.

The story of Bill Clinton's phone call and Hillary Clinton's remembrance of Trayvon Martin was many things—a rebuilding of a relationship with the black community and the *Times*. Both would be important allies as the Clintons looked at their legacy and began to eye the 2016 presidential race.

One of the reporters on the *Times* piece was Amy Chozick, a source not looked upon too keenly by old Clinton hands.

"And I just think this—you know, we have newspapers that have people devoted to doing nothing but covering a campaign that doesn't exist. So then they have to decide to create stories. You know, we don't need that. We need to focus—the American people have economic and other challenges. And our region and world have challenges. We should be focused on those things. And that's what Hillary thinks too," Bill Clinton would say, ribbing Chozick without naming her in an interview with Univision host Jorge Ramos.

Perhaps that's why Ramos got what Chozick couldn't: an exclusive and wide-ranging interview with Bill Clinton.

But Ramos also offered something the *Times* reporter couldn't: a chance to try to rebuild relationships with an ever-growing voting bloc—Hispanics.

"I think that we're trying to pass immigration reform. The country needs it," Clinton would tell Ramos, hitting on a major issue for many Hispanic voters. He'd bash Congress—always a safe bet, since their approval rating is consistently in the toilet—for not getting it done.

But Clinton would also suggest it might be hard to get it done soon. "Not this year, right?" Ramos asked. "I don't know. Next year is the election year. Not this year—2013—2014 maybe," Clinton replied.

The Clintons are usually able to use the press to their advantage—one way or another.

"The press is schizophrenic about Bill Clinton. The press was tough on Bill Clinton. They were tough on his personal foibles. They were tough on the whole Monica thing. Everything was a scandal. President Clinton, in his own unique way, turned that to his advantage by exhausting the nation with the discussion of what he did, and because everyone became so exhausted, they just wanted to move beyond it. It paradoxically helped Bill Clinton," says one former White House press secretary in an interview.

These days, Hillary Clinton gets more of the schizophrenic coverage, while Bill Clinton enjoys much more flattering coverage since leaving office more than a dozen years ago. The differences are easy to explain: Hillary is still in politics, as she is obviously considered a presidential hopeful, while former president Clinton is not. The press tends to afford a special status to former presidents, letting them rehabilitate their legacy and pursue various philanthropic goals without much scrutiny, and President Clinton is no exception.

Numerous Clinton associates, those who have known the former president for decades, have raised this question in our interviews—each separately suggesting that Bill Clinton does not want Hillary Clinton to overshadow his place in history by winning the presidency herself.

"Everybody continues to talk about how badly he wants Hillary to run. Why would he want to be the first spouse?" asks a close associate of both Clintons, and who suggests that Bill actually dreads the prospect. "What's he going to do? Live back in the White House and do the Christmas cards?" The former president, who likes to dominate any conversation, is all but certain to be frustrated being confined to the East Wing, kept out of cabinet meetings, and out of national security meetings in the Situation Room. A man who has spent the last decade doing pretty much whatever he's wanted to do suddenly will have to have his movements, trips, and associations vetted and cleared by aides to his wife for fear of conflicts of interest.

What does all this portend for 2016? A former president deeply conflicted. On the one hand motivated by the altruistic thought that his wife deserves a shot at the presidency. And on the other prone to give in to his darker qualities—selfishness and self-destructiveness.

"He'll work his ass off to get her elected," one longtime Clinton friend suggests. Taking a sip of coffee, he pauses before qualifying his statement. "But in the back of his mind he would always be thinking, 'Maybe I'd be better off if she weren't elected.'" He smiles. "He could sabotage her. And he'd be like, 'Oh, oops.' And with him, honestly, it could be subconscious, but it's there. If it's conscious, if he's purposely doing it, that's some crazy shit."

In light of the multitude of media reports about how badly Bill Clinton wants Hillary elected president, the speculation from the Clinton associate may seem farfetched, but upon closer examination it makes sense that, at a minimum, Bill Clinton has deep reservations about the role of doting first gentleman.

Bill is not the only problem for 2016. In fact, he might not even be the biggest. To some close observers that title now falls to Chelsea, who serves as Hillary's closest confidante, final arbiter, referee, advisor, and shadow campaign manager. In some sense it doesn't really matter who is named the official campaign manager for Hillary's 2016 run—even though speculation is already rampant. He or she will be answering to the candidate and the candidate's daughter (and the candidate's husband).

As *Politico* reported in early 2014, "[J]ust about every close Hillary Clinton ally, asked to describe who is at the top of her organizational chart, gives the same answer: Chelsea. Exactly what that translates into is shrouded in a bit of mystery." A 2016 campaign will make Chelsea de facto campaign manager.

"They've become beholden to her," says a longtime Clinton family associate. "Patti Solis Doyle, when she messed up, she got fired," he says, referring to a close friend of Hillary's who was relieved as her 2008 campaign manager. "But you can't fire your daughter. I mean this is unexplored territory here because all of a sudden, the person running the ship . . . you can't get rid of her." Chelsea Clinton has never come close to running a nationwide presidential effort where she must fend off attacks from all sides. As this family associate put it, Hillary may have to choose—between her family or the presidency. The choice she will make still isn't clear.

The Clintons have worked hard to build relationships with key media outlets, especially since their defeat in 2008, and have often been hugely successful. George Stephanopoulos, who has been known to hold daily calls with Clinton aides, is stationed at ABC, where Donna Brazile is now a regular. (While Stephanopoulos has been ostracized and his relationship with the Clintons is complicated, recent appearances by President Clinton on the show indicate a kind of cooling.) Virginia Moseley, whose husband (Tom Nides) was a top State Department official under Secretary of State Hillary Clinton, is at CNN, where Paul Begala seems to be back. At Fox, there's Doug Schoen and James Carville, who just signed on as a contributor. And of course Chelsea's still under contract at NBC. Which means that practically all big network and cable television stations have Clinton cronies waiting in the wings. That doesn't mean the channels will never air a negative Clinton story—but it does suggest that there will be a higher bar to air hurtful segments about Hillary Clinton than for probably any other potential candidate in the next race.

There's more unprecedented outreach this time around, too. They've welcomed two reporters into HillaryWorld by giving them unprecedented access to people and aides associated with Hillary's time at the State Department. It's a way, it's been reported, for this branch of the Clinton camp to tell *that* story in a book by the reporters—and get away from the *other* Hillary Clinton stories.

Of course, they didn't just let anyone in. In what is being presented as purely coincidental, one of the reporters, Jonathan Allen, worked for Democratic National Committee chair Debbie Wasserman Schultz—a Democratic congresswoman from Florida. He now works at Bloomberg, having jumped ship from *Politico*. The other reporter, Amie Parnes, works at the *Hill*, a Washington-based political newspaper. Even ABC chief White House correspondent Jonathan Karl panned their book—writing, "Mr. Allen and Ms. Parnes appear to have fallen in love with their subject."[8] Which would explain why ClintonWorld let them in in the first place.

Despite efforts to keep things under control, in the Clinton camp things can always spiral out of control, even for those who look most perfect and for those who appear most loyal. That is what happened to Huma Abedin in June 2011 when her husband got caught by conservative provocateur Andrew Breitbart sending lewd images of himself to young attractive women across the country.[9] The brash and obnoxious Democratic congressman Anthony Weiner lied about it, claiming at first to have been hacked.[10] Within days, the story only intensified and Weiner was forced to fess up. He resigned from Congress in shame within a month.[11]

They had only been married for a year at that point—they had tied the knot the year before in a Long Island castle. Bill Clinton had officiated at the marriage.

But not long after getting caught sending the lewd pictures, other news came out: Huma was expecting the couple's first child, a boy, who'd be born in December that year. Huma had hoped to use the birth of her child as a way to transition out of ClintonWorld. Well, not completely—her entire life and career were predicated on her close relationship with Hillary. But she saw how her comrade Doug Band had transitioned into starting his own business and making his own money and calling his own shots. And that was something that appealed to her after spending more than fifteen years at Hillary's side.

The problem was her husband. "I think Huma was trying to separate the same way; the problem is she married a fucking douche bag. You know, I think she was trying to make that same transition that Doug made," says a ClintonWorld associate. "She was transitioning out of State. She was trying to be an advisor but still make money on the side. Then her husband turned out to be the biggest fucking asshole in the world."

After she gave birth to her son, Abedin did move back to their New York City apartment. Her boss, Secretary Clinton, gave her a special status—special government employee—through a program generally given to government workers to help them transition out of the private sector and into a high-level government position. Here it was being used so Abedin could have one foot in government while she looked for work elsewhere.

"The new status made her a special government employee, which was tantamount to being a consultant," according to the source, whose information was confirmed by two other staffers familiar with the matter. "Multiple sources told *Politico* Abedin did work for other clients, which a friend of Abedin said totaled four, including the State Department, Hillary Clinton, the William Jefferson Clinton Foundation and Teneo, the firm cofounded by former Bill Clinton counselor Doug Band," *Politico* would report.[12]

Around the same time, Weiner was hoping to hop back into politics with a run for mayor of New York City. It's a coveted slot: the head of the largest American city. And one that Weiner had his eyes on for at least a decade.

It was a brilliant move. "If he runs, and even if he loses, he comes in a respectable second—if he makes a run at it and comes in second in a race of like how many people? And then he's not the guy who everyone remembers as taking creepy dick pics and tweeting them to people. Then it will be, 'Oh, he ran for mayor and came in second,'" a former aide told me. "That's why it's brilliant that he's running."

But something happened that caught ClintonWorld and Abedin completely off-guard. Weiner hadn't given up sending lewd pictures via text message to women around the country. And one of the recipients in particular decided to use the dirt she had on Weiner to try to parlay that into her fifteen minutes of fame. Which she did—to really remarkable success.

Weiner's run was over. His life was a joke. And Abedin looked to be the second part of that joke, especially when she joined Weiner at a press conference, where she looked hurt, confused—and loyal to her man.

The Clintons wanted nothing to do with Weiner, with whom they were furious . . . mainly because the scandal looked in some ways like another scandal the Clintons had for years been trying to get over: the Monica Lewinsky affair.

"They don't want anything to do with him [Anthony Weiner]. They don't want to be around him. I mean, she and her job needs to be the priority," said a Clinton aide who had worked closely with Hillary, Abedin, and Weiner.

"She'll divorce him," the aide speculated last year.

The Clintons were petrified the entire time that it would be brought up. "I think that it's just too close to home. Like if they were close to him, everyone would be talking about it like, 'Oh, the Clintons had their own problems.' Lewinsky would be in every single article. . . . You look at it now, it's never mentioned," said the aide *before* Weiner got caught in the second, and most detrimental, sexting scandal.

That's when, as the aide suspected, Lewinsky's name began to be brought up and people would compare Abedin to her mentor, Hillary Clinton. Just like Hillary she had stood by her man during a sex scandal. Now they had even more in common than before—public humiliation.

In reality, Abedin's been able to avoid divorce—at least for now. Weiner slipped away from public view. And Abedin did, too, when her boss Hillary took some time off after the State Department and before her own book launch in the summer of 2014.

The one major consequence for Abedin has been that she wasn't able to break away from ClintonWorld to start her own career in the way Doug Band was. Without someone directly pushing her out and without Weiner in view, it was hard to make a clean break—and she'd be damaged goods on the consulting market if *some* sort of relationship with Hillary were not in place.

Instead, she'd be forced into rehabilitation, to be at Hillary's side for at least another couple of years, and maybe even during a presidential run in 2016.

If there's one serious threat to Hillary Clinton's presidential primary campaign in 2016, it's the left wing of her party. They are the ones who abandoned her in 2008 for Barack Obama. They are the ones she overlooked when she voted for the Iraq War and started trying to broaden her appeal to general election voters.

She is determined not to take them for granted again. That's why, on January 1, 2014, H. Clinton and B. Clinton, as the name cards labeled the former president and (perhaps) future president, sat atop a stage for the swearing in of the new mayor of New York City, Bill de Blasio.

De Blasio was elected mayor in what many considered a progressive wave of strident liberalism returning to the Democratic Party. He unabashedly tapped into the spirit of the Occupy Wall Street protesters who pitted the 99 percent against the rich, elite 1 percent of the U.S. population.

Dressed in a long, shapeless dark overcoat, Bill Clinton had been asked to administer the oath of office to his former regional director at the U.S. Department of Housing and Urban Development and Hillary Clinton's former campaign manager for her statewide run for the U.S. Senate more than a dozen years before. Even Huma Abedin was on hand, though her husband, who had humiliated himself and his family in his primary run against de Blasio and others for the coveted office, was not.

David Axelrod, one of Obama's closest political advisors, took notice and said that President Clinton's "role" in the ceremonial inauguration "may reassure the Left" in the lead-up to the 2016 presidential election. Axelrod would also try to draw another lesson and suggest that Clinton's very presence was a "signal to the elite that new Mayor's agenda is not 'radical.'"

It would also be another sign (following Bill Clinton's boffo 2012 Democratic National Convention speech) that the Clintons were the most revered political guests to have on hand at top events. (By contrast, President Obama was on the other side of the nation that day, vacationing in Hawaii. His presence did not appear to be missed.)

In having Clinton officiate the ceremony, there of course was a glaring irony: The first modern president to be impeached after he lied to investigators looking into allegations of sexual harassment, Bill Clinton was there to administer Bill de Blasio's oath that he would faithfully uphold the U.S. Constitution and the laws of the United States and New York. Journalist Matt Drudge would take to Twitter to note, "Rehabilitation of Clinton crosses into Looney Tunes. Contempt of court, law license suspended 5 years, impeached! Now swearing in NYC mayor?"

But in fact it was a sign that the Clintons had successfully graduated from rehab. They were back.

Clinton, in a perfectly Clintonian manner, would be one of the only speakers to go out of his way to praise de Blasio's predecessor, Mayor Michael Bloomberg, whom he would credit with leaving New York City in better condition than when he arrived a dozen years before. "He made the city stronger and healthier than he found it," Clinton said of the mayor.[13] The line stood out, as all the other speakers before him had avoided directly mentioning Bloomberg—they would only criticize the state of the city and say that better days, under de Blasio, were ahead.

But the soft touch by Clinton would suggest something else: The Clintons would work to bridge the gap from the radical left (de Blasio) to the middle (Bloomberg). It wasn't just something they'd work toward in the future; it was something they claimed to have done since entering public service more than three decades before.

Bloomberg, once a nominal Republican, appeared genuinely to appreciate the praise (as would his longtime communications director, Howard Wolfson). As for Hillary, she remained a silent presence throughout the appearance, though she joined her husband and dutifully stood for photo ops with the newly sworn-in officials.

But Clinton would use the moment to appeal to the left, too. "I strongly endorse Bill de Blasio's core campaign commitment that we have to have a city of shared opportunities, shared prosperity, shared responsibilities," said Clinton, who lives outside the city limits. Some speculated that it was the most Clinton had talked about income inequality in years.

Clinton would also applaud de Blasio's diverse family. "He represents with his family the future of our city and the future of our country," Clinton said. "You know, with all respect to the television show, they're our real modern family."

It was a big moment for de Blasio. "Thank you, President Clinton, for your kind and generous words. It was an honor to serve in your administration, and we're all honored by your presence here today. And I have to note that, over twenty years ago, when a conservative philosophy seemed dominant in our nation, you broke through—and told us to still believe in a place called Hope," de Blasio began his inaugural address, turning back to face President Clinton, who quickly realized that with the mayor's glance the cameras would pan to him, seated between Hillary and Governor Andrew Cuomo. The former president reached across his wife's back and eased his hand on her shoulder, pulling her tight, as the crowd (and Mrs. Clinton) applauded him.[14]

"Thank you, Secretary Clinton. I was so inspired by the time I spent on your first campaign. Your groundbreaking commitment to nurturing our children and families manifested itself in a phrase that is now a part of our American culture—and something we believe in deeply in this city: 'It Takes a Village.' Thank you, Secretary."

Hillary's book *It Takes a Village* preaches the power of the community—and how important it is to work together toward a good cause.

And with the newly inaugurated mayor, there was a clear sign that through hard work, determination, skillful politics, and brute force, Bill and Hillary Clinton have themselves built a community of friends and allies, new and old, across the political spectrum, and even in the financial capital of the world.

That is how the impeached President Clinton was invited to New York City on that cold Wednesday last January to administer the oath, even though he himself had failed to adhere to his own oath of office after being sworn in as president of the United States. And it is how Mrs. Clinton will be able to use the village—her village—to help make her the next president of the United States.

As they sat before New York's first Democratic mayor in two decades, Bill and Hillary Clinton were happy. They were right where they wanted to be—at the center of the world's attention. The comeback was almost complete.

ACKNOWLEDGMENTS

Matt Latimer and Keith Urbahn—and the great team they've assembled at Javelin—made this possible. From start to finish, *like shepherds living with the smell of sheep*, they provided the idea behind this book, outstanding representation, and tremendous assistance in every possible way.

I'm grateful to Adam Bellow and HarperCollins for having faith in this project. Adam's perceptive ideas and sharp edits vastly improved the idea of this book and, ultimately, the final copy. I'd also like to thank Eric Meyers for helping throughout the editing process.

Everyone I work with at the *Weekly Standard* was helpful and supportive. In particular, I'm especially thankful to Bill Kristol, the boss, for giving me a job—and for offering advice and allowing me to take the time I needed from work to make this book possible. Mike Warren, John McCormack, Ethan Epstein, Jim Swift, Geoffrey Norman, Maria Santos, and Jeryl Bier made my life much easier by covering for me at work. Additionally, Fred Barnes, Richard Starr, Andrew Ferguson, Matt Labash, Steve Hayes, Vic Matus, Terry Eastland, Nick Swezey, Grace Terzian, Catherine Lowe, and Claudia Anderson gave me wise counsel and went out of their way to be helpful. And thanks to Lou Ann Sabatier.

They say that reporters are only as good as their sources, so I'm especially thankful to the many, many people who went out of their way to sit for interviews, chat on the phone, respond to my emails, and otherwise point me in the right direction. Many sources requested anonymity, so I'll stop short of naming most of them. But Ambassador Richard Carlson was outstanding—and a riveting storyteller. Thanks also to Lanny Davis, Jerome Marcus, Michael Medved, David Shuster, John McCain, Joe Lieberman, and Jason Chaffetz.

Much of the reporting for this is book built upon previous reporting by many stellar reporters and authors. Though most of these writers I've never met, I'd like to thank Maggie Haberman, Alec MacGillis, Carol Felsenthal, Amy Chozick, Vali Nasr, Sally Bedell Smith, Michael Tomasky, John Harris, Carl Bernstein, George Stephanopoulos, Mark Halperin, John Heilemann, and many others cited throughout this book.

A big thanks, also, to Ryan Lovelace (and Ben Silver) for help transcribing interviews, and Andrew Evans for fact-checking.

Reporting and writing a book takes a lot of time, of course. And I'm very appreciative of my family for their support throughout. My in-laws, Karen and Steve, provided help and support along the way. As did my sister in-law, Kimberly, and my brothers, Yehuda and Aaron, and their spouses, Sara and Mary, who rooted for the success of this project from the start. My parents have always supported in me in whatever I've wanted to do—and this project was no exception.

And of course to my wife, Lauren, who makes everything possible and worthwhile. To her—and for her—I'm eternally grateful.

NOTES

Introduction: Brand Management

1. Robert M. Gates, *Duty: Memoirs of a Secretary at War* (New York: Knopf, 2014).
2. "Clinton Cancels Middle East Trip Because of Ill Health," Reuters, December 10, 2012, http://articles.chicagotribune.com/2012-12-10/news/sns-rt-us-syria-usa-clinton bre8ba04g-20121210_1_ill-health-syrian-opposition-coalition-president-bashar-al -assad.
3. "Hillary Clinton Recovering from Fall, Working from Home," Associated Press, December 16, 2012, http://www.csmonitor.com/USA/Latest-News-Wires/ 2012/1216/Hillary-Clinton-recovering-from-fall-working-from-home.
4. Elise Labott, "Hillary Clinton Treated for Blood Clot in Her Head," CNN, January 1, 2013, http://www.cnn.com/2012/12/31/politics/hillary-clinton-hospitalized/.
5. "Hillary Clinton Faints During Speech in Buffalo," NBC, February 1, 2005, http://www.nbcnews.com/id/6890519/ns/politics/t/hillary-clinton-faints-during -speech-buffalo/#.UwuqRBZZ4Rk.
6. Kevin Robillard, "NBC Reporter Raises Hillary Clinton Questions," *Politico*, December 31, 2012, http://www.politico.com/story/2012/12/nbc-reporter-raises -hillary-questions-85611.html.
7. Selim Algar, "Big Donor Claims Bill Clinton Told Him Hillary's Running for Prez in 2016," *New York Post*, February 14, 2013, http://nypost.com/2013/02/14/big-do nor-claims-bill-clinton-told-him-hillarys-running-for-prez-in-2016/.
8. "Richard Nixon's Quiet Foreign Policy Advice to Bill Clinton Revealed in Newly Declassified Documents," Associated Press, February 14, 2013.
9. Christopher Hitchens, *No One Left to Lie To: The Values of the Worst Family* (London and New York: Verso, 1999).

10. George Stephanopoulos, *All Too Human: A Political Education* (Boston: Little, Brown, 1999).

11. Bill Richardson, *How to Sweet-Talk a Shark: Strategies and Stories from a Master Negotiator* (Emmaus, PA: Rodale Books, 2013).

12. Todd S. Purdum, "The Comeback Id," *Vanity Fair*, July 2008, http://www.vanity fair.com/politics/features/2008/07/clinton200807.

13. Kim Masters, "Bill Clinton's $20 Million Breakup," *Daily Beast*, March 29, 2010, http://www.thedailybeast.com/articles/2010/03/29/bill-clintons-20-million -breakup.html.

14. Amy Chozick and Nicholas Confessore, "Unease at Clinton Foundation Over Finances and Ambitions," *New York Times*, August 13, 2013, http://www.nytimes .com/2013/08/14/us/politics/unease-at-clinton-foundation-over-finances-and -ambitions.html.

15. Jonathan Allen and Amie Parnes, *HRC: State Secrets and the Rebirth of Hillary Clinton* (New York: Crown, 2014).

1: Hillary's Redemption

1. Hillary Rodham Clinton, *Living History* (New York: Scribner, 2004), p. 506.

2. Christopher Anderson, *Bill and Hillary: The Marriage* (New York: William Morrow, 1999).

3. Sally Bedell Smith, *For Love of Politics* (New York: Random House, 2007).

4. Gail Sheehy, *Hillary's Choice* (New York: Random House, 1999).

5. James Bennet, "The Next Clinton," *New York Times Magazine*, May 30, 1999, http://www.nytimes.com/1999/05/30/magazine/the-next-clinton.html.

6. Hillary Clinton, *Living History* (New York: Scribner, 2004), p. 292.

7. Naftali Bendavid, "Hillary-Eleanor Comparison Riles Some Fans of the Latter," *Chicago Tribune*, December 8, 1999 http://articles.chicagotribune.com/1999 -12-08/news/9912080093_1_mrs-roosevelt-franklin-d-roosevelt-memorial-mrs -clinton.

8. William Safire, "Blizzard of Lies," *New York Times*, January 8, 1996, http://www .nytimes.com/1996/01/08/opinion/essay-blizzard-of-lies.html.

9. Alana Goodman, "The Hillary Papers," *Washington Free Beacon*, February 9, 2014, http://freebeacon.com/politics/the-hillary-papers/.

10. Bennet, "The Next Clinton."

11. "Clinton's Trip to Martha's Vineyard Was Hardly a Vacation from Politics," *Los Angeles Times*, August 30, 1998, http://articles.latimes.com/1998/aug/30/news/ mn-18034.

12. See, e.g., "How Bill Clinton Neutered the Feminist Movement," *Independent*, April 4, 1998, http://www.independent.co.uk/life-style/how-bill-clinton-neutered-the -feminist-movement-1154350.html.

13. "Secretary Clinton '73 Receives Award of Merit at the Yale Law School Alumni Weekend," Yale Law School, October 5, 2013, http://www.law.yale.edu/ news/17521.htm.

14. Taylor Branch, *The Clinton Tapes: Wrestling History with the President* (New York: Simon & Schuster, 2009), p. 496.

15. Goodman, "The Hillary Papers."

16. Nancy Traver, "Choice Moments: Gail Sheehy on How Hillary Clinton Chose to Live Her Life," *Chicago Tribune,* January 26, 2000.

17. Jerry Oppenheimer, *State of a Union: Inside the Complex Marriage of Bill and Hillary Clinton* (New York: HarperCollins, 2000).

18. Gregg Birnbaum, "GOP Introduces Anti-Hill Bill to Nix Senate Bid," *New York Post,* March 9, 1999, http://nypost.com/1999/03/09/gop-introduces-anti-hill-bill-to-nix-senate-bid/.

19. Richard Perez-Pena, "Giuliani Aims Gibes at Hillary Clinton at an Upstate Dinner," *New York Times,* May 4, 1999, http://www.nytimes.com/1999/05/04/nyregion/giuliani-aims-gibes-at-hillary-clinton-at-an-upstate-dinner.html.

20. Adam Nagourney, "In a Kennedy's Legacy, Lessons and Pitfalls for Hillary Clinton; Carpetbagger Issue Has Echoes of '64, but Differences Could Prove Crucial," *New York Times,* September 10, 2000, http://www.nytimes.com/2000/09/10/nyregion/kennedy-s-legacy-lessons-pitfalls-for-hillary-clinton-carpetbagger-issue-has.html.

21. Ibid.

22. Bennet, "The Next Clinton."

23. "Home Financing for the Clintons," editorial, *New York Times,* September 28, 1999, http://www.nytimes.com/1999/09/28/opinion/home-financing-for-the-clintons.html.

24. Michael Crowley, "Bunker Hillary," *New Republic,* November 12, 2007, http://www.newrepublic.com/article/bunker-hillary.

25. Susan Dominus, "Hillary Clinton's Biggest Backer," *New York Times Magazine,* September 17, 2000, http://www.nytimes.com/2000/09/17/magazine/hillary-clinton-s-biggest-backer.html.

26. Maggie Haberman, "Chuck Schumer Hatched Secret Plan to Get Obama to Run," *New York Post,* January 10, 2010, http://nypost.com/2010/01/10/chuck-schumer-hatched-secret-plan-to-get-obama-to-run/.

27. Ibid.

28. Jura Koncius, "The Woman Behind the Room Behind Hillary Clinton," *Washington Post,* February 1, 2007, http://www.washingtonpost.com/wp-dyn/content/article/2007/01/31/AR2007013100469.html.

29. Ibid.

30. Louis J. Freeh, "Khobar Towers," *Wall Street Journal,* June 23, 2006, http://online.wsj.com/news/articles/SB115102702568788331.

31. John Solomon and Jeffrey H. Birnbaum, "Clinton Library Got Funds from Abroad," *Washington Post,* December 15, 2007, http://www.washingtonpost.com/wp-dyn/content/article/2007/12/14/AR2007121402124.html.

32. Ibid.

33. Ibid.

34. Terry Lenzner, *The Investigator: Fifty Years of Uncovering the Truth* (New York: Blue Rider Press, 2013), p. 296.

35. U.S. Government Printing Office transcript of President Clinton's remarks, available at http://www.gpo.gov/fdsys/pkg/WCPD-2001-01-15/html/WCPD-2001-01-15-Pg57.htm.

36. John Riley, "Holder as AG: Why Marc Rich Matters," *Newsday*, November 19, 2008, http://www.newsday.com/long-island/politics/spin-cycle-1.812042/holder-as-ag-why-marc-rich-matters-1.862368.

37. Ibid.

38. Jake Tapper, "Pardon Me?" ABC News, November 15, 2007, http://abcnews.go.com/Politics/Vote2008/story?id=3866786&page=1&singlePage=true.

39. Chris Matthews, *Hardball*, CNBC, January 25, 2001.

40. Maureen Dowd, "Liberties; Cats, Dogs and Grifters," *New York Times*, January 24, 2001, http://www.nytimes.com/2001/01/24/opinion/liberties-cats-dogs-and-grifters.html.

41. "Sorting Out the Pardon Mess," editorial, *New York Times*, February 23, 2001, http://www.nytimes.com/2001/02/23/opinion/sorting-out-the-pardon-mess.html.

42. Haynes Johnson, *The Best of Times: America in the Clinton Years* (New York: Harcourt, 2001), p. 546.

43. "Carter Calls Pardon of Rich 'Disgraceful,'" *Los Angeles Times*, February 21, 2001, http://articles.latimes.com/2001/feb/21/news/mn-28265.

44. Peter Slevin, "A Rush to Judgment," *Washington Post*, March 1, 2001, http://www.washingtonpost.com/wp-dyn/content/article/2008/06/11/AR2008061101245.html.

2: On Their Own

1. Gallup polling, available at http://www.gallup.com/poll/116584/presidential-approval-ratings-bill-clinton.aspx.

2. Arkansas Supreme Court Committee on Professional Conduct, filed February 21, 2001, bar number 73019, https://courts.arkansas.gov/content/200000013-suspended.

3. Ibid.

4. William Jefferson Clinton, "My Reasons for the Pardons," *New York Times*, February 18, 2001, http://www.nytimes.com/2001/02/18/opinion/my-reasons-for-the-pardons.html.

5. "Editors' Note," *New York Times*, February 19, 2001, http://www.nytimes.com/2001/02/19/opinion/editors-note-985392.html.

6. Taylor Branch, *The Clinton Tapes: Wrestling History with the President* (New York: Simon & Schuster, 2009).

7. Dianne Feinstein, "Hope for a Transformative President," *Politico*, December 12, 2013, http://www.politico.com/story/2013/12/women-rule-dianne-feinstein-hillary-clinton-hopes-for-a-transformative-president-101037.html.

8. Rebecca Johnson, "Hillary's Secret Weapon: Huma Abedin," *Vogue*, August 2007, http://www.vogue.com/magazine/article/hillarys-secret-weapon-huma-abedin/#1.

9. Andrew C. McCarthy, "The Huma Unmentionables," *National Review Online*, July 24, 2013, http://www.nationalreview.com/corner/354351/huma-unmentionables-andrew-c-mccarthy.

10. Ibid.

11. Brianna Gurciullo, "FBI Tailed Terrorist Anwar Al-Awlaki as He Ordered Pizza, Took Classes at GW," *GW Hatchet*, July 3, 2013, http://blogs.gwhatchet.com/newsroom/2013/07/03/fbi-tailed-terrorist-anwar-al-awlaki-as-he-ordered-pizza-took-classes-at-gw/.

12. Johnson, "Hillary's Secret Weapon."

13. "Hillary Clinton Aide Tells Reporter to 'Fuck Off' and 'Have a Good Life,'" *Buzz-Feed*, September 24, 2012, http://www.buzzfeed.com/buzzfeedpolitics/hillary-clinton-aide-tells-reporter-to-fuck-off.

14. Jason Horowitz, "Longtime Keeper of Hillary Clinton's Image Has Forged a Loyal Badge of His Own," *Washington Post*, June 12, 2011, http://www.washingtonpost.com/lifestyle/style/longtime-keeper-of-hillary-clintons-image-has-forged-a-loyal-badge-of-his-own/2011/05/31/AGLAu9RH_story.html.

15. Jeff Gerth and Don Van Natta Jr., *Her Way: The Hope and Ambitions of Hillary Rodham Clinton* (Boston: Little, Brown, 2007).

16. Janet Maslin, "Books of the Times: Clintons' 'Good Soldier' Explains All Those Messes," *New York Times*, May 15, 2003, http://www.nytimes.com/2003/05/15/books/books-of-the-times-clintons-good-soldier-explains-all-those-messes.html.

17. David Maraniss, "First Lady Launches Counterattack," *Washington Post*, January 28, 1998, http://www.washingtonpost.com/wp-srv/politics/special/clinton/stories/hillary012898.htm.

18. Matt Bai, "Notion Building," *New York Times Magazine*, October 12, 2003.

19. Neera Tanden, email to supporters, December 27, 2013.

20. Robert Dreyfuss, "An Idea Factory for the Democrats," *Nation*, March 1, 2004, p. 18.

21. Media Matters website: http://mediamatters.org/about.

22. David Brock, "His Cheatin' Heart: Living with the Clintons: Bill's Arkansas Bodyguards Tell the Story the Press Missed," *American Spectator*, January 1994, http://spectator.org/print/49976.

23. Noel Sheppard, "Hillary Clinton Told YearlyKos Convention She Helped Start Media Matters," Newsbusters.org, October 1, 2007, http://newsbusters.org/blogs/noel-sheppard/2007/10/01/hillary-clinton-told-yearlykos-convention-she-helped-start-media-matt.

24. Kevin Hassett, "Hillary Clinton Reigns as Queen of Federal Pork," Bloomberg, October 8, 2007, http://www.bloomberg.com/apps/news?pid=newsarchive&sid=aXWIZU3DOyr4.

25. Michael R. Blood, "McCain Says He'll Fight Clinton's 'Pork,'" Associated Press, June 14, 2007.

26. Charlie Savage, "A Donor's Gift Soon Followed Clinton's Help," *New York Times*, January 3, 2009, http://www.nytimes.com/2009/01/04/washington/04clinton.html.

27. Ibid.

28. Leslie Wayne, "From Campaign Trail to Celebrity Circuit," *New York Times*, April 18, 2004, http://www.nytimes.com/2004/04/18/us/from-campaign-trail -to-celebrity-circuit.html.

29. Ibid.

30. "Excerpts from the Deposition of L. D. Brown," March 13, 1998, WashingtonPost.com, http://www.washingtonpost.com/wp-srv/politics/special/pjones/docs/brown031398.htm.

31. http://lencolasullivan.com/about.html.

32. Accessible on Roel P. Verseveldt's LinkedIn profile: http://nl.linkedin.com/in/ roelpverseveldt.

33. Thomas M. DeFrank, *Write It When I'm Gone: Remarkable Off-the-Record Conversations with Gerald R. Ford* (New York: G. P. Putnam's Sons, 2007).

34. John M. Broder and Patrick Healy, "How a Billionaire Friend of Bill Helps Him Do Good, and Well," *New York Times*, April 23, 2006, http://www.nytimes.com/2006/04/23/ nyregion/23burkle.html.

35. Alisson Clark, "The Gator Behind Bill Clinton," Gainesville.com, February 4, 2009, http://www.gainesville.com/article/20090204/MAGAZINE01/902040257.

36. Alec MacGillis, "Scandal at Clinton Inc.: How Doug Band Drove a Wedge Through a Political Dynasty," *New Republic*, September 22, 2013, http://www .newrepublic.com/article/114790/how-doug-band-drove-wedge-through- clinton-dynasty.

37. Ibid.

38. Carol Felsenthal, *Clinton in Exile: A President Out of the White House* (New York: William Morrow, 2008).

39. William Jefferson Clinton, *My Life* (New York: Knopf, 2004), p. 11.

40. Martin Kasindorf, "Reagan's Fall From Grace: The $2-Million Japan Tour, Nancy's Vengeful Memoirs and Legal Battles Over the Iran-Contra Affair Have Made His Retirement Anything but Restful," *Los Angeles Times*, March 4, 1990, http://articles .latimes.com/1990-03-04/magazine/tm-2327_1_nancy-reagan-foundation.

3: Charm Offensives

1. Peter Baker, *The Breach: Inside the Impeachment and Trial of William Jefferson Clinton* (New York: Scribner, 2000).

2. Raymond Hernandez, "Not the Mrs. Clinton Washington Thought It Knew," *New York Times*, January 24, 2002, http://www.nytimes.com/2002/01/24/nyregion/ not-the-mrs-clinton-washington-thought-it-knew.html.

3. Josh Green, "Take Two: Hillary's Choice," *Atlantic*, November 2006, http://www .theatlantic.com/magazine/archive/2006/11/take-two-hillarys-choice/305292/.

4. Robert M. Gates, *Duty: Memoirs of a Secretary at War* (New York: Knopf, 2014).

5. Josh Delreal, "Bill Clinton Recalls Lessons from Nelson Mandela," *Politico*, December 6, 2013, http://www.politico.com/story/2013/12/bill-clinton-nelson -mandela-lessons-100810.html.

6. "Gingrich Attacks Clinton on Lewinsky Matter, Foreign Policy," CNN, May 18, 1998, http://www.cnn.com/ALLPOLITICS/1998/05/18/gingrich.clinton/index.html.

7. Ibid.

8. Baker, *The Breach*.

9. Phil Gramm, "Announcement of Candidacy," CNN, February 24, 1995, http://www.cnn.com/ALLPOLITICS/1996/candidates/republican/withdrawn/gramm.announcement.shtml.

10. Hudson Union Society, "Senator Trent Lott on President Clinton," video, You-Tube, February 19, 2009, http://www.youtube.com/watch?v=BQH24KqHYyg.

11. Josh Gerstein, "Bill Clinton: Spec. Prosecutors 'All Got Waxed,'" *Politico*, February 23, 2010, http://www.politico.com/blogs/joshgerstein/0210/Bill_Clinton_spec_prosecutors_all_got_waxed.html.

12. Bill Richardson, *How to Sweet-Talk a Shark: Strategies and Stories from a Master Negotiator* (Emmaus, PA: Rodale Books, 2013).

13. Ray Paulick, "Clinton with Stronachs at Preakness: Funny Cide 'No Fluke,'" Blood-Horse.com, May 17, 2003, http://www.bloodhorse.com/horse-racing/articles/15869/clinton-with-stronachs-at-preakness-funny-cide-no-fluke.

14. Robert Fife, "Rumours Abound as Clinton 'Befriends' Billionaire Socialite: Former U.S. President Seen Frequently with Magna CEO," *Vancouver Sun*, CanWest News Service, June 12, 2003, p. D1.

15. Patrick Healy, "For Clintons, Delicate Dance of Married and Public Lives," *New York Times*, May 23, 2006, http://www.nytimes.com/2006/05/23/nyregion/23clintons.html.

16. Ibid.

17. Ibid.

18. Ronald Brownstein, "Old Divides Growing in Dean, Centrist Rift," *Los Angeles Times*, December 24, 2003, http://articles.latimes.com/2003/dec/24/nation/na-dlc24.

19. Maggie Haberman, "Hillary Clinton's Shadow Campaign," *Politico*, January 5, 2014, http://dyn.politico.com/printstory.cfm?uuid=F9AE51A4-3E0D-4604-B08F-2E63DE4F600A.

4: Seducing the Bushes

1. Tony Freemantle, "Bush, Clinton Form Unlikely Bond on Tsunami Tour," *Houston Chronicle*, March 7, 2005, http://www.chron.com/news/nation-world/article/Bush-Clinton-form-unlikely-bond-on-tsunami-tour-1931175.php.

2. Kevin Bohn, "George H. W. Bush on Bonding with Bill Clinton," CNN, March 5, 2013, http://politicalticker.blogs.cnn.com/2013/03/05/george-h-w-bush-on-bonding-with-bill-clinton/.

3. Charles Green and R. A. Zaldivar, "Bush, Clinton Trade Insults, Ignore Perot While Perot Made His Only Appearance of the Day on CNN, Bush Called the Democrats 'Bozos,' and Clinton Warned That the President Lacked Conviction," *Philadelphia Inquirer*, October 30, 1992, http://articles.philly.com/1992-10-30/news/25996985_1_democrat-bill-clinton-clinton-and-bush-ross-perot.

4. Doro Bush Koch, *My Father, My President* (New York: Grand Central, 2006).

5. George W. Bush, *Decision Points* (New York: Crown, 2010), p. 50.

6. Ibid.

7. Freemantle, "Bush, Clinton Form Unlikely Bond on Tsunami Tour."

8. Barbara Bush, *A Memoir* (New York: Charles Scribner's Sons, 1994), p. 457.

9. Koch, *My Father, My President*.

10. Herbert S. Parmet, *George Bush: The Life of a Lone Star Yankee* (New Brunswick, NJ: Transaction, 2000).

11. Koch, *My Father, My President*.

12. Robert Draper, *Dead Certain: The Presidency of George W. Bush* (New York: Free Press, 2007), p. 91.

13. Taylor Branch, *The Clinton Tapes: Wrestling History with the President* (New York: Simon & Schuster, 2009).

14. See, e.g., President Clinton's Remarks at a Luncheon for Representative Patrick J. Kennedy in Barrington, Rhode Island, July 28, 2000, http://www.presidency.ucsb.edu/ws/index.php?pid=1512&st=gay&st1.

15. Tom Raum, "Bush Snaps Back at Clinton Barbs," Associated Press, August 2, 2000.

16. Karl Rove, *Courage and Consequence: My Life as a Conservative in the Fight* (New York: Threshold Editions, 2010), p. 220.

17. Lanny Davis, "Book Discussion on Crisis Tales," video, C-SPAN, April 17, 2013, http://www.c-span.org/video/?312719-1/book-discussion-crisis-tales.

18. "President Bush Welcomes President Clinton and Senator Clinton," June 14, 2004, transcript, http://georgewbush-whitehouse.archives.gov/news/releases/2004/06/20040614-2.html.

19. Davis, "Book Discussion on Crisis Tales."

20. Simmie Knox, "Painting Clinton's White House Portrait," NPR, June 14, 2004, http://www.simmieknox.com/press2.asp.

21. "Transcript from Portrait Unveiling Ceremony," June 14, 2004, http://www.washingtonpost.com/wp-dyn/articles/A40670-2004Jun14_3.html.

22. Rove, *Courage and Consequence*, p. 467.

23. See, e.g., Eliana Johnson, "Clinton's Fixer," *National Review*, May 10, 2013.

24. Jonathan Lemire, "Barbara Bush Gushes About Bill Clinton, Says He Treats George H. W. Bush Like a Father," *New York Daily News*, July 13, 2012, http://www.nydailynews.com/news/politics/barbara-bush-gushes-bill-clinton-treats-george-h-w-bush-father-article-1.1113917.

25. "Clinton Criticizes Bush's Hitler, Lenin Analogy," CNN, November 2, 2007.

26. Patrick Gavin, "Bush: 'Clinton and I Are Buddies,'" *Politico*, November 14, 2010, http://www.politico.com/click/stories/1011/bush_clinton_and_i_are_buddies.html.

27. Koch, *My Father, My President*.

28. Taylor Berman, "Hacker Exposes Bush Family Emails, Photos, and George W. Bush's Amazing Self-Portraits," *Gawker*, February 7, 2013, http://gawker.com/5982694/hacker-exposes-bush-family-emails-photos-and-george-w-bushs-amazing-self-portraits.

29. Marie Loiseau, "At Georgetown, John Kerry, Hillary Clinton and Laura Bush Urge Continued Support for Afghan Women," *Georgetowner*, November 18, 2013.

5: Death Defiers

1. Bob Herbert, "Hillary Can Run, but Can She Win?" *New York Times*, May 18, 2006, http://www.nytimes.com/2006/05/18/opinion/18herbert.html.

2. Ibid.

3. John F. Harris, "Policy and Politics by the Numbers; For the President, Polls Became a Defining Force in His Administration," *Washington Post*, December 31, 2000.

4. Gail Sheehy, "Hillaryland at War," *Vanity Fair*, August 2008, http://www.vanity fair.com/politics/features/2008/08/clinton200808.

5. Mike Allen, "Clinton Told to Portray Obama as Foreign," *Politico*, August 10, 2008, http://www.politico.com/news/stories/0808/12420.html.

6. "Clinton's Lead in Historical Perspective," Gallup.com, October 22, 2007, http://www.gallup.com/poll/102265/clintons-lead-historical-perspective.aspx.

7. Maureen Dowd, "Obama's Big Screen Test," *New York Times*, February 21, 2007, http://www.nytimes.com/2007/02/21/opinion/21dowd.html.

8. Patrick Healy, "Clinton Deputy Campaign Manager Quits," *New York Times*, February 12, 2008.

9. Paul Steinhauser, "Poll: Obama Opens Double-Digit Lead over Clinton," CNN, January 7, 2008, http://www.cnn.com/2008/POLITICS/01/06/nh.poll/index.html?eref=rss_topstories.

10. Ibid.

11. Ed Quillen, "Are Politicians' Kids Off-limits?" *Denver Post*, September 7, 2009, http://www.denverpost.com/opinion/ci_10384065.

12. Joshua Green, "Take Two: Hillary's Choice," *Atlantic*, November 1, 2006, http://www.theatlantic.com/magazine/archive/2006/11/take-two-hillarys-choice/305292/.

13. Ben Smith, "Clinton Campaign Kills Negative Story," *Politico*, September 24, 2007, http://www.politico.com/news/stories/0907/5992.html.

6: Out of Control

1. John R. Emshwiller, "Bill Clinton May Get Payout of $20 Million," *Wall Street Journal*, January 22, 2008, http://online.wsj.com/news/articles/SB120097424021905843.

2. Michael Luo, Jo Becker, and Patrick Healy, "Donors Worried by Clinton Campaign Spending," *New York Times*, February 22, 2008, http://www.nytimes.com/2008/02/22/us/politics/22clinton.html.

3. Andrea Mitchell, "Hillary's $5 Million Loan," NBC News, February 6, 2008, http://firstread.nbcnews.com/_news/2008/02/06/4424720-hillarys-5-million-loan?lite.

4. Peter Nicholas, "Tug of War Among Staffers Is a Drag on Clinton Candidacy," *Los Angeles Times*, March 3, 2008, http://articles.latimes.com/2008/mar/03/nation/na-clintoncamp3.

5. Patrick Healy, "In S. Carolina, It's Obama vs. Clinton. That's Bill Clinton," *New York Times*, January 22, 2008, http://www.nytimes.com/2008/01/22/us/politics/22clinton.html.

6. Jason Linkins, "*L.A. Times* Captures Clinton Camp In-Fighting, Fingers Bill, Penn," *Huffington Post*, March 28, 2008, http://www.huffingtonpost.com/2008/03/03/la-times-captures-clinton_n_89555.html.

7. Jason Horowitz, "Four Key Hillary Clinton Staffers from 2008 Unlikely to Sign On for 2016 Bid," *Washington Post*, May 19, 2013, http://www.washingtonpost.com/lifestyle/style/four-key-hillary-clinton-staffers-from-2008-unlikely-to-sign-on-for-2016-bid/2013/05/19/c9e43908-be4a-11e2-89c9-3be8095fe767_story.html.

8. Gail Sheehy, "Hillaryland at War," *Vanity Fair*, August 2008, http://www.vanityfair.com/politics/features/2008/08/clinton200808.

9. David Montgomery, "The Sex Scandal from Outer Space," *Washington Post*, June 26, 2004, http://www.washingtonpost.com/wp-dyn/articles/A6778-2004Jun25.html.

10. Christi Parsons, "Keyes' Loss Resets Bar on Margins of Victory," *Chicago Tribune*, November 4, 2004, http://articles.chicagotribune.com/2004-11-04/news/0411040199_1_republican-alan-keyes-senate-race-democrat-barack-obama.

11. Mark Mooney, "Bubba: Obama Is Just Like Jesse Jackson," ABC News, January 26, 2008, http://abcnews.go.com/blogs/politics/2008/01/bubba-obama-is/.

12. Mark Mooney, "Bill Clinton: Obama Played Race Card on Me," ABC News, April 22, 2008, http://abcnews.go.com/blogs/politics/2008/04/bill-clinton-ob-2/.

13. "Off-Color 'Joke' Is a Hot Potato," *New York Post*, December 10, 2007, http://nypost.com/2007/12/10/off-color-joke-is-a-hot-potato/.

14. "Bill Clinton Argues with ABC Reporter over Nevada Caucuses," video, uploaded by jkq2ery8046, January 17, 2008, http://www.youtube.com/watch?v=zqSFFU8rrWQ.

15. Sheehy, "Hillaryland at War."

16. Vaughn Ververs, "Analysis: Bill Clinton's Lost Legacy," CBS News, January 26, 2008, http://www.cbsnews.com/news/analysis-bill-clintons-lost-legacy/.

17. Ann E. Kornblut, "Bill Clinton: Obama Campaign 'Played the Race Card on Me,'" *Washington Post*, April 22, 2008, http://voices.washingtonpost.com/44/2008/04/22/bill_clinton_obama_campaign_pl.html.

18. Ben Smith, "Daschle: WJC 'Not Presidential,'" *Politico*, January 22, 2008, http://www.politico.com/blogs/bensmith/0108/Daschle_WJC_not_presidential.html.

19. Bill Richardson, *How to Sweet-Talk a Shark: Strategies and Stories from a Master Negotiator* (Emmaus, PA: Rodale Books, 2013).

20. Patrick Healy, "Carville Stands by 'Judas' Remark," *New York Times*, March 24, 2008, http://thecaucus.blogs.nytimes.com/2008/03/24/carville-stands-by-judas-remark/.

21. Jeff Zeleny and Carl Hulse, "Kennedy Chooses Obama, Spurning Plea by Clintons," *New York Times*, January 28, 2008.

22. Ryan Lizza, "Let's Be Friends," *New Yorker*, September 10, 2012, http://www.newyorker.com/reporting/2012/09/10/120910fa_fact_lizza.

23. "Sen. Kennedy Endorses Barack Obama," Associated Press, January 28, 2008, http://www.nbcnews.com/id/22873162/ns/politics-decision_08/t/sen-kennedy -endorses-barack-obama/.

24. Ibid.

25. "Gore Endorses Obama, Helps Court Michigan," Associated Press, June 17, 2008, http://usatoday30.usatoday.com/news/politics/election2008/2008-06-16 -gore_N.htm.

26. Kate Zernike, "Clinton Discusses What She Wants, but Not What She Will Do," *New York Times*, June 4, 2008, http://www.nytimes.com/2008/06/04/us/politics/ 04clinton.html.

27. Ibid.

28. "Obama Apologizes over 'Hillary Clinton (D-Punjab)' Memo," *New York Times*, June 19, 2007.

29. Christopher Hitchens, *No One Left to Lie To: The Values of the Worst Family* (London and New York: Verso, 1999).

30. John Tomasic, "Clinton Calls for 'Cathartic' First-Ballot Nomination," *Huffington Post,* August 1, 2008.

31. Rebecca Traister, "Angry PUMAs on the Prowl in Denver," *Salon.com*, August 26, 2008, http://www.salon.com/2008/08/26/pumas_3/.

32. Sara Just, "Clinton Demands Florida, Michigan Votes Count," ABC News, May 21, 2008, http://abcnews.go.com/blogs/politics/2008/05/clinton-demands/.

33. Jim Rutenberg and Raymond Hernandez, "In an About-Face, Howard Wolfson Now Works for Mayor Bloomberg," *New York Times*, July 10, 2009, http://www.nytimes .com/2009/07/12/nyregion/12wolfson.html?pagewanted=1&sq&st=nyt&scp=46.

34. Lindsey Ellerson, "Bill Clinton: Hillary Never Wanted to Be Obama's VP," ABC News, September 22, 2008, http://abcnews.go.com/blogs/politics/2008/09/bill-clinton-hi-2/.

7: The Bubble

1. "Senate Confirms Clinton as Secretary of State," Associated Press, January 21, 2009, http://nypost.com/2009/01/21/senate-confirms-clinton-as-secretary-of-state/.

2. "P. J. Crowley: Bradley Manning Treatment 'Counterproductive and Stupid,'" *Huffington Post*, March 11, 2011, http://www.huffingtonpost.com/2011/03/11/pj -crowley-bradley-manning-treatment-_n_834611.html.

3. Jonathan Allen and Amie Parnes, *HRC: State Secrets and the Rebirth of Hillary Clinton* (New York: Crown, 2014).

4. Mark Landler, "Lost in Translation: A U.S. Gift to Russia," *New York Times*, March 6, 2009, http://www.nytimes.com/2009/03/07/world/europe/07diplo.html.

5. Robin Toner, "PUBLIC LIVES; For a Tough Clinton Lawyer, a Tough Decision to Leave," *New York Times*, August 16, 1999, http://www.nytimes.com/1999/08/16/ us/public-lives-for-a-tough-clinton-lawyer-a-tough-decision-to-leave.html.

6. "From the Desk of Judicial Watch," email newsletter, Judicial Watch, February 20, 2009, http://www.judicialwatch.org/press-room/weekly-updates/09-loathsome -and-inadequate/.

7. Naftali Bendavid, "White House Counsel Earns Praise," *Chicago Tribune*, January 21, 1999, http://articles.chicagotribune.com/1999-01-21/news/9901210163_1_white-house-cheryl-mills-beth-nolan.

8. Amie Parnes, "Gatekeeper: Cheryl Mills," *Politico*, April 24, 2009, http://www.politico.com/news/stories/0409/21584.html.

9. Toby Harnden, "Hillary Clinton: My Husband Bill Clinton Is Not Secretary of State," *Telegraph*, August 11, 2009, http://www.telegraph.co.uk/news/worldnews/northamerica/usa/6011874/Hillary-Clinton-my-husband-Bill-Clinton-is-not-secretary-of-state.html.

10. Patrick E. Tyler, "Hillary Clinton, in China, Details Abuse of Women," *New York Times*, September 6, 1995, http://www.nytimes.com/1995/09/06/world/hillary-clinton-in-china-details-abuse-of-women.html.

11. "Remarks at China University for Women," remarks by Melanne Verveer, U.S. Department of State, June 2, 2012, http://www.state.gov/s/gwi/rls/rem/2012/191765.htm.

12. "Meeting with Chinese Women Civil Society Leaders," remarks by Hillary Rodham Clinton, U.S. Department of State, May 26, 2010, http://www.state.gov/secretary/20092013clinton/rm/2010/05/142288.htm.

13. "Message to LGBT Youth," remarks by Hillary Rodham Clinton, U.S. Department of State, October 19, 2010, http://www.state.gov/secretary/20092013clinton/rm/2010/10/149681.htm.

14. "Transcript of Bill Clinton's Speech to the Democratic National Convention," *New York Times*, September 5, 2012, http://www.nytimes.com/2012/09/05/us/politics/transcript-of-bill-clintons-speech-to-the-democratic-national-convention.html.

15. Olivier Knox, "Bill Clinton Stars in New Obama Ad," Yahoo News, August 23, 2012, http://news.yahoo.com/blogs/ticket/bill-clinton-stars-obama-ad-122603501.html.

16. Kyle Campbell, "White Tie and Jokes: Top Ten Obama, Romney Zingers from Al Smith Dinner," *Houston Chronicle*, October 19, 2012, http://blog.chron.com/txpotomac/2012/10/white-tie-and-jokes-obama-romney-exchange-zingers-at-al-smith-dinner-video/.

17. "Secretary of State Hillary Clinton's Remarks at Transfer of Remains Ceremony for Americans Killed in Libya," September 14, 2012, transcript, http://www.washingtonpost.com/politics/decision2012/secretary-of-state-hillary-clintons-remarks-at-transfer-of-remains-ceremony-for-americans-killed-in-libya-transcript/2012/09/14/54fc64c0-fea2-11e1-8adc-499661afe377_story.html.

18. David Lerman, "Ambassador Died in Smoke While Agents Searched for Him," Bloomberg, October 10, 2012, http://www.bloomberg.com/news/2012-10-10/ambassador-died-in-smoke-while-agents-searched-for-him.html.

19. John T. Bennett, "Amid Political Barbs, Realization of Africa-Based Threats Emerges," *DefenseNews*, January 23, 2013, http://www.defensenews.com/article/20130123/DEFREG02/301230023/Amid-Political-Barbs-Realization-Africa-Based-Threats-Emerges.

20. "Chris Matthews: 'I Felt This Thrill Going Up My Leg' As Obama Spoke," *Huffington Post*, March 28, 2008, http://www.huffingtonpost.com/2008/02/13/chris-matthews-i-felt-thi_n_86449.html.

21. Jeff Poor, "Chris Matthews on Clinton Hearing: 'Hillary, Hillary, Hillary—She Never Looked Better,'" *Daily Caller*, January 23, 2013, http://dailycaller .com/2013/01/23/chris-matthews-on-clinton-hearing-hillary-hillary-hillary -she-never-looked-better/.

8: The Deal

1. Sally Bedell Smith, *For Love of Politics* (New York: Random House, 2007).
2. "Obama on Clinton: I'm Going to Miss Her," transcript, CBS News, January 25, 2013, http://www.cbsnews.com/news/obama-on-clinton-im-going-to-miss-her/.
3. Lauren Ashburn, "Hillary Clinton and Barack Obama's Lovefest on '60 Minutes,'" *Daily Beast*, January 28, 2013, http://www.thedailybeast.com/articles/2013/01/28/ hillary-clinton-and-barack-obama-s-lovefest-on-60-minutes.html.
4. Max Read, "BFFs Barack Obama and Hillary Clinton Say Giddy Goodbye on 60 Minutes," *Gawker*, January 27, 2013, http://gawker.com/5979404/bffs-barack -obama-and-hillary-clinton-say-giddy-goodbye-on-60-minutes.
5. Philip Elliot, "In TV Interview, Obama, Clinton Chat, Avoid 2016," Associated Press, January 28, 2013.
6. Tom McKay, "Hillary Clinton 2016: Obama Basically Endorses Clinton for President on '60 Minutes,'" PolicyMic, January 28, 2013, http://www.policymic .com/articles/24301/hillary-clinton-2016-obama-basically-endorses-clinton-for -president-on-60-minutes.
7. Jason Easley, "Obama Delivered a Not Too Subtle Hillary 2016 Endorsement in 60 Minutes Interview," PoliticusUSA, January 27, 2013, http://www.politicususa .com/2013/01/27/obama-delivered-subtle-hillary-2016-endorsement-60-minutes -interview.html.
8. Kevin Cirilli, "Jiltin' Joe? Obama Does '60 Minutes' with Hillary Clinton," *Politico*, January 25, 2013.
9. Dean Chambers, "CBS 60 Minutes Interview Suggests Obama Support for Hillary in 2016," Examiner.com, January 28, 2013, http://www.examiner.com/article/cbs -60-minutes-interviews-suggests-obama-support-for-hillary-2016.
10. John Heilemann and Mark Halperin, *Game Change* (New York: HarperCollins, 2010).
11. Ken Strickland and Andrea Mitchell, "Clinton, Obama 'Memo of Understanding,'" NBC News, December 18, 2008, http://firstread.nbcnews.com/_news/2008/12/18/4 426618-clinton-obama-memo-of-understanding.
12. Cheryl K. Chumley, "New Book: Bill Clinton Forges Secret Deal with 'Incompetent' Obama," *Washington Times*, June 3, 2013, http://www.washingtontimes .com/news/2013/jun/3/new-book-bill-clinton-forges-secret-deal-incompete/.
13. "Bill Clinton Basically Endorses Mitt Romney," transcript, RushLimbaugh.com, June 1, 2012, http://www.rushlimbaugh.com/daily/2012/06/01/bill_clinton_ basically_endorses_mitt_romney.
14. Mark Leibovich, "Voice Is Strained, but Support on the Trail Unstinting," *New York Times*, November 4, 2012, http://www.nytimes.com/2012/11/05/us/ politics/bill-clinton-presses-on-in-campaign-for-barack-obama.html?_r=0.

15. Josh Rogin, "McCain: Is Bill Clinton Preparing for a Hillary Run in 2016?" *Foreign Policy*, October 23, 2012, http://thecable.foreignpolicy.com/posts/2012/10/23/mccain_is_bill_clinton_preparing_for_a_hillary_run_in_2016.

16. Kevin Cirilli, "Newt Gingrich: Bill Clinton 'Collecting IOUs' for 2016," *Politico*, November 5, 2012, http://www.politico.com/news/stories/1112/83375.html.

17. Xuan Thai and Ted Barrett, "Biden's Description of Obama Draws Scrutiny," CNN, February 9, 2007, http://www.cnn.com/2007/POLITICS/01/31/biden.obama/.

18. Adam Nagourney, "Biden Unwraps His Bid for '08 With an Oops!" *New York Times*, January 31, 2007, http://www.nytimes.com/2007/01/31/washington/02cnd-biden.html?pagewanted=print.

19. "Biden's Description of Obama Draws Scrutiny," CNN, February 9, 2007, http://www.cnn.com/2007/POLITICS/01/31/biden.obama/.

20. Ibid.

21. "Joe Biden's Weird Relationship with Obama: A Mix of Condescension, Awe," *Time*, September 6, 2012.

22. Mark Leibovich, "For a Blunt Biden, an Uneasy Supporting Role," *New York Times*, May 7, 2012.

23. Dylan Stableford, "Biden on Gay Marriage: 'Absolutely Comfortable with Men Marrying Men, Women Marrying Women,'" ABC News, May 6, 2012.

24. Rick Klein, "Obama: 'I Think Same-Sex Couples Should Be Able to Get Married,'" ABC News, May 9, 2012, http://abcnews.go.com/blogs/politics/2012/05/obama-comes-out-i-think-same-sex-couples-should-be-able-to-get-married/.

25. Daniel Halper, "Obama on Biden: 'Got Out a Little Bit over His Skis,'" *Weekly Standard*, May 10, 2012, https://www.weeklystandard.com/blogs/obama-biden-got-out-little-bit-over-his-skis_644325.html.

26. John Heilemann and Mark Halperin, *Double Down: Game Change 2012* (New York: Penguin, 2013).

27. Kevin Cirilli, "David Plouffe: Hillary Clinton 'Probably the Strongest' for 2016," *Politico*, March 18, 2013, http://www.politico.com/story/2013/03/hillary-clinton-2016-plouffe-88978.html.

28. Alex Roarty and Niraj Chokshi, "Axelrod: Hillary Clinton 'First Among Equals' for 2016 Nomination," *National Journal*, December 13, 2012, http://www.nationaljournal.com/politics/axelrod-hillary-clinton-first-among-equals-for-2016-nomination-20121213.

29. Jake Tapper and Sherisse Pham, "Rahm Emanuel: If Hillary Runs in 2016, I'm There," CNN, October 30, 2013, http://thelead.blogs.cnn.com/2013/10/30/rahm-emanuel-nsa-obamacare-2016-hillary/.

30. Heather Ginsberg, "Obama Campaign Manager and Former Bill Clinton Aide to Head Hillary Clinton Project," Townhall.com, November 13, 2012, http://townhall.com/tipsheet/heatherginsberg/2013/11/13/obama-campaign-manager-and-former-bill-clinton-aide-to-head-hillary-clinton-project-n1745947.

31. Maggie Haberman, "Hillary Clinton's Answer to the Has-Been Charge," *Politico*, July 8, 2013, http://www.politico.com/story/2013/07/hillary-clinton-2016-93801 .html.

32. "Press Briefing by Deputy Press Secretary Josh Earnest," transcript, Whitehouse.gov, July 29, 2013, http://www.whitehouse.gov/photos-and-video/video/2013/07/29/press-briefing-deputy-press-secretary-josh-earnest#transcript.

33. "Obama Awards Presidential Medals of Freedom," transcript, CNN, November 20, 2013, http://transcripts.cnn.com/TRANSCRIPTS/1311/20/cnr.06.html.

34. "Remarks by the President at the 50th Anniversary of the Presidential Medal of Freedom," transcript, November 20, 2013, Whitehouse.gov, http://www.white house.gov/the-press-office/2013/11/20/remarks-president-50th-anniversary -presidential-medal-freedom.

35. Earle Earle, White House Pool Report email to White House listserv, November 20, 2013.

36. Michael D. Shear, "Obama, George W. Bush and Hillary Clinton Share Flight to South Africa," *New York Times*, December 10, 2013, http://www.nytimes .com/2013/12/11/world/africa/mandela-obama-bush-clinton.html.

9: Daddy's Little Girl

1. Video of event available at http://www.bloomberg.com/video/bill-clinton-urges -white-house-to-do-more-in-syria-51D3W1X_SHud6NKNxlO_3w.html.

2. Ibid.

3. See, e.g., Jeffrey Lord, "Bill Clinton and the Reagan Consensus," *American Spectator*, June 7, 2012.

4. Hillary Clinton, *It Takes a Village* (New York: Simon & Schuster, 2003)

5. Lloyd Grove, "Chelsea's Morning," *New York*, February 24, 2008, http://nymag .com/nymag/rss/politics/44454/.

6. Jim Frederick, "Q&A With Chelsea Clinton," *Time*, September 26, 2012, http:// ideas.time.com/2012/09/26/q-a-with-chelsea-clinton/.

7. Ibid.

8. Tony Freemantle, "Bush, Clinton Form Unlikely Bond on Tsunami Tour," *Houston Chronicle*, March 7, 2005, http://www.chron.com/news/nation-world/article/ Bush-Clinton-form-unlikely-bond-on-tsunami-tour-1931175.php.

9. James P. Steyer, *Talking Back to Facebook: The Common Sense Guide to Raising Kids in the Digital Age* (New York: Scribner, 2012), p. xii.

10. Todd S. Purdum, "Chelsea Clinton, Still a Closed Book," *New York Times*, June 17, 2001, http://www.nytimes.com/2001/06/17/us/chelsea-clinton-still-a-closed-book.html.

11. Ibid.

12. Taylor Branch, *The Clinton Tapes: Wrestling History with the President* (New York: Simon & Schuster, 2009), p. 601.

13. Ibid.

14. Ibid.

15. Ibid.
16. Ibid.
17. Ibid., p. 496.
18. Ronda Kaysen, "Power Punk: Chelsea Clinton," *New York Observer*, December 15, 2013, http://observer.com/2003/12/power-punk-chelsea-clinton/.
19. Stuart Jeffries, "The Firm," *Guardian*, February 21, 2003, http://www.theguardian.com/education/2003/feb/21/mbas.highereducation.
20. "Chelsea Clinton Joins New York Hedge Fund," Reuters, November 3, 2006, http://www.nbcnews.com/id/15549672/ns/business-us_business/t/chelsea-clinton-joins-new-york-hedge-fund/.
21. Profile of Marc Lasry, *Forbes*, http://www.forbes.com/profile/marc-lasry/.
22. Frederick, "Q&A with Chelsea Clinton."
23. Ibid.
24. Clip of event posted on YouTube, October 11, 2012, http://www.youtube.com/watch?v=r71NjJFjdV0.
25. "Chelsea's Exes," *Daily Beast*, http://www.thedailybeast.com/galleries/2010/07/26/chelsea-s-exes.html#slide2.
26. "Chelsea's Exes," *Daily Beast*, http://www.thedailybeast.com/galleries/2010/07/26/chelsea-s-exes.html#slide4.
27. Noel Sheppard, "Chelsea Clinton Interviews . . . the GEICO Gecko?" Newsbusters.org, April 27, 2013, http://newsbusters.org/blogs/noel-sheppard/2013/04/27/chelsea-clinton-interviewsthe-geico-gecko.
28. Michael Hastings, "Chelsea Clinton, TV's Dork Diva, Struggles at NBC," *BuzzFeed*, April 16, 2012, http://www.buzzfeed.com/mhastings/chelsea-clinton-tvs-dork-diva-struggles-at-nb.
29. Sara Stewart, "Love After the Storm," *New York Post*, July 15, 2010, http://nypost.com/2010/07/15/love-after-the-storm/.
30. Joseph Rhee and Drew Sandholm, "Will Father of the Groom Be Welcome Figure at Chelsea Clinton's Wedding?" ABC News, December 1, 2009, http://abcnews.go.com/Blotter/father-groom-figure-chelsea-clintons-wedding/story?id=9211229.
31. Bob Shrum, *No Excuses: Confessions of a Serial Campaigner* (New York: Simon & Schuster, 2007).
32. "Senior Advisors," TeneoHoldings.com, http://www.teneoholdings.com/senior-advisor/.
33. Alec MacGillis, "Scandal at Clinton Inc.: How Doug Band Drove a Wedge Through a Political Dynasty," *New Republic*, September 22, 2013, http://www.newrepublic.com/article/114790/how-doug-band-drove-wedge-through-clinton-dynasty.
34. Ibid.
35. Ibid.
36. Ibid.
37. Ibid.
38. Ibid.

39. Catherine Herridge, "'Revolving Door'? Ties Between Consultancy, Gov't Raise Questions about Benghazi Probe," Fox News, March 24, 2014, http://www.fox news.com/politics/2014/03/24/revolving-door-ties-between-consultancy-govt -raise-questions-about-benghazi/.

40. Michael Shnayerson, "The Follieri Charade," *Vanity Fair*, October 2008, http:// www.vanityfair.com/style/features/2008/10/follieri200810.

41. MacGillis, "Scandal at Clinton Inc."

42. "FoundationSearch," Metasoft Systems, January 2014, http://www.foundation search.com/.

43. Ibid.

44. Ibid.

45. Ibid.

46. MacGillis, "Scandal at Clinton Inc."

10: Chasing Hillary

1. Christopher Wills, "Obama's Thin, but Varied Record," Associated Press, January 16, 2008, http://usatoday30.usatoday.com/news/politics/2008-01-16-2414012588_x.htm.

2. *This Week*, transcript, ABC News, August 11, 2013, http://abcnews.go.com/ThisWeek/ week-transcript-lon-snowden-donald-trump/story?id=19926953&page=6.

3. Jim Galloway, "Hearsay from Hillary Clinton: On Joe Biden and the Osama bin Laden Raid," *Atlanta Journal-Constitution*, October 15, 2013, http:// www.ajc.com/weblogs/political-insider/2013/oct/15/hearsay-hillary- clinton-theres-more-life-slim-jims/.

4. Mark Z. Barabak, "Jerry Brown, Urged to Run for President, Won't Rule Out 2016 Bid," *Los Angeles Times*, December 17, 2013, http://articles.latimes.com/2013/ dec/17/news/la-pn-jerry-brown-president-2016-20131217.

5. Jane C. Timm, "RNC, DNC Narrow Crosshairs on Hillary, Christie," MSNBC, December 5, 2013, http://www.msnbc.com/morning-joe/gop-focusing-clinton.

6. Amy Chozick and Bill Carter, "CNN and NBC Scrap Projects on Hillary Clin- ton," *New York Times*, September 30, 2013.

7. Charles Ferguson, "Why I Am Cancelling My Documentary on Hillary Clinton," *Huffington Post*, September 30, 2013, http://www.huffingtonpost.com/charles -ferguson/hillary-clinton-documentary_b_4014792.html.

8. Stephen Dinan, "Rand Paul Demands Dems Return Money Raised by 'Sexual Pred- ator' Bill Clinton," *Washington Times*, February 7, 2014, http://www.washingtontimes .com/news/2014/feb/7/rand-paul-demands-democrats-return-money-raised-se/.

9. Alana Goodman, "The Hillary Papers," *Washington Free Beacon*, February 9, 2014, http://freebeacon.com/politics/the-hillary-papers/.

10. Christopher Hitchens, *No One Left to Lie To* (New York, Verso, 1999), 114–16.

11. Sheryl Stolberg, "Clinton Due Back at White House Today," *Los Angeles Times*, March 16, 1997, http://articles.latimes.com/1997-03-16/news/mn-39035_1_white-house.

12. Richard H. Curtiss, "Report of Israeli Eavesdropping on White House Telephones Gets Varying Media Treatment," *Washington Report*, July 2000.

13. David Johnston, "Israeli Spy Inquiry Finds Nothing, Officials Say," Associated Press, May 6, 2000, http://www.nytimes.com/2000/05/06/us/israeli-spy-inquiry -finds-nothing-officials-say.html.

14. James Risen and Steven Erlanger, "C.I.A. Chief Vowed to Quit if Clinton Freed Israeli Spy," *New York Times*, November 11, 1998, http://www.nytimes .com/1998/11/11/world/cia-chief-vowed-to-quit-if-clinton-freed-israeli-spy.html.

15. Ibid.

16. Jorge Ramos, "Bill Clinton Interviewed by Jorge Ramos [Full Transcript]," December 3, 2013, Fusion, http://fusion.net/america_with_jorge_ramos/story/bill -clinton-interviewed-jorge-ramos-full-transcript-278503.

17. R. W. Apple Jr., "The Capital Spotlight; Anguished Words from Dead Clinton Aide Make Washington Think About Its Values," *New York Times*, August 13, 1993, http://www.nytimes.com/1993/08/13/us/capital-spotlight-anguished-words -dead-clinton-aide-make-washington-think-about.html.

18. Hillary Rodham Clinton, *Living History* (New York: Scribner, 2004), p. 506.

11: The Road to Coronation

1. Maggie Haberman, "Hillary Clinton's Shadow Campaign," *Politico*, January 5, 2014, http://dyn.politico.com/printstory.cfm?uuid=F9AE51A4-3E0D-4604-B08F -2E63DE4F600A.

2. Rick Klein, "In Secret Letter, Senate Democratic Women Rally Behind Hillary Clinton," ABC News, October 30, 2013, http://abcnews.go.com/blogs/politics/ 2013/10/in-secret-letter-senate-democratic-women-rally-behind-hillary-clinton/.

3. "N.Y. Gov. Andrew Cuomo: Hillary Clinton No Bearing on 2016 Thinking," Associated Press, April 29, 2013, http://www.politico.com/story/2013/04/andrew -cuomo-hillary-clinton-2016-90742.html.

4. Frederick U. Dicker, "If Hillary Is Running for Prez, I'm Out," *New York Post*, April 29, 2013, http://nypost.com/2013/04/29/if-hillary-is-running-for-prez-im-out/.

5. "Secretary Hillary Rodham Clinton," Clintonfoundation.org, accessed June 2013, http://www.clintonfoundation.org/about/secretary-hillary-rodham-clinton.

6. Jim Rutenberg and Amy Chozick, "In Hamptons Again, Clintons Get to Work on Their Vacation," *New York Times*, August 22, 2013, http://www.nytimes.com/2013/08/23/ nyregion/back-in-hamptons-clintons-get-to-work-on-their-vacation.html.

7. Amy Chozick and Jonathan Martin, "Eye on 2016, Clintons Rebuild Bond with Blacks," *New York Times*, November 30, 2013, http://www.nytimes.com/2013/12/01/ us/politics/eye-on-2016-clintons-rebuild-bond-with-blacks.html.

8. Jonathan Karl, "Book Review: 'HRC' by Jonathan Allen and Amie Parnes," *Wall Street Journal*, February 10, 2014, http://online.wsj.com/news/articles/SB100014240 5270230349680457936723428837144.

9. Jonathan Allen and Ben Smith, "Anthony Weiner: Hackers Posted Lewd Photos on Twitter," *Politico*, May 28, 2011, http://www.politico.com/news/stories/0511/55877 .html.

10. Ibid.

11. Jonathan Karl, Jake Tapper, and Devin Dwyer, "Anthony Weiner Announces Resignation from Congress," ABC News, June 16, 2011, http://abcnews.go.com/Politics/anthony-weiner-resign-huma-abedin-return/story?id=13855468.

12. Maggie Haberman, John Bresnahan, and Glenn Thrush, "Huma Abedin Allowed to Represent Clients While at State," *Politico*, May 16, 2013, http://www.politico.com/story/2013/05/huma-abedin-consultant-state-91503.html.

13. Mara Gay and Michael Howard Saul, "Mayor Bloomberg Stoic at de Blasio Inauguration," *Wall Street Journal*, January 1, 2014, http://online.wsj.com/news/articles/SB10001424052702303870704579294843755086018.

14. "2014 New York City Inauguration," video posted by NYC Mayor's Office, January 1, 2014, https://www.youtube.com/watch?v=cvqfn3RYc9U.

INDEX

Note: The abbreviations CVC, HRC, and WJC stand for Chelsea Victoria Clinton, Hillary Rodham Clinton, and William Jefferson Clinton respectively.

role of CVC, 277–78

vice president selection, 243, 265–66

voter sympathy for HRC, 245–46

See also Clinton, Hillary Rodham (presidential candidate)

2016 presidential challengers

Amy Klobuchar, 242, 266

Andrew Cuomo, 242, 264–65

Biden aspirations, 191–92, 204

Brian Schweitzer, 243–44

Elizabeth Warren, 244

Jerry Brown, 244

Martin O'Malley, 242–43

Rahm Emanuel, 207–8

Rand Paul, 249

Republican opposition, 244–46

U

University of Virginia, 233

U.S. Department of Veterans Affairs, 66–67, 93

U.S. Drug Enforcement Administration, 65

U.S. Supreme Court, 63, 102, 274

U.S.-Afghan Women's Council, 111–12

V

Vancouver Sun, 86

Vanity Fair, 55–56, 86, 115, 137, 232

Van Natta, Don, 46

Verveer, Melanne, 112

Vignali, Carlos, 36

Violence Against Women Act, 72

Vitter, David, 155

Vogue, 43

Voting Rights Act, 274

W

Wade, Richard, 9

Walker, Martin, 256

Walters, Barbara, 250, 272

War on Women, xi

Warner, Mark, 265

Warren, Elizabeth, 244, 262

Washington Free Beacon, 249

Washington Monthly, 132

Wattenberg, Ben, 69–70

Weekly Standard, xviii, xxiv

Wehner, Pete, 108

Weiner, Anthony, 45, 76, 128, 279–82

Whitewater scandal, 4, 5, 9–10, 60, 129

Whouley, Michael, 261

WikiLeaks, 164

Willey, Kathleen, 168

William J. Clinton Foundation. *See* Clinton Foundation

Williams, Maggie, xvii, 57

Wolfson, Howard, 20, 36, 122, 124, 127–28, 137, 142, 150, 284

Women in Islam (Abedin), 44

women-in-combat, x–xi

women's rights, x, 169, 172–74, 249

Wonder, Stevie, 53

Woodward, Bob, 161

Write It When I'm Gone (DeFrank), 55

Wye River Memorandum (1998), 252–53

Y

Yankelovich, Daniel, xvii

"The Year Everyone Gave Hillary Clinton an Award," 263

Yeltsin, Boris, 252

Young, Andrew, 139

Young, Charlie, 56

YouTube, xii, 139, 182, 185, 273

Z

Zogby, John, 3

Zucker, Jeff, 129

ABOUT THE AUTHOR

Daniel Halper is the online editor of the *Weekly Standard* and one of the most widely read political bloggers and reporters.